The Sound of STEVE HACKETT - Vol. 1

The Complete Guitar Transcriptions of

Voyage of the Acolyte

by

Paulo De Carvalho

To my family
Maluh, Gabriel, Giulia,
Rose, Monique, and Nando,
and to all friends
who came aboard on this Voyage

CONTENTS

FOREWORD BY STEVE HACKETT   7

PREFACE   8

A VOYAGE BEFORE THE VOYAGE   10

THE STUDIO OF VOYAGE OF THE ACOLYTE   14

MEETING WITH JOHN HACKETT   16

MEETING WITH SALLY OLDFIELD   20

MEETING WITH PETE CORNISH   22

STEVE'S GUITARS: LES PAUL 24.   YAIRI 25.   ZERMAITIS 12-STRING 26.   24

VOYAGE OF THE ACOLYTE   27

    ACE OF WANDS   28

    HANDS OF THE PRIESTESS PART I   58

    A TOWER STRUCK DOWN   67

    HANDS OF THE PRIESTESS PART II   81

    THE HERMIT   98

    STAR OF SIRIUS   119

    THE LOVERS   161

    SHADOW OF THE HIEROPHANT   167

PHOTO GALLERY   204

ABOUT THE AUTHOR   205

FOREWORD

Voyage of the Acolyte was an important album for me, the first solo record. Of course I had the help of many gifted musos - some from rock, some from classical. With influences ranging from folk to jazz, the pan-genre approach was adopted from the outset...

The input from the late John Acock was also invaluable. I felt it was a team of friends working way into the night which gave the project its character, none more important than John Hackett making his own stunning debut on this first collaboration between two brothers. It was great to have Mike and Phil on board too, as the rhythmic engine underpinning everything.

Along with John Acock, Robin Miller and John Gustavson have now also passed on, which makes this musical memory all the sweeter - an unrepeatable moment in time, a confluence of magical things.

I remember a hot Summer, a hot band, a nervous guitarist (me) hovering over unfinished tapes like a chain-smoking expectant father living on soup from the studio dispensing machine. The price was very little sleep but rather a kind of euphoric delirium...

I was finally captain of my own ship, loving every last note, grappling with the rigging, storms unleashed from beneath the strings of my guitar, haunted by the wailing of distant mellotrons - I was at sea, a sea of sound and in my element completely for the first time…

Steve Hackett

April 3rd, 2018.

PREFACE

In continuation of *The Sound of Steve Hackett: A Selection of Guitar Transcriptions from His Solo Career*, the present book *The Sound of Steve Hackett: The Complete Guitar Transcriptions of Voyage of the Acolyte* is the first volume of a collection of complete guitar transcriptions of Steve Hackett's solo career albums. As its predecessor, it keeps the innovative style of being a mix of a book and a songbook along with having the differentiating mark of being a pioneer work, containing the first complete guitar transcriptions ever published on Steve's debut solo album *Voyage of the Acolyte* (released in October 1975), featuring notes, tablatures, and chords. Both the music sheet and the text in this first volume were also a result of live meetings between Steve Hackett himself and me. Steve reviewed these materials, making it, once again, a very reliable source for guitar players.

Photo 1: Paulo De Carvalho (left) and Steve Hackett (right) in Steve's home in London, U.K., 2017

Besides interviews with Steve, other sources were the communications with people that were part on the making of *Voyage of the Acolyte* having worked directly with Steve, including: John Hackett, Steve's youngest brother, a flautist, composer, guitarist and keyboard player; Sally Oldfield, singer; and Pete Cornish, who has built pedalboards for Steve throughout his career.

The work brings previously unpublished information on how Steve first conceptualized *Voyage of the Acolyte*, recorded while he was still a member of Genesis - and the history of how Steve, as composer and instrumentalist, and the other musicians started recording the album all the way until its release.

The previously unpublished charts of the instruments and gears that Steve used in each song of the album is another fact of relevance in this first volume. These charts were put together by me upon thorough investigation. They are the first evidence, in my opinion, of how Steve creates his unique and differentiate sound - as per the name of this collection - along with his remarkable technique, previously detailed in *The Sound of Steve Hackett: A Selection of Guitar Transcriptions from His Solo Career*.

Voyage of the Acolyte is undoubtedly one of the most important records of prog rock of all time, merging elements from classical music, using instruments such as: flute, oboe, cor anglais, cello, acoustic guitars, as well as electric guitars, keyboards, bass, and drums. This range of instruments and musical ideas clearly demonstrate the composer's eagerness to express a series of high quality compositions that had been often stunted. All the songs on the album were composed by Steve Hackett. *A Tower Struck Down* was written in partnership with John Hackett, and *Shadow of the Hierophant*, with Mike Rutherford.

The book includes unpublished photographs taken by me of the original instruments that Steve used on *Voyage* along with Steve's hands on the guitar showing details of parts of some songs in the album. You will also find unpublished photos taken by me of John Hackett's original manuscripts of parts of the songs included in the album.

1975, the year in which *Voyage of the Acolyte* was recorded and released, was a distressful year in Steve Hackett's life. One year before, he had recorded the album *The Lamb Lies Down on Broadway* with Genesis and he went on a long tour playing this entire double album, aware, as well as all the other bandmates, that Peter Gabriel would leave the band right at the end of the tour.

I bought the record *Voyage of the Acolyte* as soon as it was released in Brazil, and I had a "problem" with that vinyl: I could not stop listening to it until the last song was finished. Genesis' single and duo guitars were one of the most impressive things that appeared to me, and I was curious to know how Steve would explore his solo career. I was extremely grateful to hear the album because I felt delighted from the very first notes of it. The songs and arrangements were very concise, there was not a single note out of context, and all the lines were written in a sense of harmony. At that time I was a fourteen-year-old teen.

I picked up my only guitar, an acoustic one, and the first song I tried playing was *Hands of the Priestess Part I*, and that was when I realized that I had to find a flute player to play that song along with me. Later on I bought an electric guitar and I tried playing *Ace of Wands*. That is how I began transcribing music: playing for fun, listening to Steve's recordings and trying to play his music on the guitar. Because of that, I can say with confidence that *Voyage* was my own voyage to the beginning of my career as a composer and arranger - and I am immensely grateful to Steve for that.

I must conclude acknowledging that, in the process of creating this book/songbook, I had valuable contributions from generous souls. Without them it would be impossible to transcribe the songs with so many details: Steve and Jo Hackett, who brought so much enlightenment to my work - as great friends do, they were always there to help me with the project; John Hackett, who spent hours talking and playing with me at his home in Northern England, revealing some subtle musical aspects of *Voyage of the Acolyte*, as well as giving me access to all the scores he himself wrote for the recording sessions of the album; Sally Oldfield, who kindly explained in details her performance; and Pete Cornish, with his amazing knowledge of electric guitar effects,

Photo 2: *Steve Hackett (left) and Paulo De Carvalho (right) in London, U.K., 2017*

not to mention: Dr. Marcos Nogueira, composer, professor of Graduate Studies at the School of Music of Federal University of Rio de Janeiro, who reviewed the music sheet with the careful vision of a great musician that he is; Kim Poor, for courteously disposing the rights of her art work in the cover of *Voyage of the Acolyte*; Mike King, Warner Bros/De Lane Lea operational manager; Nick Myerscough, production manager at Raindirk; Alex Teixeira, friend, Gabriel and Giulia De Carvalho, my dearest kids - on text revision; Sergio Lestingi, for overall revision; and Maluh De Felice, a violinist, my life partner and soulmate, who was the first one to encourage me towards this work.

I hope you will enjoy reading it as much as I did doing it.

Paulo De Carvalho

A VOYAGE BEFORE THE *VOYAGE*

Peter Gabriel's final gig with Genesis was at the end of *The Lamb* tour, in Besançon, France, at the Palais des Sports, on May 22ⁿᵈ, 1975. The band knew for quite a while that Peter would leave the band right after that, but news broke out about it only on August 15ᵗʰ, 1975.

Peter Gabriel was on his way to do what he always wanted to do. Mike Rutherford was invited to participate in Anthony Phillips' first solo album, even though Mike would not complete his collaboration due to Genesis' agenda. Phil Collins was playing with different musicians, giving priority to his personal and professional desires. Since the future of the band was uncertain, Steve also decided to pursue other paths.

Near the end of 1973, with a Mellotron at home, Steve started composing a lot of new material which he did not primarily think on introducing to Genesis, as the band was very competitive about their compositions. He composed freely, without any restrictions or concerns about the band liking or not his new works. Even though it was a prolific material, Steve did not think on recording an album at that time. While touring with the band, which would often last seven months or more, Steve continued composing in his hotel room in order to relax, escape, and maintain his peace of mind.

But two weeks after the end of Genesis' nine-month *The Lamb* tour, Steve felt fresh and started thinking on getting into a studio with his own material. At that time, he wasn't sure if he would produce a variety of different outtakes or a complete album. With a band, he shared the ups and downs, success and failure, but it would be significantly different if he would be also in charge of the production, on the top of having musicians waiting for his directions. Nevertheless, it didn't take too long for Steve to feel encouraged. He told Tony Smith, Genesis' manager, that he was sure about making a solo album, and that he knew it would be a good one.

He entered the studio more organized than ever, with plenty of material to work on. After the first night recording *Hands Part I* with his brother John Hackett, Steve felt even more confident to tackle the project.

Soon after that, the director of Charisma Records Tony Stratton-Smith (not to be confused with Genesis' manager Tony Smith) approved the project. Steve had the right musicians, the studio, and the schedule in mind. On this project he wanted to create something more instrumental. The material was solid, and he was ready to go.

The recordings would take place at *Kingsway Recorders* at Aviation House, a Government Building in Kingsway, London. By law, they could only start recording after 6:00 pm as there were employees working in the building during the day. In addition, one could hear the trains passing. Because of these, the schedule of recording was set daily between 6 pm and 4 am. The night-time mood can definitely be felt in the album.

The album was originally intended to be named *Premonitions*, but Charisma Records didn't like it. Tony Stratton Smith suggested *Voyage of the Acolyte*, which Steve thought linked well enough with his original idea of writing the lyrics based on the Tarot cards.

Steve tended to create the melody first, so he explained:

I felt that basing the lyrics on the meaning of the cards would give the album a cohesiveness and a sense of a journey. In the case of the instrumentals, sometimes the title is all you have of indication. I found the Tarot intriguing and I was interested in its meaning. It held up an interesting psychological mirror and it also had a sense of mystery. Some people called it the Oracle whilst, others referred to it as the Devil's Picture-book. For me it was a mystical reflection of life's challenges and experiences which indicated different possible pathways. The different energies of the cards gave a sense of musical scope and variety between tracks.

On the first night Steve recorded *Hands of the Priestess Part I* was recorded with John Hackett on the flute on the first night. Steve played a twelve-string guitar borrowed from Mike Rutherford, and a Mellotron from Tony Banks - since by this time he had already sold his Mellotron. John was on the flute. They used an EMT 140 plate reverb and echo chamber. The performance and the reverb were magical. This kind of reverb were never used on Genesis albums. That was just the perfect start for the glorious sound of the album.

As John mentioned: *Steve was obviously writing melodies and we would try them out. Things like "Hands" was written as a flute tune as was "The Hermit". There were little guitar things, little harmony bits; descending passages and things that I had and Steve would do something with it. We were messing around with tape recorders and I had a Tandberg; a stereo tape recorder and we just played tapes backwards and things like that and I was trying the flute backwards and the kinds of things we used in the song The Lovers. Steve had always loved classical music as well and because I was very much into classical flute by then; thence the classical influence on the album.*

John Hackett, on the flute, and Steve Hackett had already played *The Hermit* for Phil Henderson, with whom Steve had worked already in the band *Quiet World*. Phil had suggested that a flute would be replaced by an oboe. Although John Hackett, in charge of writing the melodies for all orchestral instruments on the album, didn't realize at the time that the melody was outside the range of an oboe - the melody was high for an oboe. The legendary Robin Miller, principal oboe of the BBC Symphony Orchestra, managed to record it precisely.

Steve had asked Mike Rutherford and Phil Collins if they wanted to play on his album, to which they replied "sure!". So on the second night, they recorded *Ace of Wands* together. Before they began recording, Steve told them that recording *Voyage of the Acolyte* would be a different experience from recording a Genesis record. Steve's vision was clear. He showed Phil and Mike how he wanted the arrangement, and they instantly got it. Steve wanted his band mates to be comfortable since they already

had a "code" that only they themselves knew. It was a killer rhythm section.

Steve chose Phil Collins to sing *Star of Sirius* because he liked Phil's voice very much. Phil had previously sang and collaborated with the lyrics in *For Absent Friends*, a song Steve had written for Genesis. As a matter of fact, Steve was the first one to suggest Phil to become Genesis' lead singer after Peter Gabriel left the band.

Steve mentioned that at the time of the recording of *Voyage of the Acolyte*, he didn't get much sleep. He was living in his parent's house, where there was drilling going on in the early mornings, and as he normally left the studio at around 3 or 4 am, he kept going for an entire month basically with pure adrenaline, cigarettes, and chicken soup from the vending machine of the studio to keep up the energy. *But I had a really good time doing this album* - Steve commented.

The recording lasted three weeks, and the fourth one was devoted to editing the album. One of the things that had to be done was to shorten *Star of Sirius*, which was originally much longer then *Shadow of the Hierophant*.

Voyage of the Acolyte is definitely one of the masterpieces of progressive rock. The album was released on October 1975. It reached number 26 in the U.K. and number 191 in America. It eventually went silver in the U.K.

After the album was finished, Steve immediately started working back with Genesis, with whom he would record two more studio albums - one after another in addition to a live one.

Voyage of the Acolyte

1 - Ace of Wands (Steve Hackett)

2 - Hands of the Priestess Part I (Steve Hackett)

3 - A Tower Struck Down (Steve Hackett, John Hackett)

4 - Hands of the Priestess Part II (Steve Hackett)

5 - The Hermit (Steve Hackett)

6 - Star of Sirius (Steve Hackett)

7 - The Lovers (Steve Hackett)

8 - Shadow of the Hierophant (Steve Hackett, Mike Rutherford)

Players/Instruments:

Steve Hackett: Gibson Les Paul Gold Top 1957, Zemaitis Custom 12-string, Steel 6-string Yamaha acoustic, Danelectro baritone guitar, Yairi Nylon, Mellotron, EMS Synthi Hi-Fli, Harmonium, Autoharp, Tubular bells, Vocals

John Hackett: Flute Yamaha YFL 21S, Flute Armstrong, Arp Odyssey (Monophonic Synth), Tubular bells, Mellotron

John Acock: Elka-Rhapsody Synth, Mellotron

Sally Oldfield: Vocals

Robin Miller: Oboe, Cor anglais

Nigel Warren-Green: Cello

Mike Rutherford: Bass, Vox bass pedals, fuzz 12-string guitar

Percy Jones: Fretless Bass

Johnny Gustafson: Bass

Phil Collins: Drums, Vibraphone, Percussion, Vocals on *Star of Sirius*

Engineering by John Acock
Assistant engineers: Louie Austin (in *Hierophant* only), Paul Watkins, Rob Broglia
Equipment: Tex Read, Geoff Banks, Steve Baker
Organization: Tony Smith, Alex Sim

THE STUDIO OF *VOYAGE OF THE ACOLYTE*

The studio where *Voyage of the Acolyte* was recorded was called *Kingsway Recorders*. It was owned by Deep Purple's lead singer Ian Gillan, but originally owned by De Lane Lea. The studio was located in the basement of the Civil Aviation Authority in London.

Photo 3: Civil Aviation Authority in London, building below where Kingsway Recorders used to be in 1975.
Photo by Paulo De Carvalho, London, England, October 2017

Kingsway Recorders had a 24-track recording console from Raindirk. Ian Gillan asked designer Cyril Jones to put it together. This console was also used at Kingsway to record Deep Purple, and Paul McCartney with his band Wings during the London recording of *Band on the Run*, among others.

Besides the 24 channels, the Raindirk console has 16 tracks, and separated mixing outputs. The microphone channel amplifier has full equalization. There are four echo sends and three auxiliary feeds each, with a level control and pre/off/post fader switches. At the time, it also had an EMT plate connected for stereo and remote.

Photo 4: the original 24-track console of Kingsway Recorders in 1975, still in use in Dusseldorf nowadays. Photo kindly provided by Nick Myerscouh from Raindirk

Kingsway Recorders also had a 24-track Studer, a stereo Studer, an Ampex four track, and two Ampex stereo. It used an EMI TR90 mono machine for editing. For echo, the studio had an EMT 140 stereo plate with remote control and an EMT 240 plate. It had an echo room, as well as four Universal Audio Limiters, an Altec 436 compressor, a Fairchild 666 compressor, and JBL 4350 monitor speakers - each one with a Crown D150.

Photo 5: Altec 436 compressor

EMT 140

Photo 6: EMT 140 stereo plate

Photo 8: the original 24-track console of Kingsway Recorders in 1975.

Photo kindly provided by Nick Myerscough from Raindirk

Photo 7: What once was the entrance of Midland bank, in which basement was Kingsway Recorders in 1975, now is the entrance of a Pharmacy on 129 KIngsway, London, England.

Photo by Paulo De Carvalho, 2017

Photo 9: EMI TR 90

MEETING WITH JOHN HACKETT

*Photo 10: Paulo De Carvalho (left) and John Hackett (right)
in Sheffield, England, October, 2017.*

I started with the guitar when I was 12 by buying a guitar for 5 pounds from a friend of Steve's and Steve taught me how to play House of the Rising Sun, which was a great piece to learn when you start, and with this song he taught me how to use the plectrum (pick). We used to play a lot together, the blues, improvising, and we listened to Eric Clapton, Jeff Beck, and The Beatles.

Then the flute came into my life when I saw a King Crimson concert with Ian McDonald playing the instrument on "I Talk to the Wind". I loved that sound, it was amazing to hear it through a PA system with echo and reverb, such a fantastic sound! Steve and I both liked the flute, so we bought an English flute for 25 pounds, but I was the one who stayed with it even though it was really hard in the beginning when you don't know how to play it.

John Hackett

Nigel Warren-Green, who played cello on *Voyage of the Acolyte*, was John's friend at school, and he suggested John to take lessons with a teacher he knew, whose main instrument was the clarinet but who also played the flute. Later on, John studied with a more specialized flute instructor named Paul Chapman, who was very enthusiastic and helped him a lot.

It was about this time that John switched his focus from rock to classical. He lived in Victoria, in the middle of London, and he was lucky to have the Central Music Library nearby, where he was able to borrow lots of flute sheet music and started building a record collection. One of the first records he bought was one by the fantastic French flute player Jean-Pierre Rampal playing Bach's D minor flute concerto - a very difficult piece and a source of inspiration to John. Despite still appreciating rock, John wanted to improve his flute playing by exploring classical pieces.

John got high marks on his Grade 8 flute exam, playing advanced pieces which involved difficult techniques such as double-tonguing, a technique he would explore in pieces such as *Hands of the Priestess* and later on in *Jacuzzi*.

John practised nearly every day, because the lip muscles weaken with inactivity, which interferes in the tone quality. *If you don't play for 3 days you're done* - he told me. John also sang, played the guitar and the keyboard, but he has always kept the flute as a priority, so that his most heartfelt, serious efforts have always gone towards playing the flute.

The sound John produces on the flute does not come as an accident, but through a tenacious effort. For him the most important aspect of training is continuously achieving good tone. He had a teacher who encouraged him to do many different exercises to achieve these results. He also learned a lot from a book called *De La Sonorité* by Marcel Moyse, who was sort of a "guru" in the flute world, and who taught techniques to practise tone with long notes. For John, tone means everything, and he continues to work on this; it is a never ending pursuit. Vibrato is also very important for John. On *Hands of the Priestess* one can hear this technique clearly as the identity of a musician.

At age 19 John went to Cambridge University to study French and German, though he eventually left. It was a very difficult decision but he wanted to be a musician. Soon after that, John received a call from Mike Rutherford asking if he would record a project with him and Anthony Phillips on the album that later became *The Geese and The Ghost*. John took this as a sign that he had made the right decision on dropping his foreign language degree so he accepted the invitation.

During a session, Anthony handed John a crazy flute part, with lots of high and low notes and wild combinations of ninths, elevenths, and so forth. Later on, Anthony admitted it was a joke, and gave John the real part.

What really struck John about *Voyage*, probably more than any later album of Steve, was its classical influence mixed with rock, unusual at the time, in addition to the way Steve used the twelve-string guitar, which produced a sound much like a harpsichord.

John and Steve used to listen to the music of the Italian composer Giuseppe Domenico Scarlatti (1685-1757). Steve had an album of Scarlatti's Harpsichord Sonatas, played by John Beckett on the flute, and which contained remarkable performances. John believes this recording influenced Steve's twelve-string guitar tone.

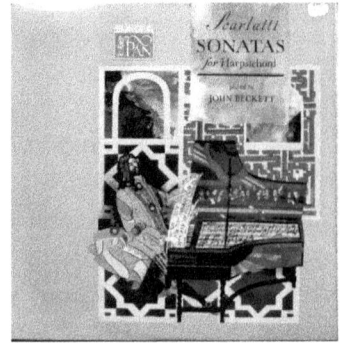

Acolyte is an amazing album for someone who was 25 at the time with no musical training, with all the beautiful unusual harmony and interesting modulations. The quality of his writing is unusual and created completely by ear. A truly gifted musician (…).

Everyone can improve but he is definitely a natural talent. It's amazing how the classical passages go into rock very smoothly which is very difficult to do. The sound of the album is transparent because of the way it was arranged.

John Hackett

Part of the creative process on *Voyage of the Acolyte* was the use of a stereo reel-to-reel tape recorder - which helped with the double tracking, echo effects, and the experimentation on guitar parts such as in *Ace of Wands*, in addition to the harmony part of *The Hermit*, and the backward effect used in *The Lovers*.

Photo 11: Paulo De Carvalho (left) and John Hackett (right), in John's home in Sheffield, England, October, 2017.

Steve composed the first part of the riff for *The Tower* on the guitar. John wrote the middle riff, which Steve then extended. The oboe part of *The Hermit* was a melody which John and Steve had previously played together for Peter Gabriel and Tony Banks at the Hackett's flat during Steve's audition to enter Genesis.

Hands Part I was recorded by Steve and John Hackett on the first night at Kingsway, and *it was great* - John commented. For John, the quality of the recording was not like anything he had ever done before. *Hands' melody is not obvious, but it is beautiful* - John added. John and Steve still perform together this song in concerts. John has also recorded it with Italian organist Marco Lo Muscio of *Playing the History*. The piece still sounded fresh.

The flute in the opening track *Ace of Wands* was recorded in half time then sped up to sound like a piccolo. John never used this effect again.

On *Voyage* John used two flutes. One was an Armstrong, an open hole model with in line G French style not offset, so that all the keys are in a straight line, meaning the third finger, left hand, has to stretch a little further. It was an ordinary silver-plated student model, which John used on *Priestess I* and *II*. For the other songs, John used a Yamaha that was also silver-plated, model YFL 21S, and which is a very popular, standard, student flute.

John is very proud of how he played the counter melody in *Shadow*. In this song he created a guide before the singing, then an overdub. What stayed with him was that anything was possible. He also remembers occasionally hearing tube trains rumbling in the distance as the studio was in the basement of Aviation House, near Holborn station.

In addition, on *Voyage*, John wrote some of the music for Nigel Warren-Green to play the cello, and Robin Miller to play the oboe and the cor anglais. Robin Miller played *Star of Sirius* accurately, despite the fact that, for not knowing that the cor anglais was a transposing instrument, John had written it in a key for non-transposing instruments such as the flute.

Photo 13:Yamaha YFL 21S

Photo 12: Armstrong Open Hole Flute

Some months later after *Voyage* was finished, John began studying music at Sheffield University, where he stayed from 1975 to 1978. During his last year, Steve and him were recording Steve's second solo album *Please Don't Touch*, which meant frequent trips to London. John worked very closely with Steve both on *Voyage of the Acolyte* and on *Please Don't Touch*. After John left the university, he continued his flute studies with Paul Chapman and later on with Edward Beckett and David Butt, the lead flute player of the BBC Symphony Orchestra.

When Steve left Genesis to form his own band and go on the road, he asked John if he wanted to join him, which John happily accepted. Having finished the University in the summer allowed John to play with Steve in their first gig in Oslo in October 1978. John mentioned that playing some of the songs live for the first time was a fantastic experience. He played flute, guitar, and bass pedals (using his hands), but did not sing in those days.

Pete Cornish helped John to change the on/off of the Roland Space Echo to immediately cut the sound when John played live, and suggested that John used a bass amp as monitor live on stage.

For recording purposes, John has never liked to have the mic too close to the flute, choosing to hear the ambience of the instrument, not just the attack. Nowadays he is using a Shure SM58 because he sings as well.

It was a wonderfully creative period and so much good music came from that experience.

John Hackett

MEETING WITH SALLY OLDFIELD

Sally Oldfield was born in Dublin, Ireland. At the age of four she began studying ballet, having winning competitions in different dance styles. Later on she studied classical piano and became friends with singer Marianne Faithful in school.

As a singer and a guitar player, she founded the duo The Sallyangie, with her brother Mike Oldfield, who was also on the vocals and the guitar, having recorded together the album *Children of the Sun* in August 1968.

In 1973 she was part of the Girlie Chorus, who participated in the album *Tubular Bells* by her brother. Later she added more vocals in Mike's future albums such as *Hergest Ridge*, *Ommadawn*, and *Incantations*.

Steve Hackett heard Sally singing in The Sallyangie duo and eventually met her at Mike's Gloucestershire's home during the 70's, when Mike was working on his *Ommadawn*. Mike had just completed his home studio and during that period he met Steve.

Sally was living nearby Mike at that time, and she often visited him. That was how she happened to meet Steve.

In 1975 Steve asked Sally to sing on *Shadow of the Hierophant* and gave her a demo cassette of the song along with the lyric sheet. She rehearsed it on her own, singing along with a piano, until she knew it by heart.

I was working on some sessions for Mike Oldfield at the time, so sometimes I would rehearse Steve's song on the lovely Kawai piano in Mike's house.

Sally Oldfield

When Sally and Steve met for the recording session, Steve gave her some directions on how he felt the part should be sung.

The song has a deep spiritual element which is important to me in my own music, so I felt a close affinity with it. The lyrics are beautiful and echo the Romantic Poets of the eighteenth century, which was the period of literature I studied at school and at the University such as Keats, Shelley and Coleridge. These poets often wrote of beauty amidst pain and suffering and "Shadow of the Hierophant" deals with a similar theme.

Tears fill the fountains breaking their promise to heal,
Rippling the waters mirror an ended ideal
(From *Shadow of the Hierophant*)

I felt it was an honor to be asked to sing on an album that was to become an iconic one for the golden era of Progressive Rock Music and I felt inspired by the experience. I never got the chance to sing this song again - but I guess it might have been a nice idea to have included it on one of my concert tours.

Sally Oldfield

In 1978 Sally released her album *Water Bearer*, whose song "Mirrors" reached number 12 in the U.K. In total she has released 15 solo albums so far.

MEETING WITH PETE CORNISH

One of the most important people in the rock industry, pedalboard builder Pete Cornish have a huge list of clients such as: Genesis, Paul McCartney, Queen, Pink Floyd, King Crimson, Pete Banks (Yes), Camel, Black Sabbath, Dire Straits, Asia, Moody Blues, Eric Clapton, Marillion, ELP, John McLaughlin, Jimmy Page, The Who, Carlos Santana, Paul Simon, Metallica, and The Police.

According to Cornish's notes, the first pedalboard that he built for Steve Hackett was delivered on August 13th, 1973, and the second was built on October 25th, 1973. As far as he remembers they were both the same and them ordered by Steve Hackett's tech, David Jacobson.

The routing order was: GTR>Colorsound Octivider>Marshall Supa Fuzz>Shaftesbury Duo Fuzz>Cry Baby>Pete Cornish Preamp (NB-3 preset to +10dB)>Schaller F121 Volume pedal>Echo Send/Return>Single output to amp.

The size of the pedalboard was 44 x 18 inches, and it was the first totally powered main system featuring stabilized +9vdc, and also stabilized -9vdc supplies for the effects. There were three extra footswitches: master effects bypass, Echo S/R bypass and Duo Fuzz Tone. Each pedal on it had its own bypass footswitch and there was no LED or any other light indicator for the effects - just a main "power on" neon indicator. The *AC Power in* was on a *Bulgin 3* pin plug as used on HiWatt Amps. The input voltage was fixed at 240 vac.

Pete Cornish is nowadays selling the buffered NB-3. The difference between his current NB-3, is that it has now variable gain 0 ~ +30dB, in contrast to its earlier version built specially for Steve , in which had fixed gain at +10dB. Pete included this preamp to compensate for the losses in the circuit.

In later pedalboards he added a separate variable gain preamp to each effect so that he could compensate for individual pedal losses rather than an overall boost.

Photo 14: Peter Cornish (right) showing Paulo De Carvalho, in his office in Northern England, the signal path of Steve's pedalboards, September, 2016

Pedal Board built by Pete Cornish

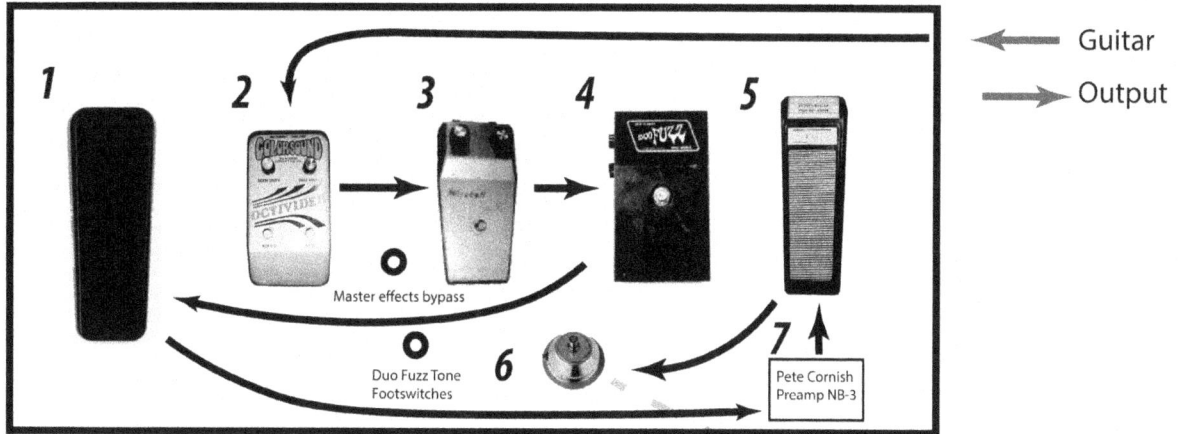

Guitar
Output

Master effects bypass

Duo Fuzz Tone
Footswitches

Pete Cornish
Preamp NB-3

1 - Cry Baby Wah-Wah
2 - Colorsound Octivider
3 - Marshall Supa Fuzz
4 - Shaftesbury Duo Fuzz
5 - Schaller Volume Pedal F121
6 -Pedal Switch for Echoplex EP-3
7 - Pream NB-3
8 - Echoplex EP-3 Tape Echo

Signal Routing:

Gtr1 → Octivider → Supa Fuzz → Duo Fuzz → Cry Baby → (Preamp) Peter Cornish NB-3 → Schaller F121 Volume Pedal → Echo Send/Return (Echoplex EP-3 → Output

STEVE'S GUITARS

Gibson Les Paul Gold Top

It was my favorite choice of electric guitar for album. I played it live many times with Genesis. I still have it to this day. It has a beautiful tone and a superb action.

Steve Hackett

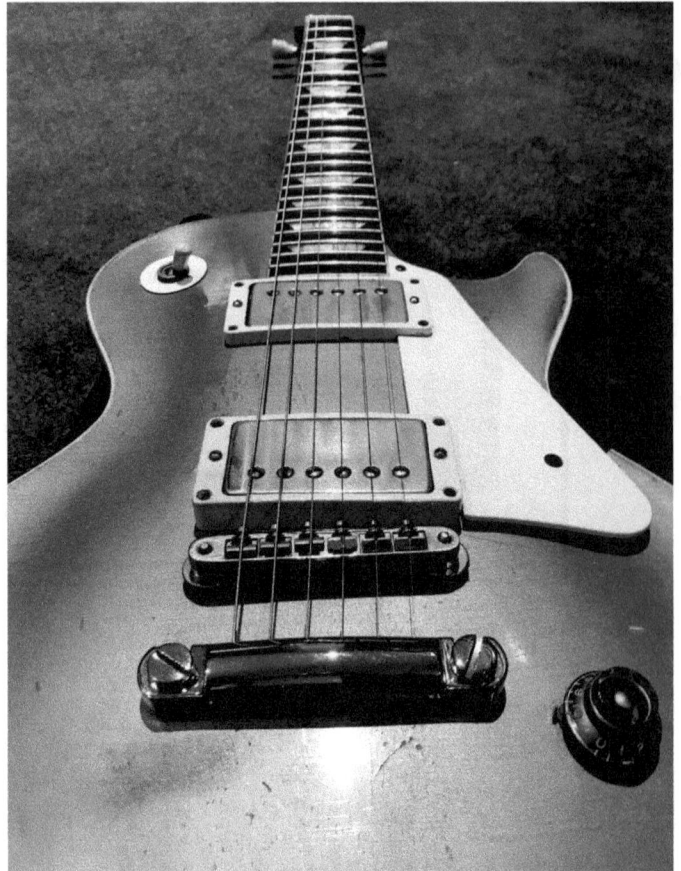

Photos 15 & 16:
Steve Hackett's original 1957 Gibson Les Paul Gold Top
Photos by Paulo De Carvalho, 2017

Yairi Nylon

When I bought this, it was the loudest classical guitar I had ever heard. It sounded almost more like a piano. Hardly a day goes past without me still playing this wonderful guitar.

Steve Hackett

Photos 17 & 18: Steve Hackett's original Yairi Nylon
Photos by Paulo De Carvalho, 2017

25

Zermaitis Custom 12-String

On this album I borrowed Mike Rutherford's Zemaitis, whilst my own one was still being constructed by Tony Zemaitis who made these beautiful 12-string for many famous people including George Harrison, Bob Dylan and Greg Lake. The one I have has the best tone of any I have ever played. It has a lovely glassy ringing quality.

Steve Hackett

Photos 19-22: Steve Hackett's original Zermaitis Custom 12 String
Photos by Paulo De Carvalho, 2017

VOYAGE OF THE ACOLYTE

ACE OF WANDS

The first track of *Voyage of the Acolyte* was actually the second song recorded for the album, and the first time that Phil Collins and Mike Rutherford went to a studio under Steve's guidance.

For the song *Ace of Wands* Steve used his Gibson Les Paul guitar, H&H overdriven amp - melody played in octaves; a Fender Champ with Echoplex; Coloursound Fuzz box and Shaftesbury Duo Fuzz - both connected in sequence, in addition to a Yamaha acoustic guitar recorded at half speed and reversed with repeat echo. For the final phrases he used an MXR Phase 90.

I was using Sound City strings, standard set starting 011 on the top and using a small Fender pick. I was using an H&H amp, but also a Fender Champ.

Steve Hackett

Steve explained why he chose the Tarot card "Ace of Wands":

The card means the beginning of a new venture/project, which for me was this solo album – my first one. The mixture of genres on the first track links in with the world of possibilities inherent in that card. The process of seeing a new album unfolding for the first time was incredibly exciting. I marveled at little ideas could become wonderfully developed and magical.

Steve also wrote the bass line. Later on, Tony Banks, Genesis' keyboard player, praised Steve on that matter, as he was not aware that Steve could create such a bass line.

Players/Instruments:

Steve Hackett: Gibson Les Paul Gold Top 1957, Zemaitis Custom 12-string, Steel 6-string Yamaha acoustic, Mellotron

John Hackett: Flute Yamaha YFL 21S, Arp Odyssey (Monophonic Synth), Tubular bells

John Acock: Elka-Rhapsody Synth, Mellotron

Mike Rutherford: Bass

Phil Collins: Drums, Percussion

Studio Gears : Ace of Wands - Voyage of the Acolyte

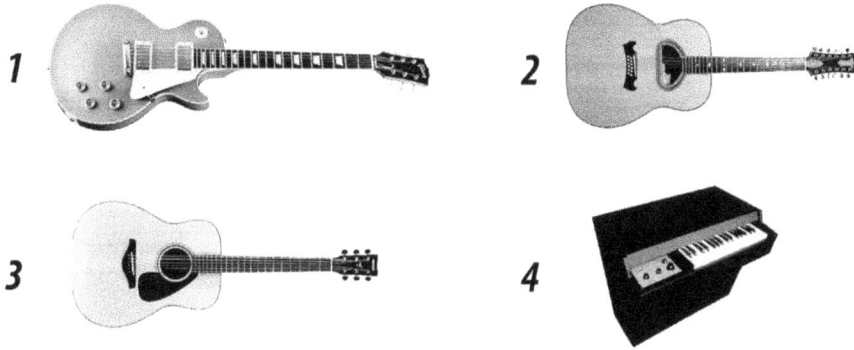

1

2

3

4

Pedal Board built by Pete Cornish

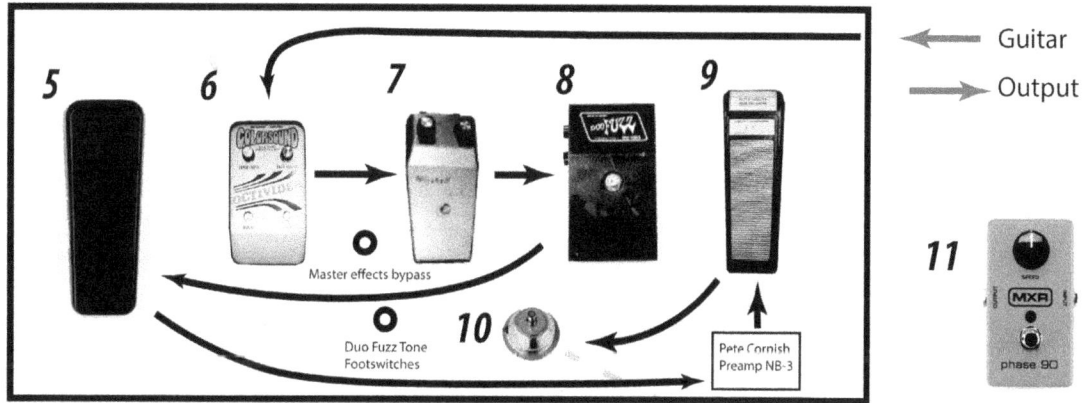

5

6

7

8

9

← Guitar

→ Output

Master effects bypass

Duo Fuzz Tone
Footswitches

10

Pete Cornish
Preamp NB-3

11

1 - Gibson Les Paul Gold Top 1957
2 - Zemaitis Custom 12 String
3 - Steel 6 String Yamaha Acoustic
4 - Mellotron
5 - Cry Baby Wah-Wah
6 - Colorsound Octivider
7 - Marshall Supa Fuzz
8 - Shaftesbury Duo Fuzz
9 - Schaller Volume Pedal F121
10 -Pedal Switch for Echoplex EP-3
11 - MXR Phase 90
12 - Echoplex EP-3 Tape Echo
13 - HH 100w IC100
14 - Hiwatt 150w 4x12 Cabinets SE 4123
15 - Fender Champ
16 - Coloursound Tonebender (Fuzz)

13

14

12

15

16

Signal Routing:

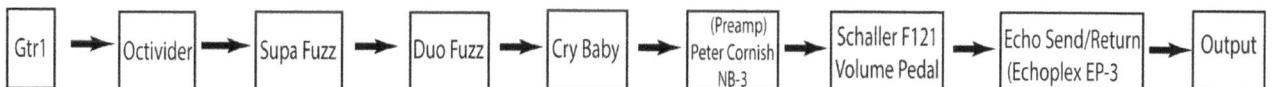

Gtr1 → Octivider → Supa Fuzz → Duo Fuzz → Cry Baby → (Preamp) Peter Cornish NB-3 → Schaller F121 Volume Pedal → Echo Send/Return (Echoplex EP-3 → Output

Photo 23: John Hackett's original manuscripts of Ace of the Wands. Kindly provided by John Hackett.
Photo by Paulo De Carvalho, October 2017.

Photo 24: : John Hackett's original manuscripts of the flute part of Ace of the Wands. Kindly provided by John Hackett.
P.S.: the song was recorded at halftime, then sped up to double time to make it sound like a Piccolo.
Photo by Paulo De Carvalho, October 2017.

Fi

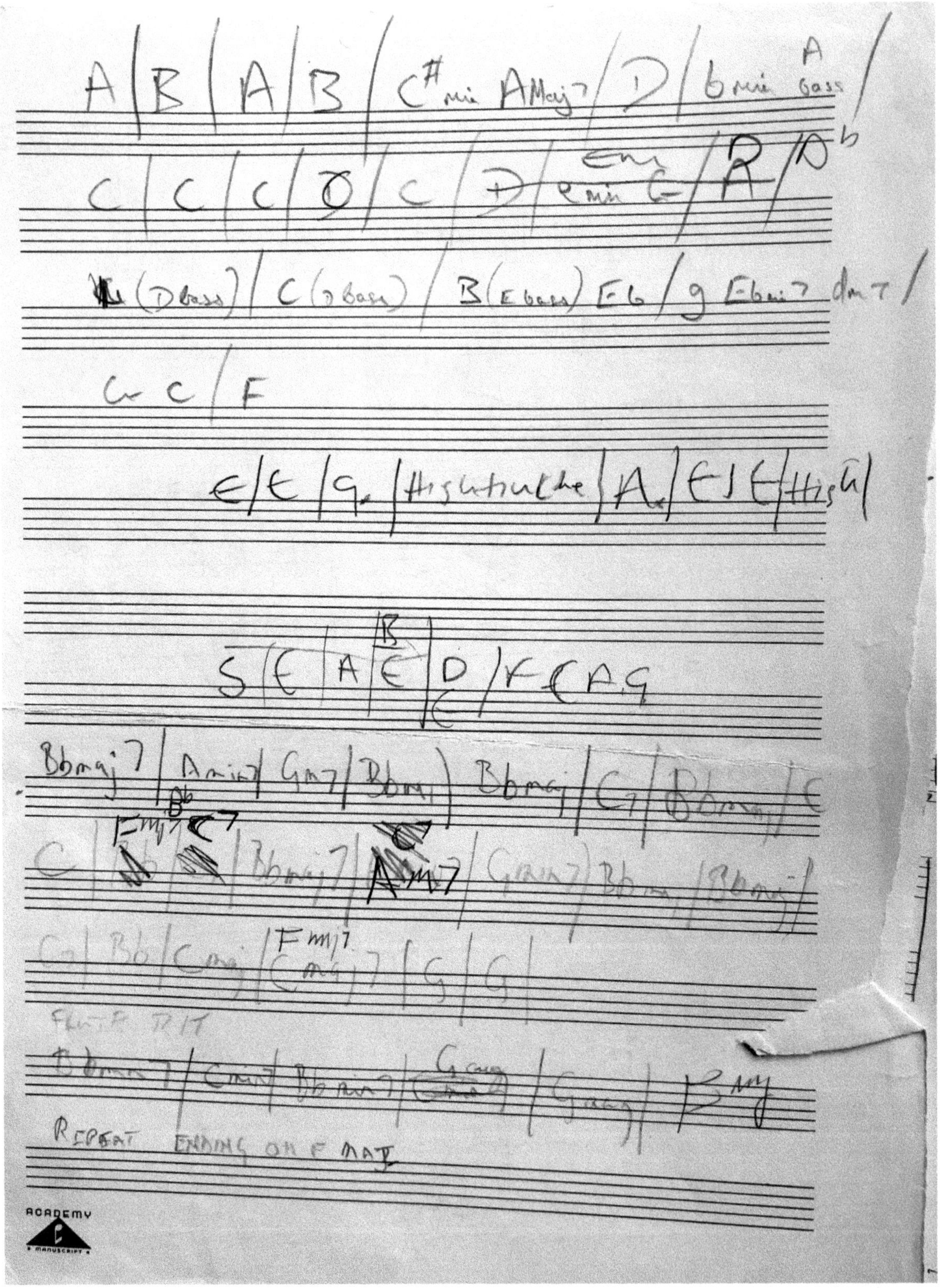

Photo 25: : John Hackett's original manuscripts including the chords of the second part of Ace of the Wands and the second part of Hands of the Priestess Part 2. Kindly provided by John Hackett.

Photo by Paulo de Carvalho, October 2017.

Intro of *Ace of Wands*

Photo 26: Steve showing the beginning of the intro. *Photo by Paulo De Carvalho*

Photo 27: Steve showing the middle part of the intro. *Photo by Paulo De Carvalho*

Photo 28: Steve showing the end of the intro. *Photo by Paulo De Carvalho*

from Steve Hackett - *Voyage of the Acolyte*

Ace of Wands

by Steve Hackett

Transcribed by Paulo De Carvalho

* Gibson Les Paul Golden Top 1957

** Gibson Les Paul Golden Top 1957

*** Zamaitis Custom 12 strings

**** Bass arr. for gtr.

*Chords symbols reflect overall harmony.

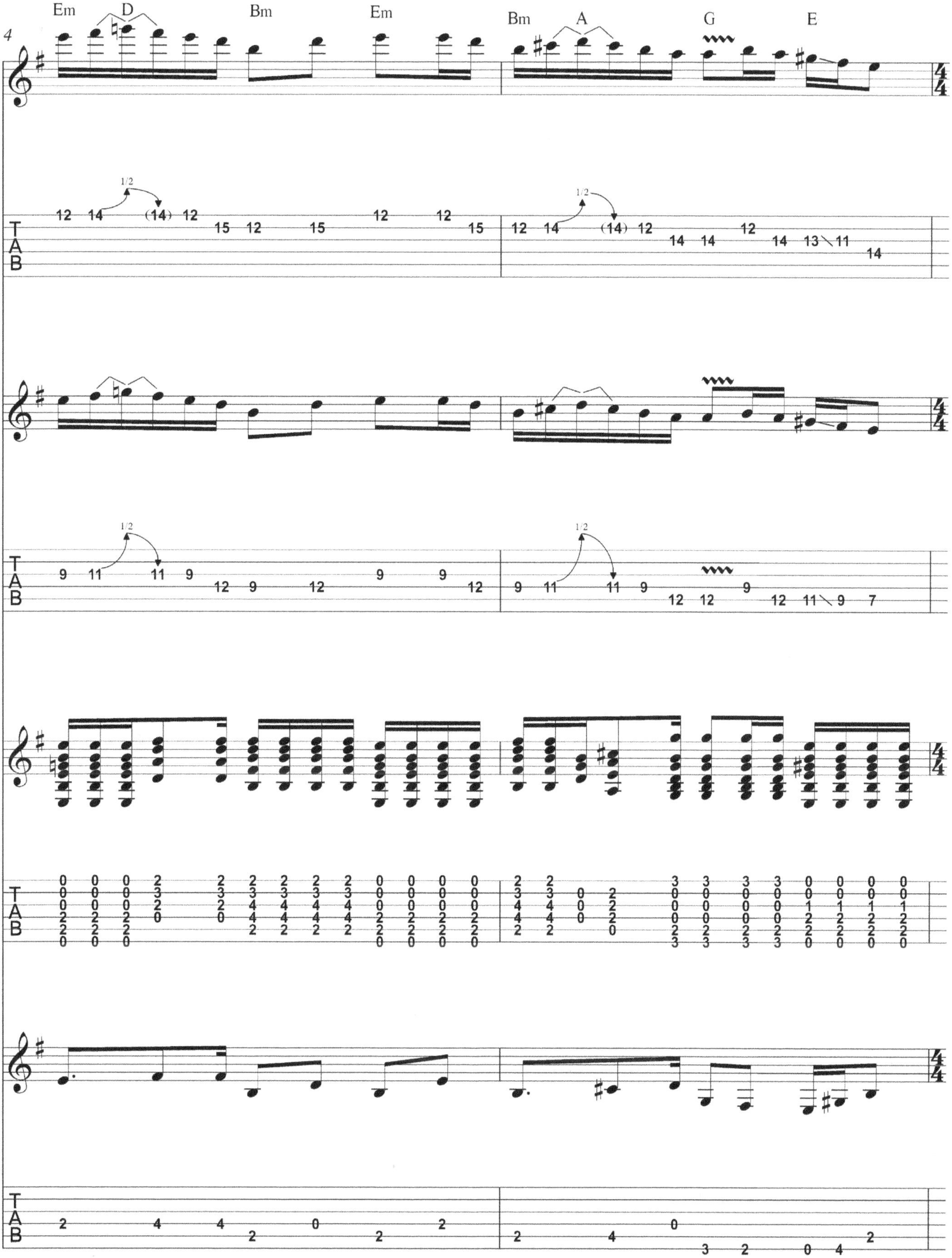
Em
D
Bm
Em
Bm
A
G
E

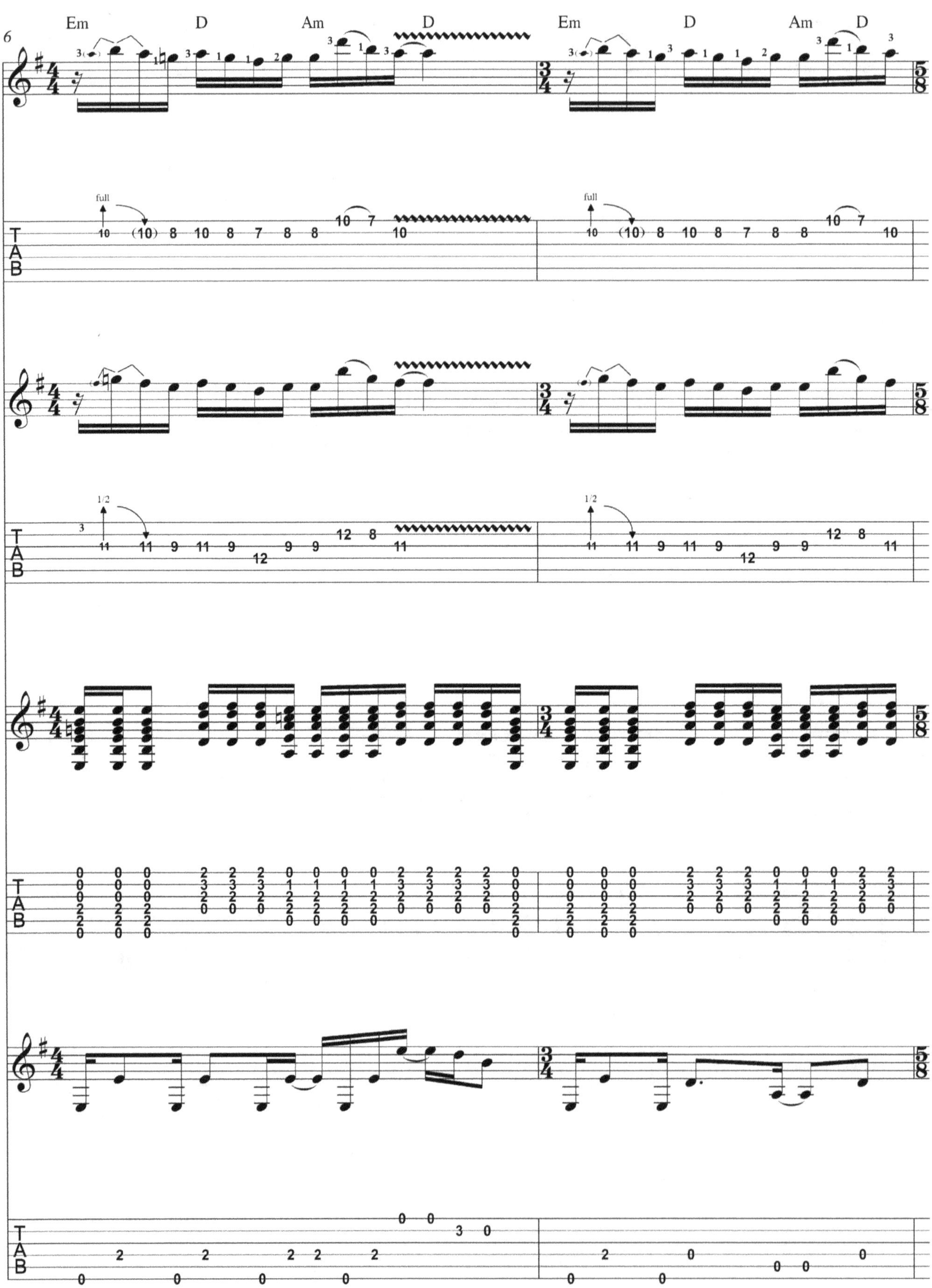
6
Em
D
Am
D
Em
D
Am
D
full
full
1/2
1/2

*Synth Arp Odyssey (John Hacket) arr. for gtr.

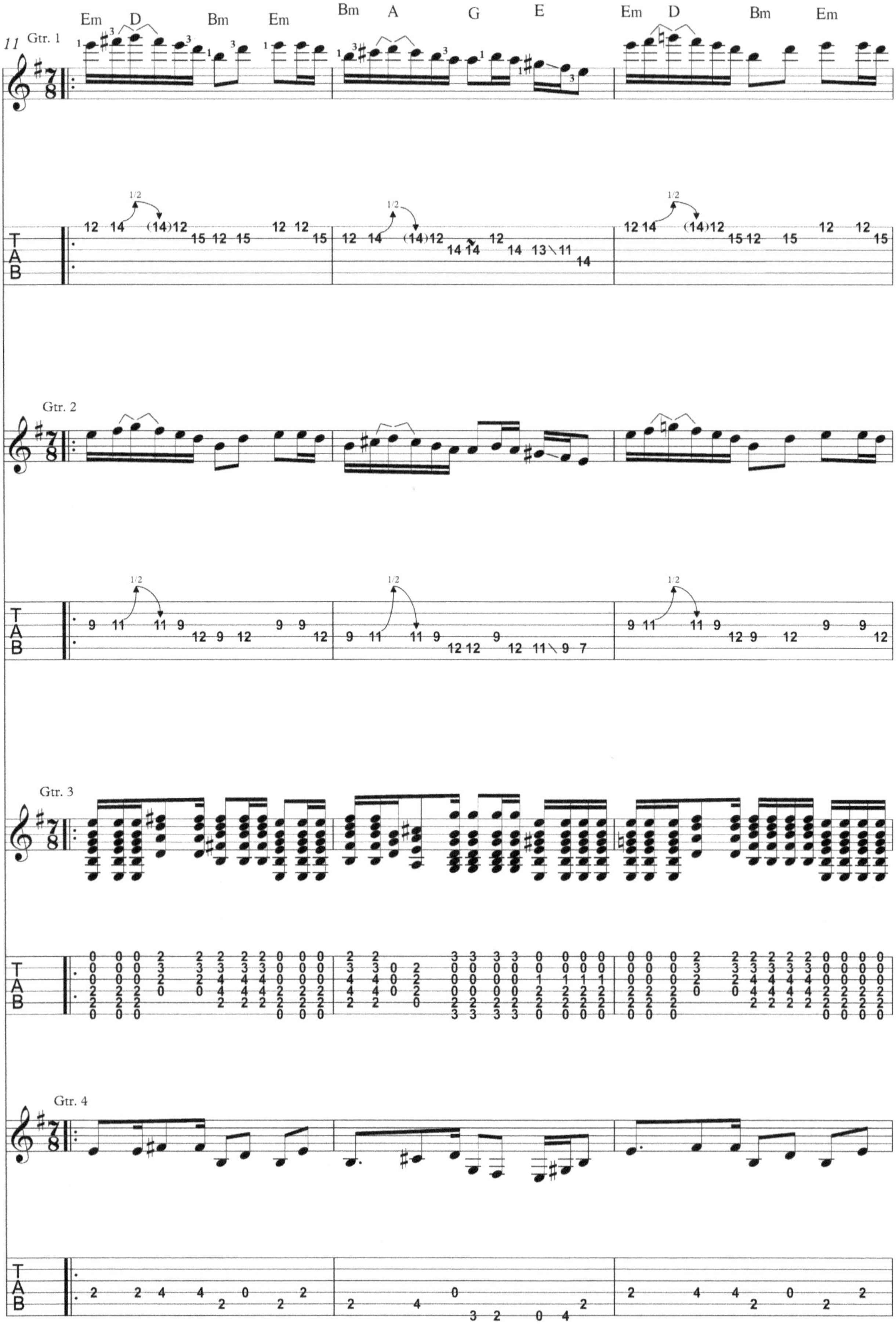
Em D Bm Em Bm A G E Em D Bm Em
11 Gtr. 1
Gtr. 2
Gtr. 3
Gtr. 4

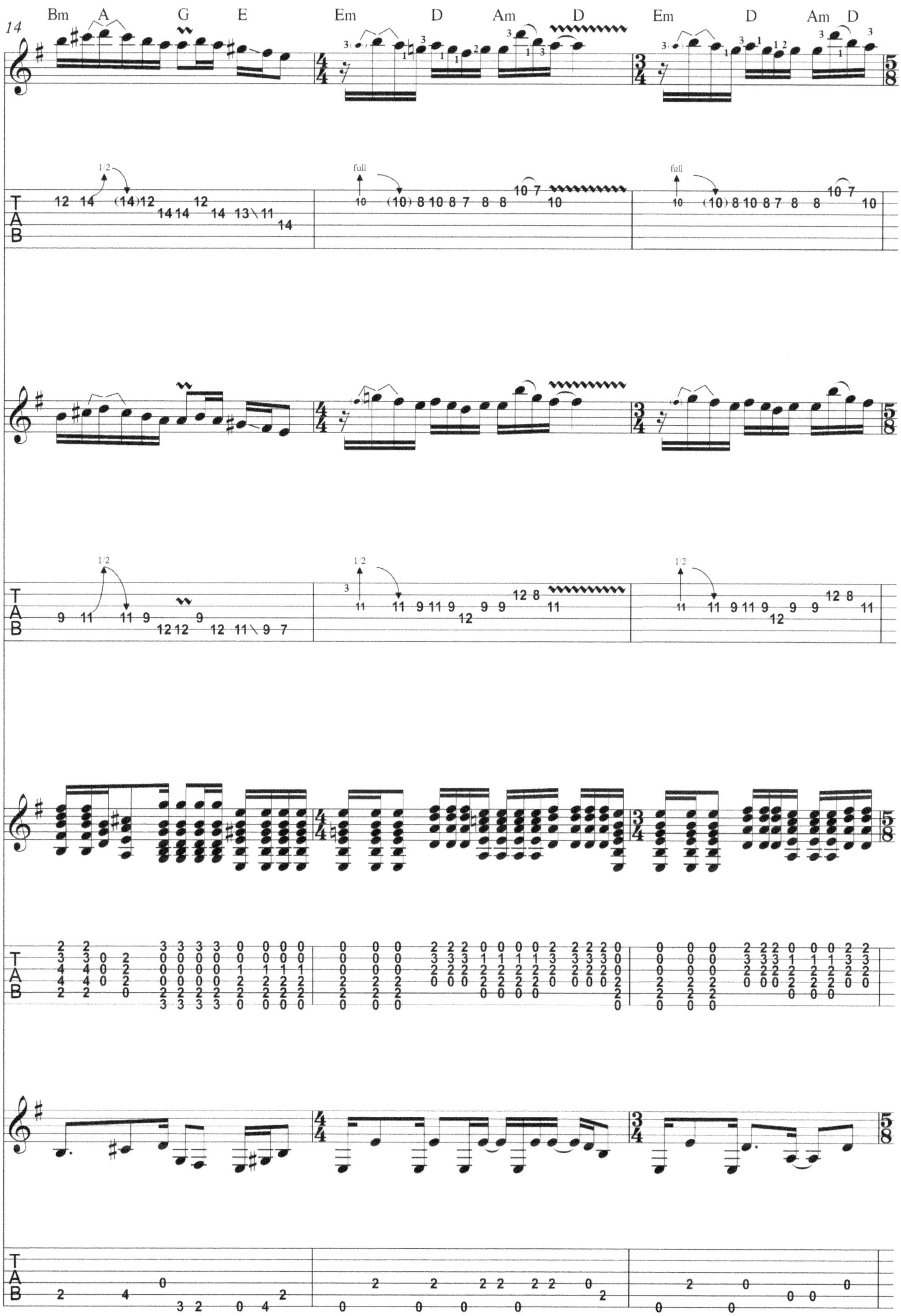
14
Bm A G E
Em D Am D
Em D Am D
1/2
full
full
1/2
1/2
1/2

Em D Bm G Am7(add2) G/B G/C F(add9)
17
Gtr. 5
Gtr. 1
gliss.
Gtr. 2
gliss.
Gtr. 3
Gtr. 4

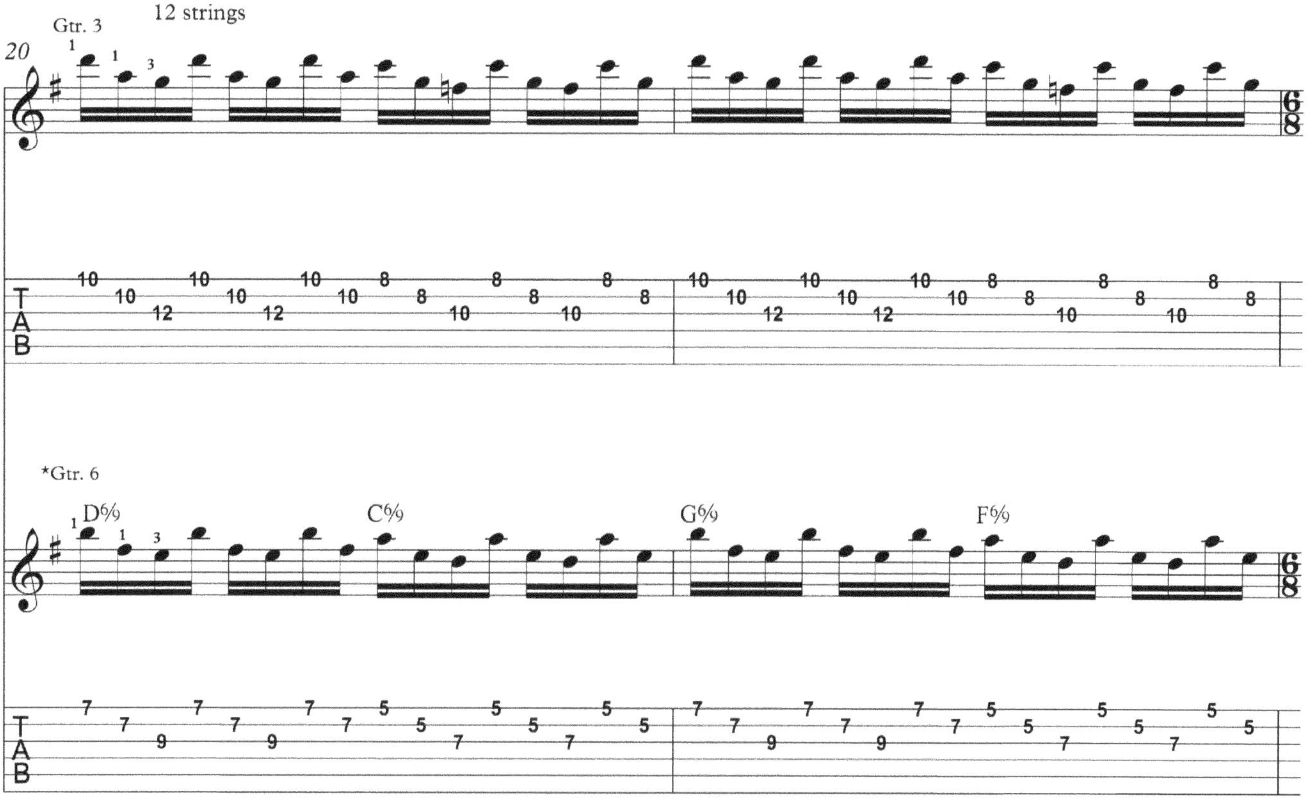

*Zemaitis Custom 12 strings

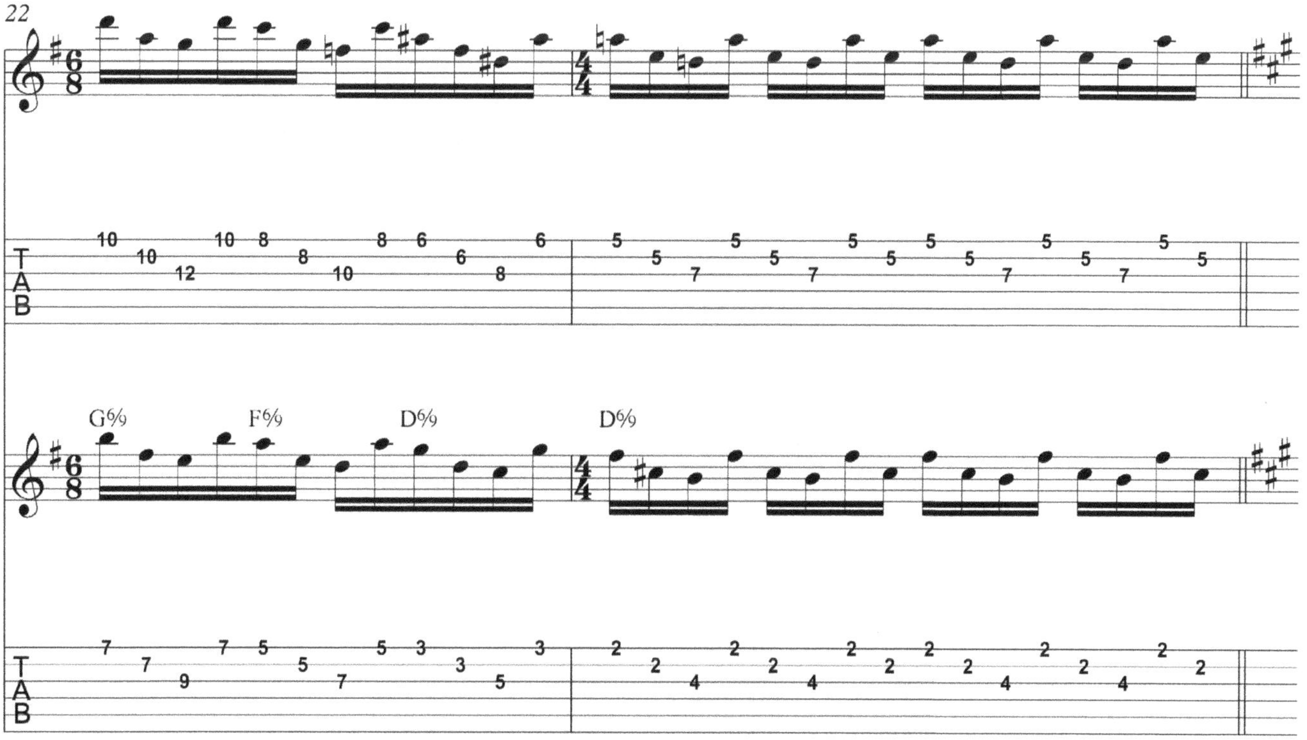

24 *Gtr. 7 A B/A

*Flute Yamaha (John Hackett) arr. for gtr.
Musical Notation for fl. but tab notation transposte for gtr.s (Music note for the guitar is written an octave higher)

*Gtr. 8

*Mellotron (Steve Hackett) arr. for gtr.

25 A B/A

*Tubular Bells(John Hackett) arr. for gtr.

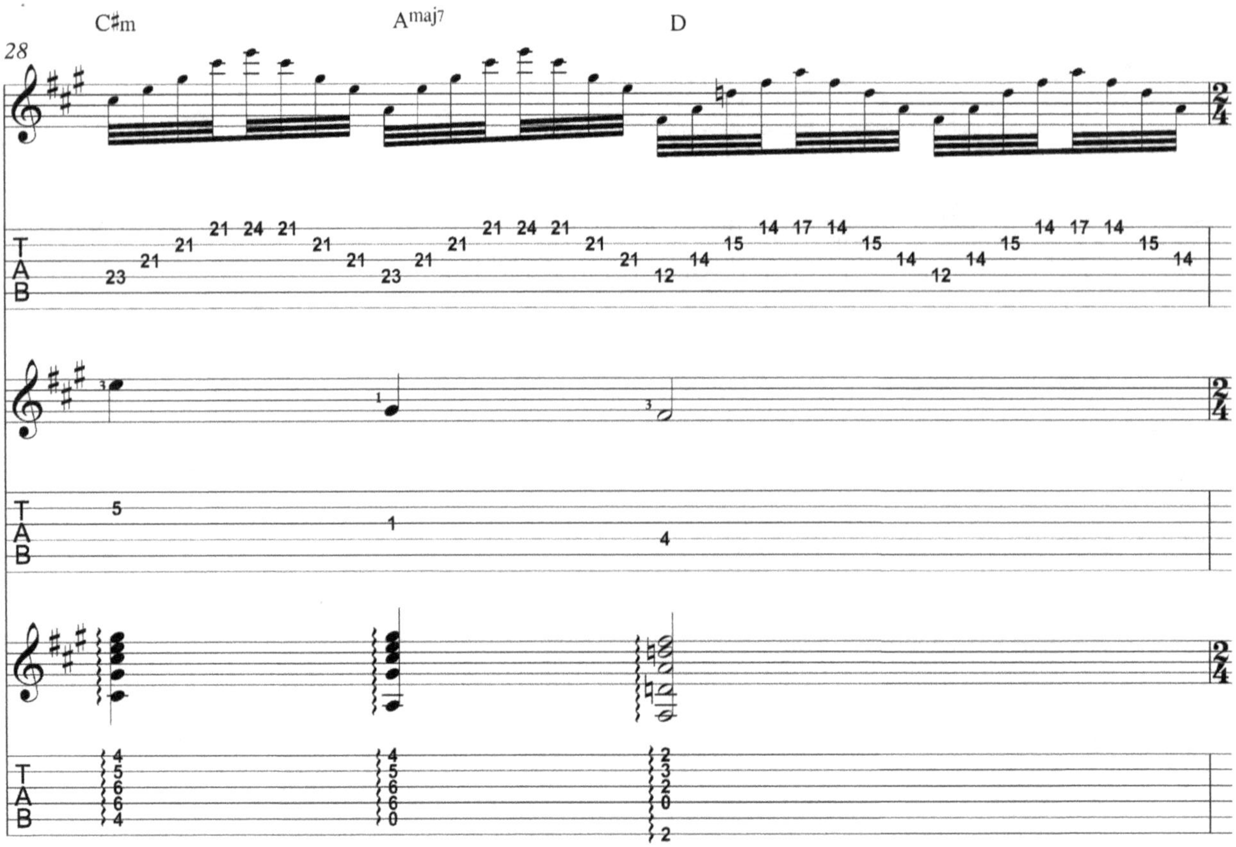
C#m
A maj7
D
28

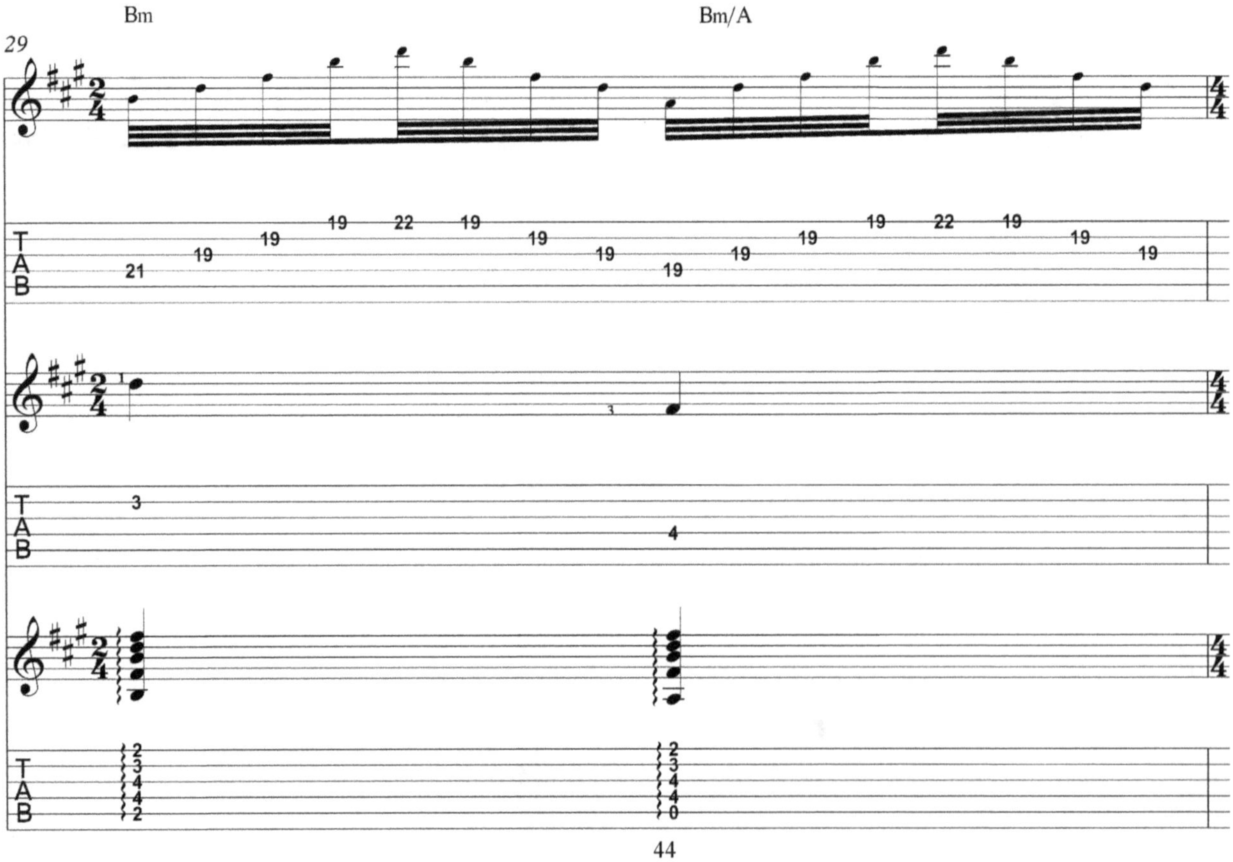
Bm
Bm/A
29

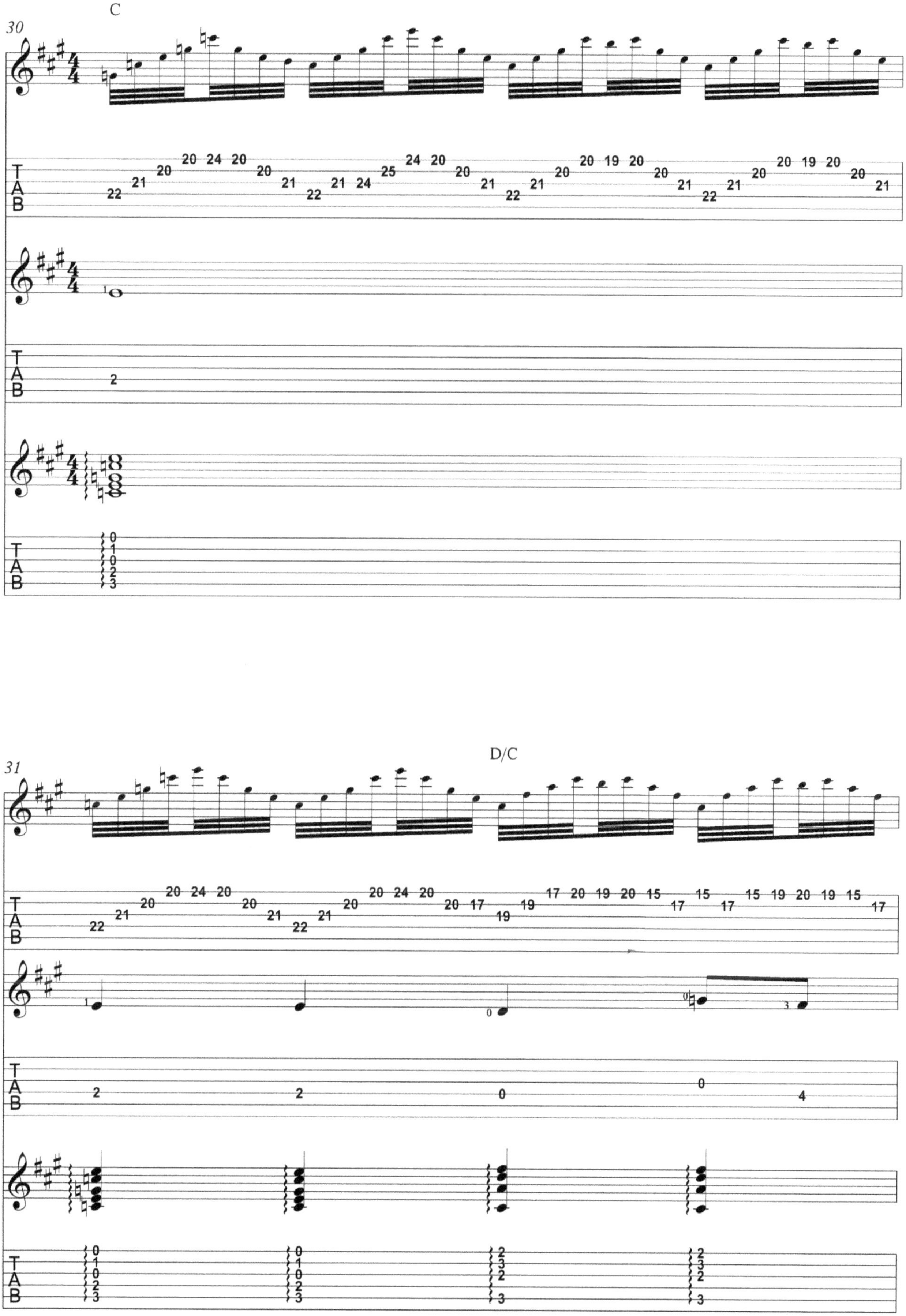
C
30
31
D/C

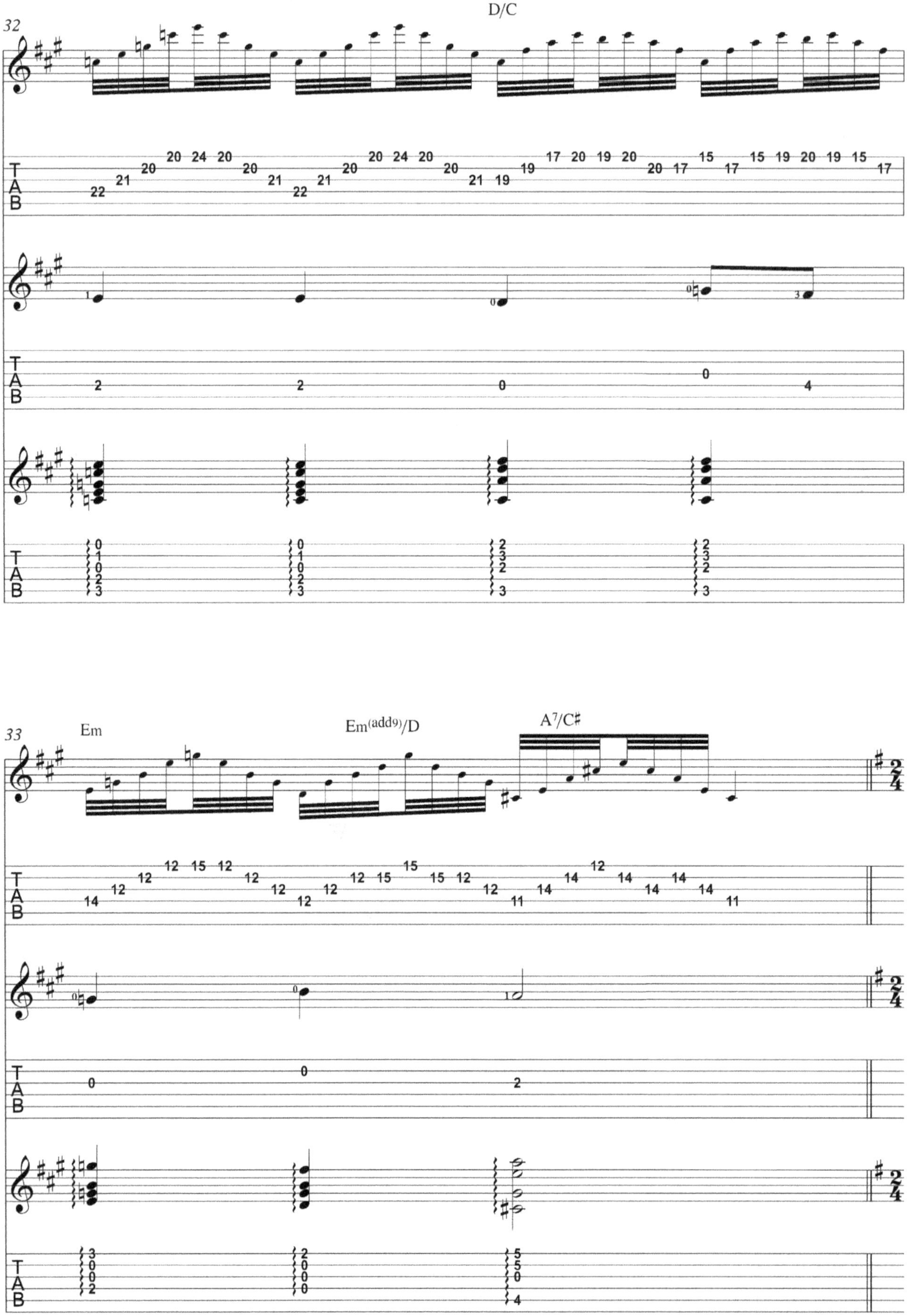
32
D/C
33
Em
Em(add9)/D
A7/C♯

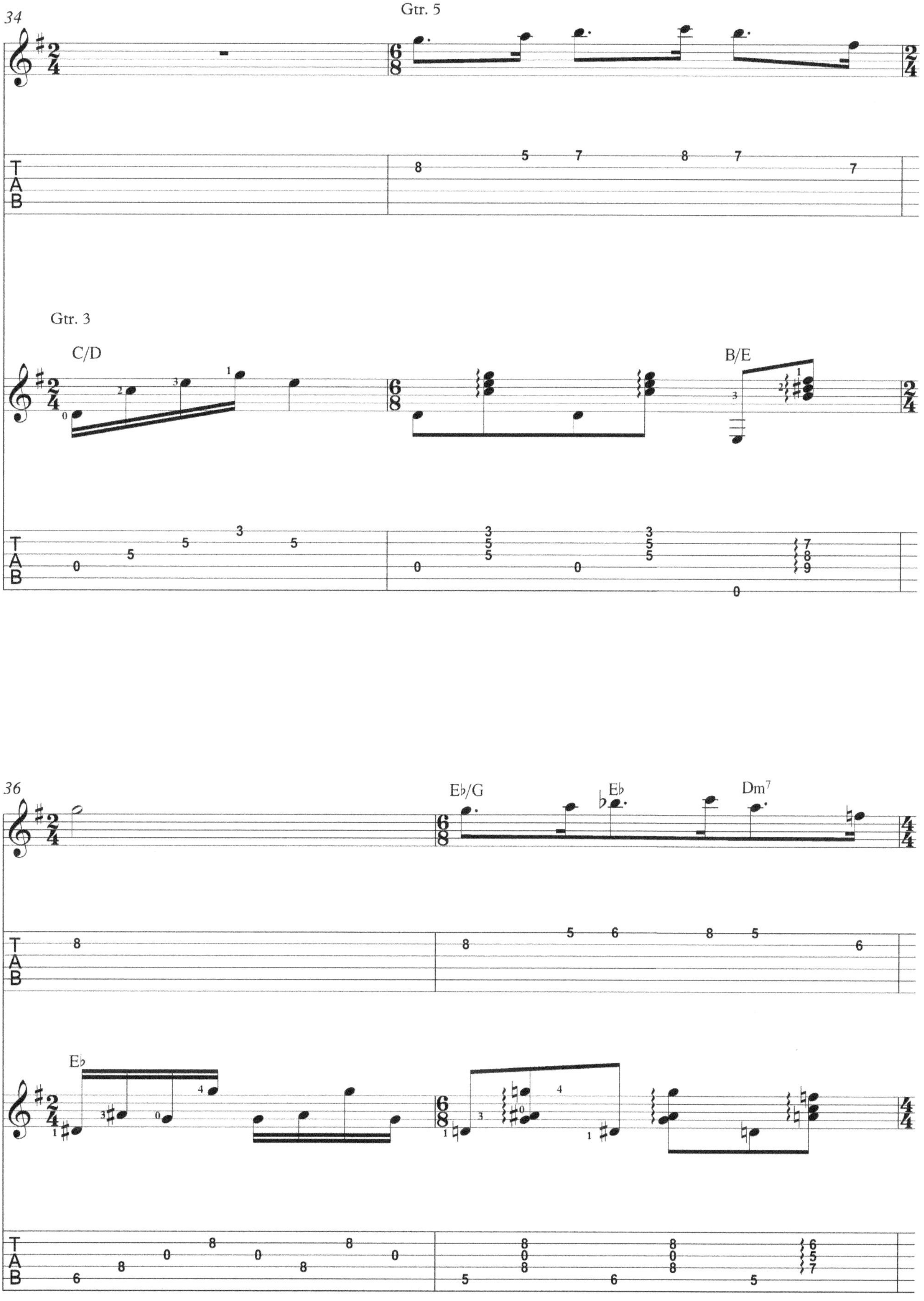
34
Gtr. 5
Gtr. 3
C/D
B/E
36
E♭/G
E♭
Dm7
E♭

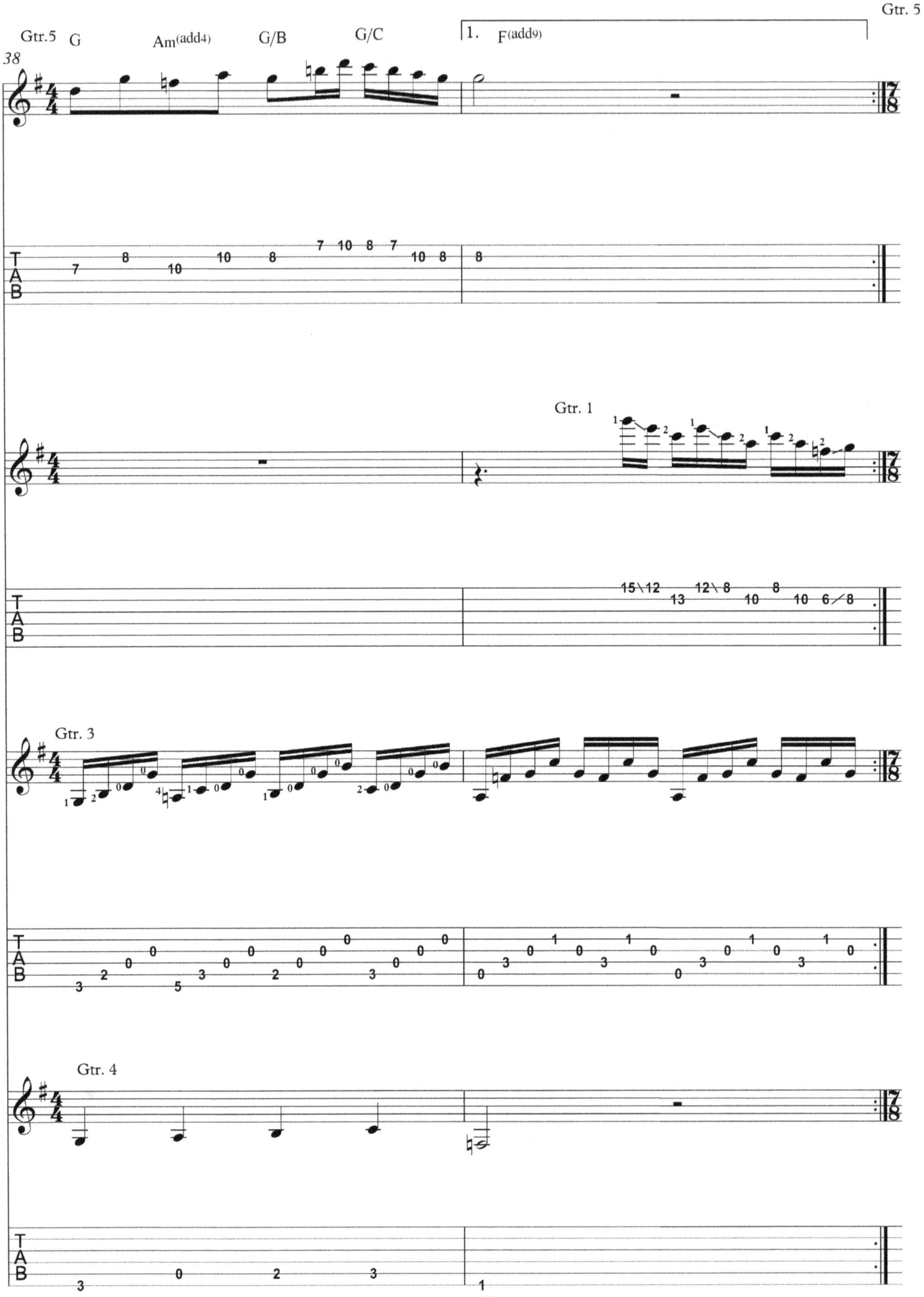
Gtr. 5
Gtr.5
G
Am(add4)
G/B
G/C
1. F(add9)
38
Gtr. 1
Gtr. 3
Gtr. 4

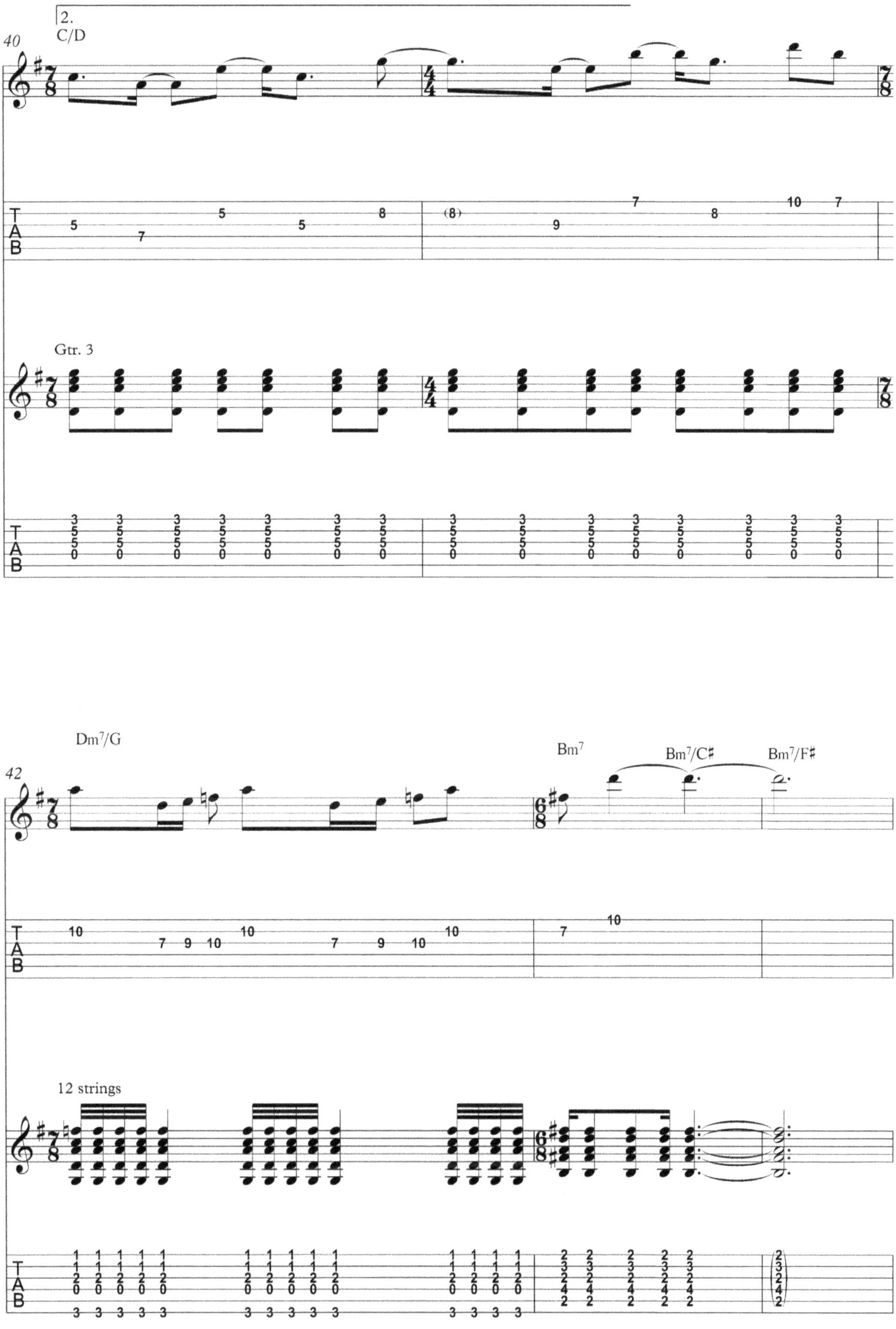
40
2.
C/D
Gtr. 3
42
Dm7/G
Bm7
Bm7/C♯
Bm7/F♯
12 strings

* Steel 6 string Yamaha acoustic

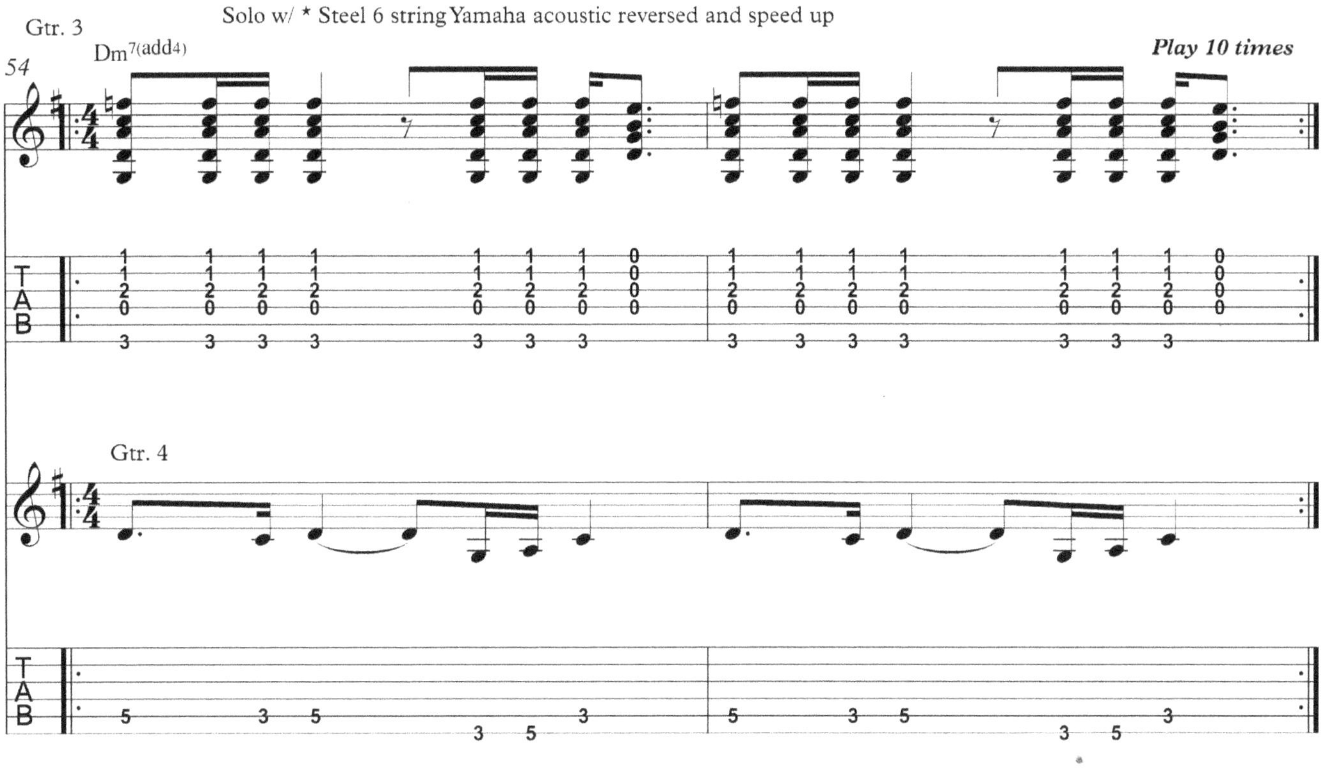
Gtr. 3
Solo w/ * Steel 6 string Yamaha acoustic reversed and speed up
Dm7(add4)
54
Play 10 times
Gtr. 4

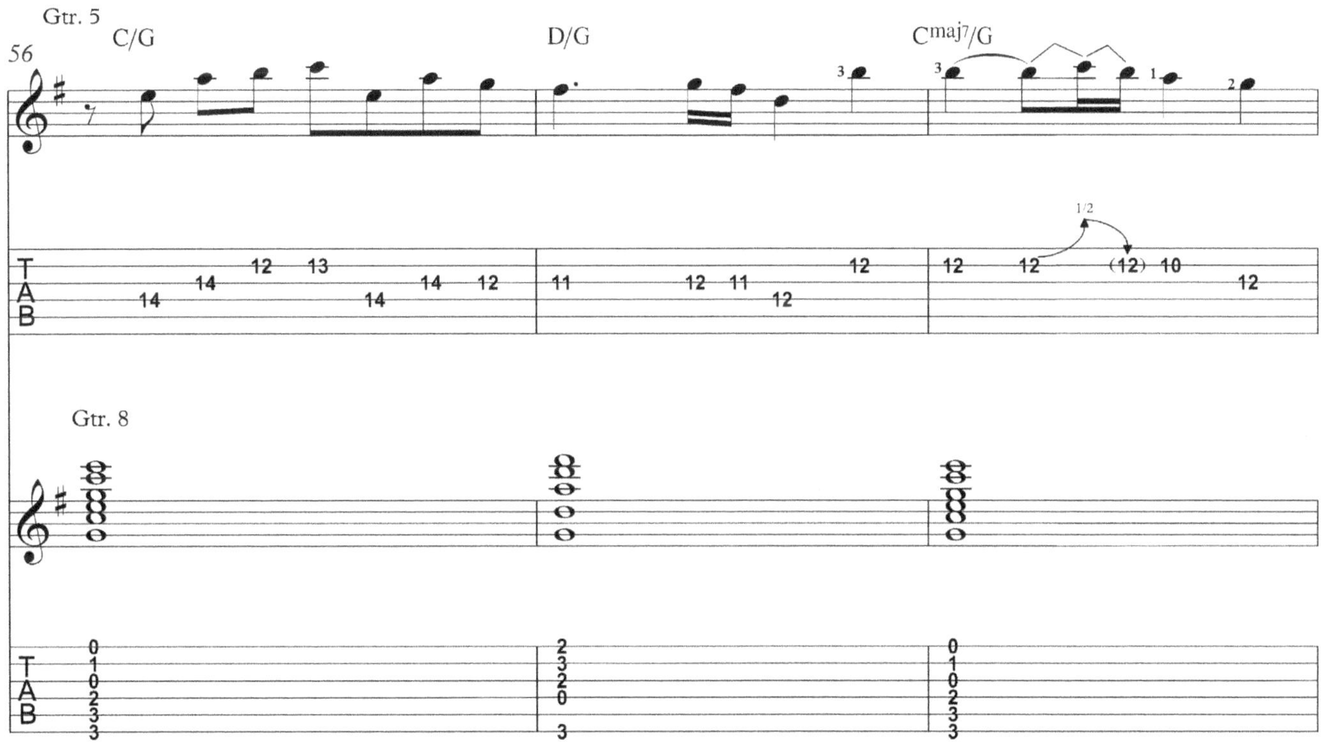
Gtr. 5
C/G
D/G
Cmaj7/G
56
1/2
Gtr. 8

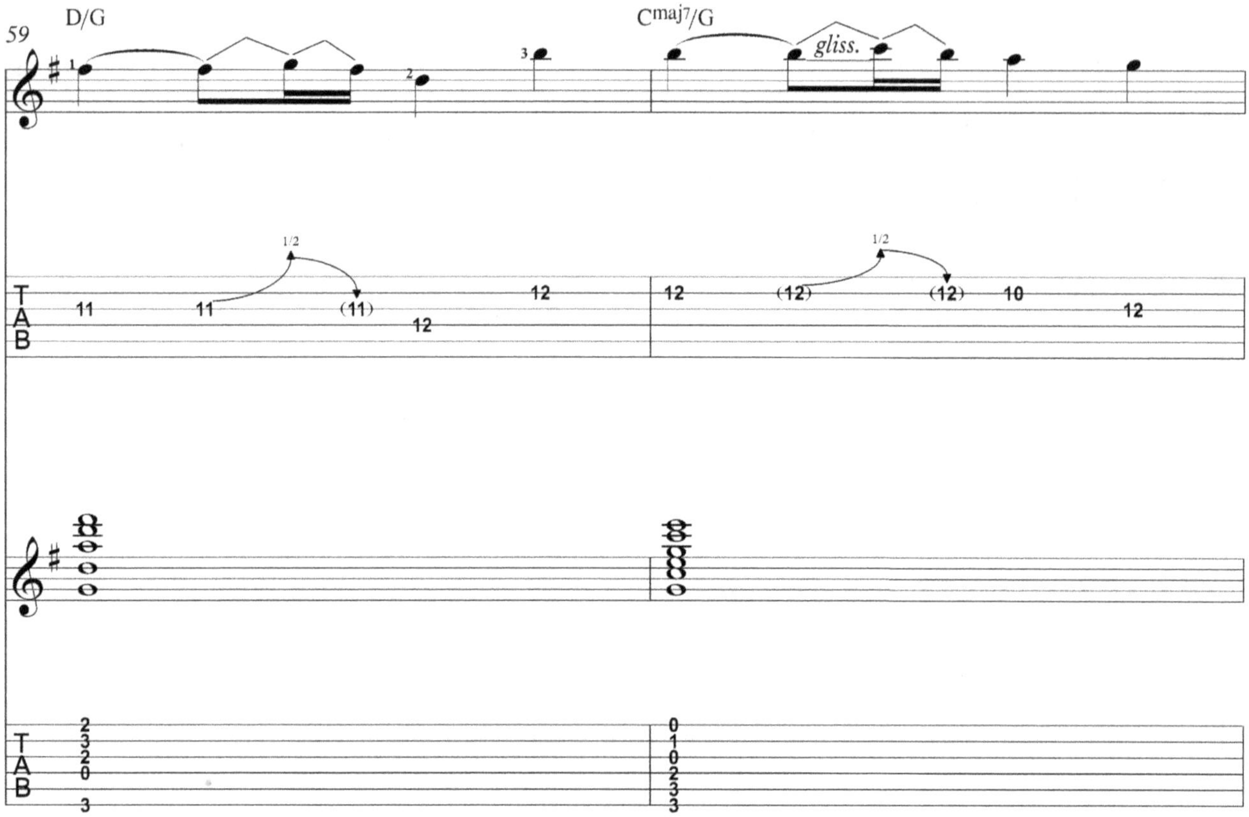
59
D/G
Cmaj7/G
gliss.

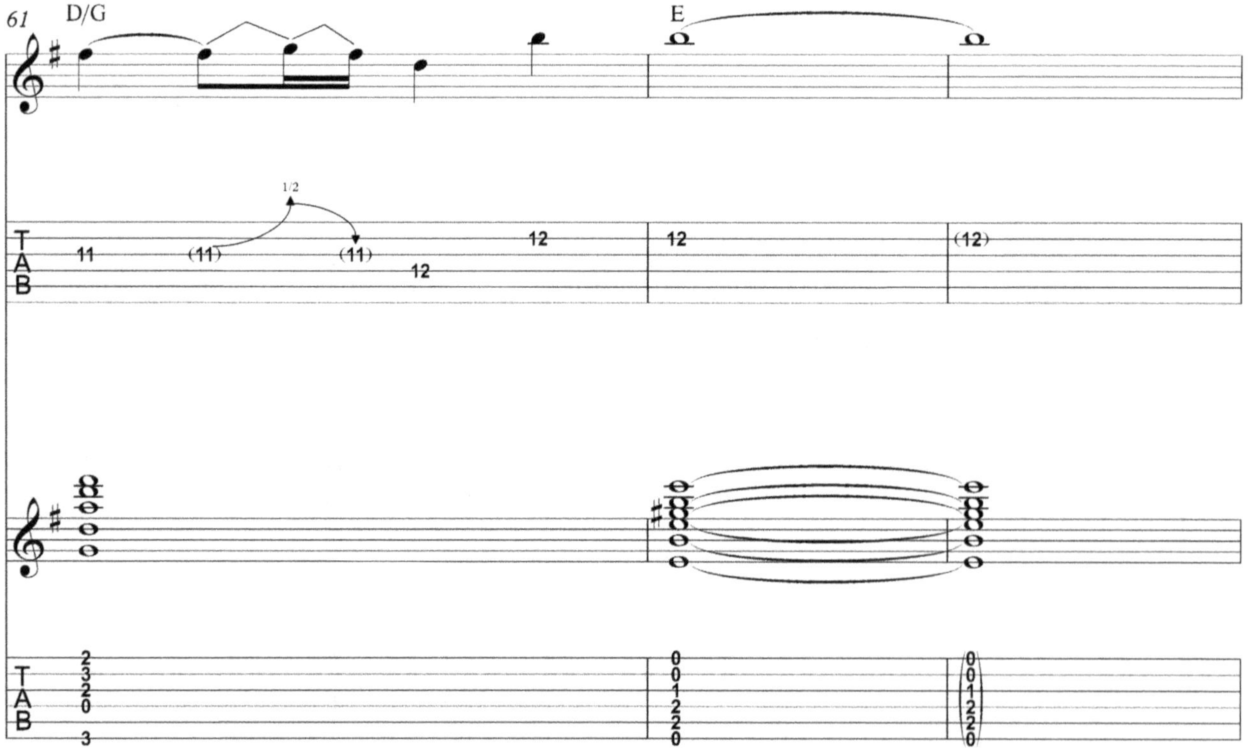
61
D/G
E

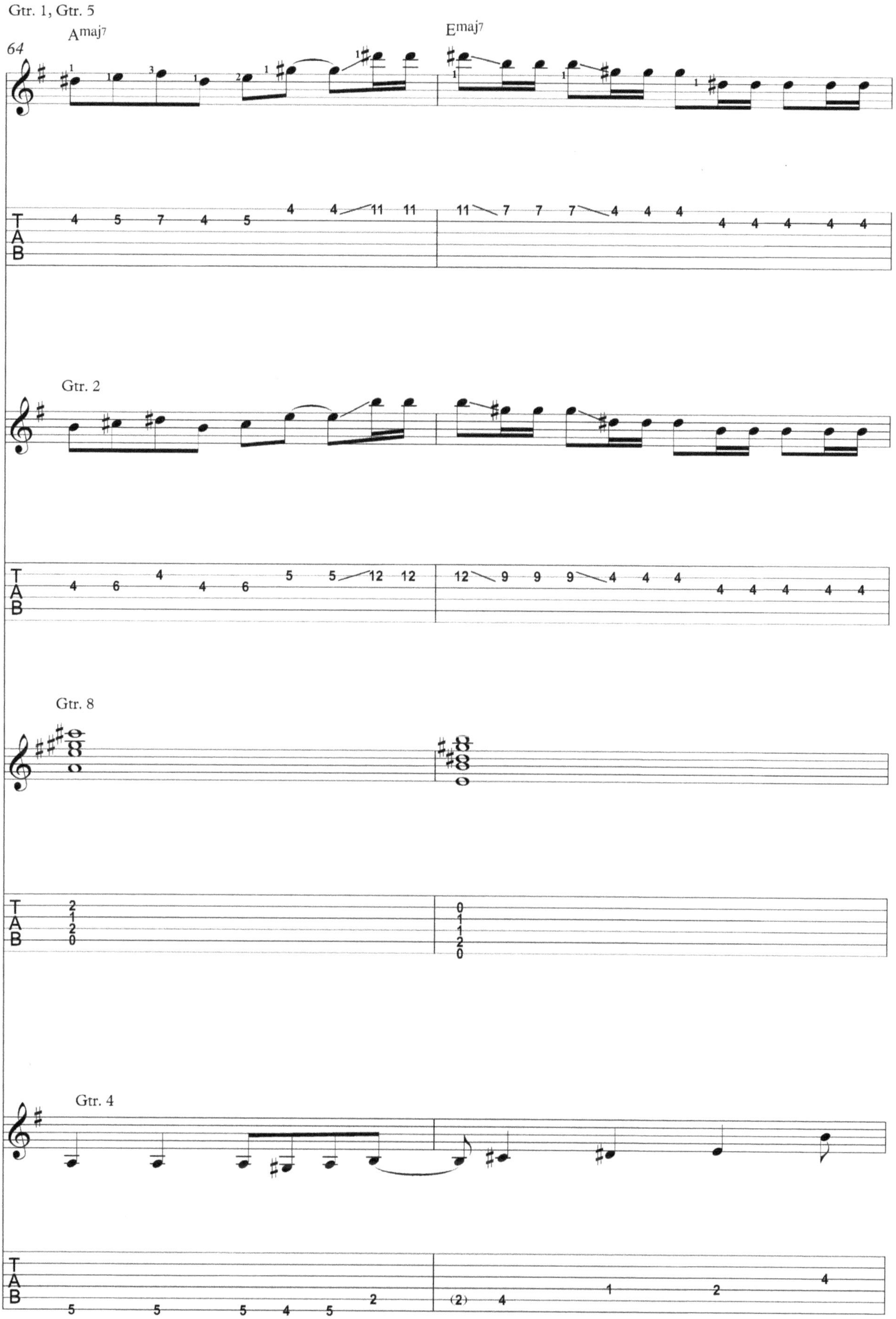
Gtr. 1, Gtr. 5
Amaj7
Emaj7
64
Gtr. 2
Gtr. 8
Gtr. 4

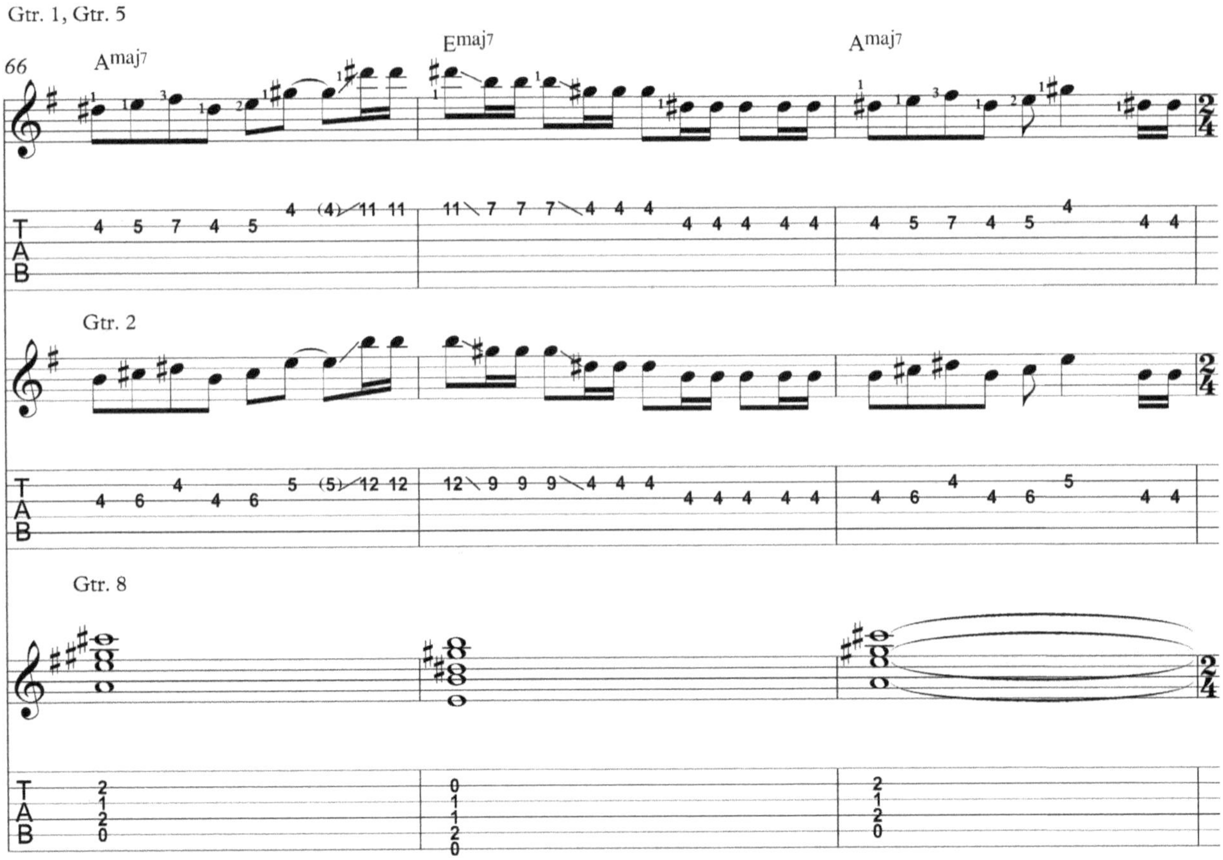
Gtr. 1, Gtr. 5
66
Amaj7
Emaj7
Amaj7
Gtr. 2
Gtr. 8

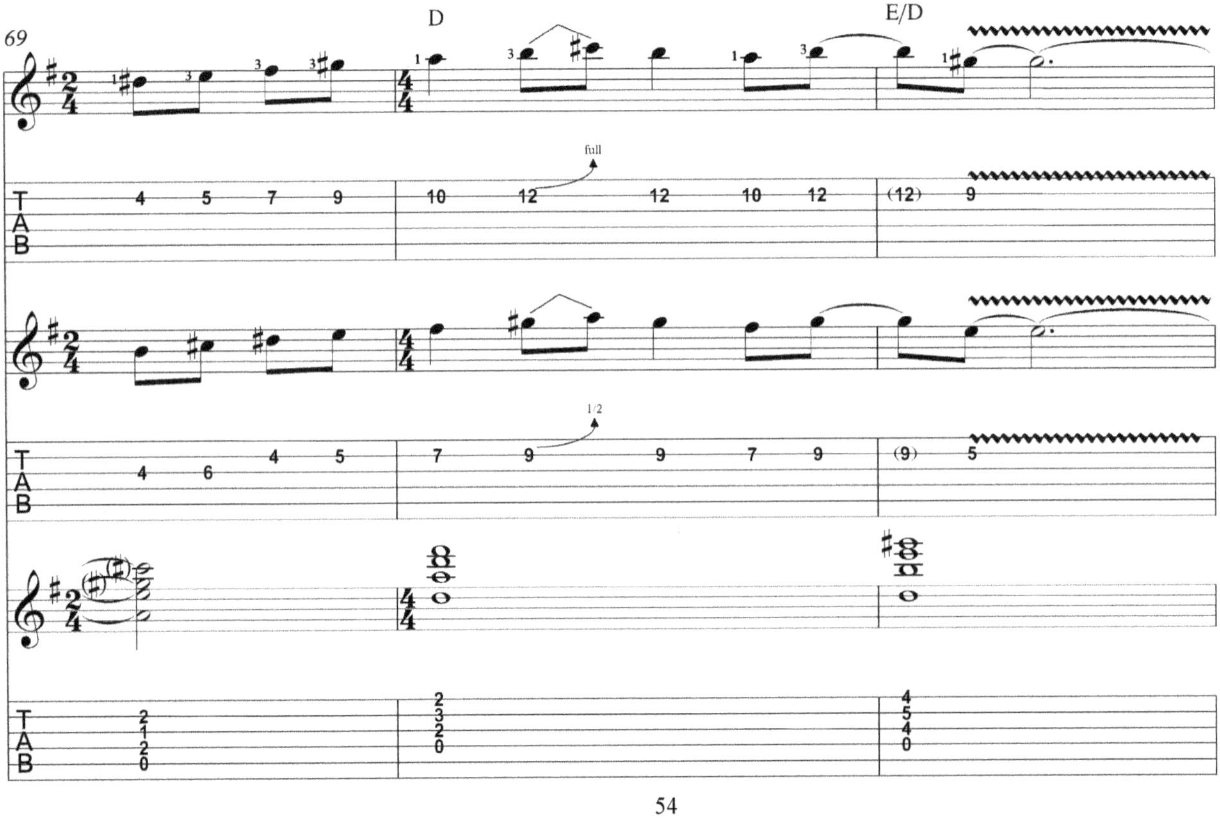
69
D
E/D
full
1/2

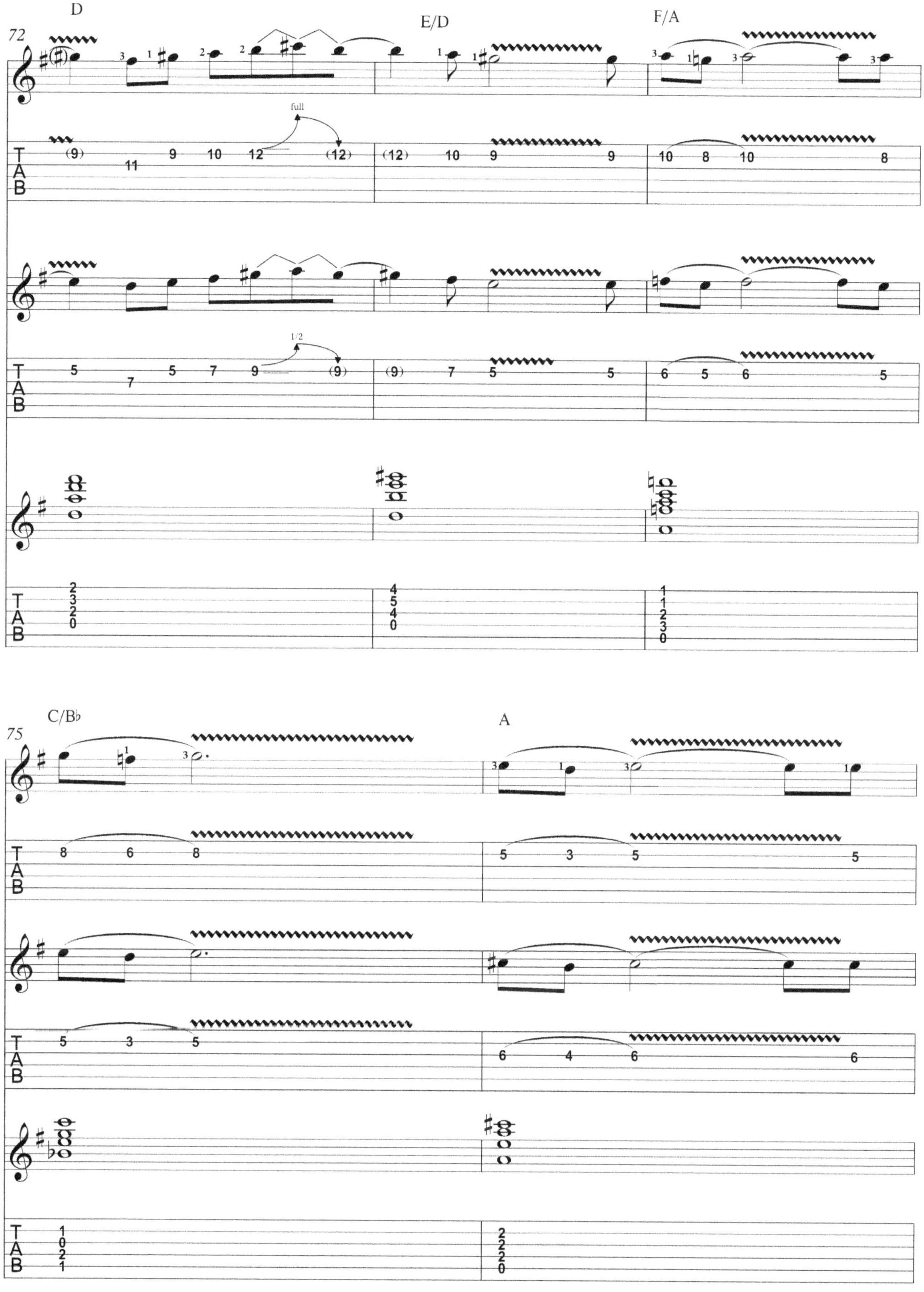
72
D
E/D
F/A
full
1/2
75
C/B♭
A

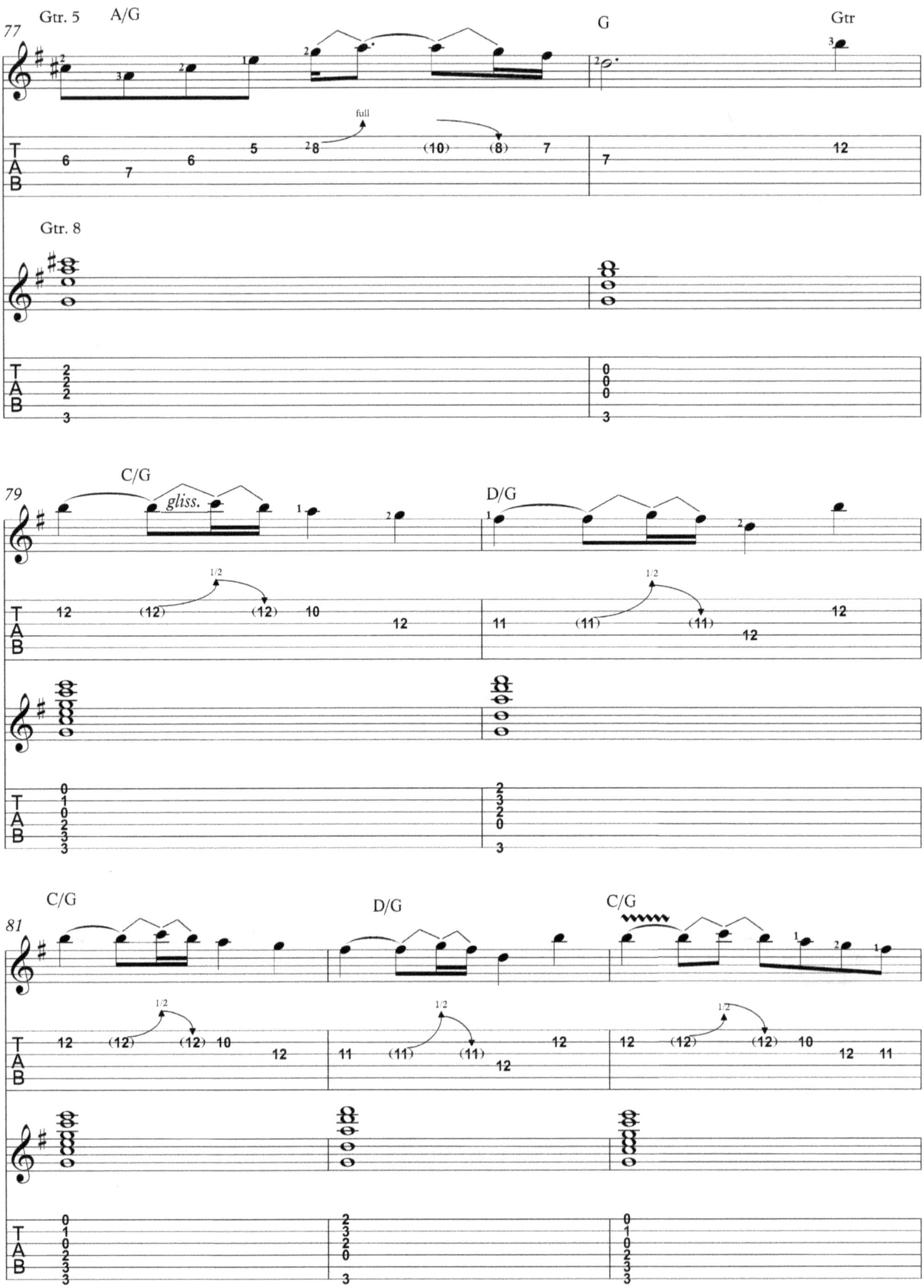
77
Gtr. 5
A/G
G
Gtr
full
Gtr. 8
79
C/G
gliss.
D/G
1/2
81
C/G
D/G
C/G
1/2

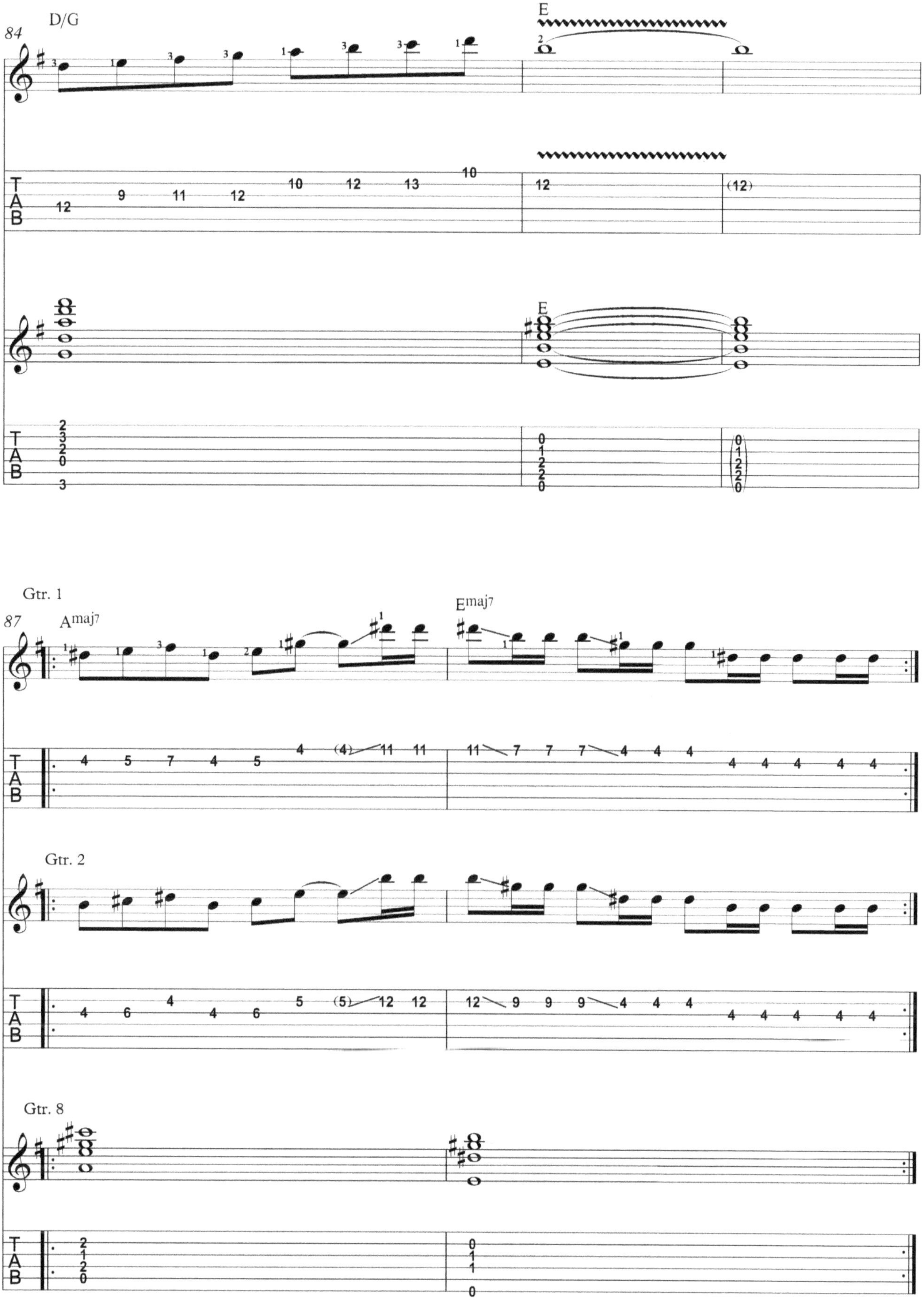
84
D/G
E
Gtr. 1
87
Amaj7
Emaj7
Gtr. 2
Gtr. 8

HANDS OF THE PRIESTESS PART 1

This was the first song recorded on this album, being recorded by just Steve and his brother John. It was a great start that gave Steve the confidence of doing something really special.

Steve divided the song into two parts (Part I and Part II) which are the second and fourth tracks of *Voyage of the Acolyte*. He chose the Tarot card "The High Priestess" as per his comment:

I thought she [the card] was both feminine and mysterious. She evoked magical music.

Steve Hackett

Steve recorded this piece with a microphone on a Yamaha acoustic six string, a Les Paul with the Fender Champ, an Echoplex and a Tone Bender. It was double tracked.

He recorded the Yamaha guitar in reverse using the same chords of the harmony, then flipped the track and matched it to fit the chords.

John Hackett used a new Armstrong flute on this track.

Players/Instruments:

Steve Hackett: Zemaitis Custom 12-string, Gibson Les Paul Gold Top 1957, Mellotron, Steel 6 string Yamaha acoustic (reverse fx)

John Hackett: Flute Armstrong

Phil Collins: Percussion (Bell Tree)

Studio Gears : Hands of The Priestess Part I - Voyage of the Acolyte

1

2

3

4

5

6

1 - Zemaitis Custom 12 String
2 - Steel 6 String Yamaha Acoustic
3 - Gibson Les Paul Gold Top 1957
4 - Mellotron
5 - Coloursound Tonebender (Fuzz)
6 - Echoplex EP-3 Tape Echo
7 - Fender Champ

7

from Steve Hackett - *Voyage of the Acolyte*

Hands of Priestess Part I

by Steve Hackett

Transcribed by Paulo De Carvalho

* Zamaitis Custom 12 strings
**Chords symbols reflect overall harmony.

*Mellotron (Steve Hackett) arr. for gtr.

7
*Gtr. 3
E
Gtr. 1
E
Am/E
*Flute (John Hackett) arr. for gtr.
Gtr. 2
Play just 2nd time
10
Am/E
E
Am/E

*steel guitar using same chords
but with reverse tape until bar 18

* Gibson Les Paul Gold Top 1957

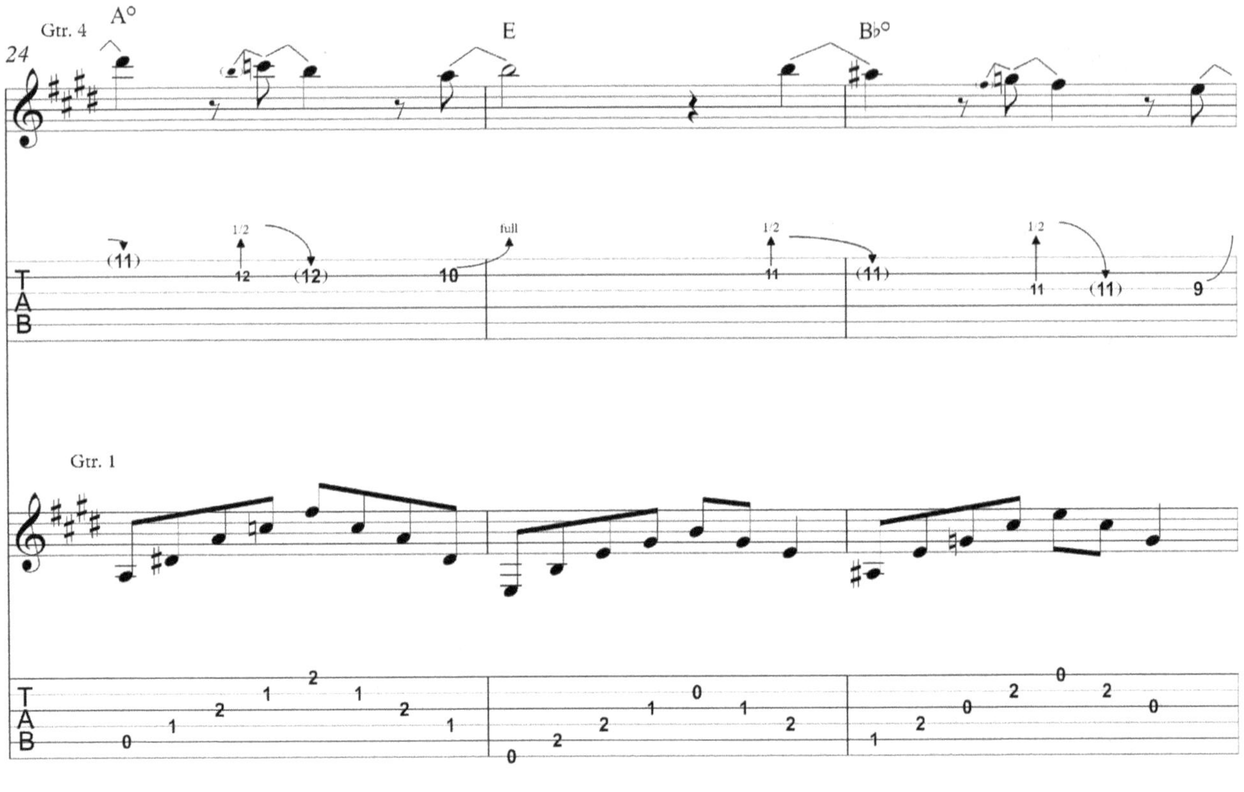
Gtr. 4
24
A°
E
B♭°
1/2
full
1/2
1/2
T
A
B
Gtr. 1
T
A
B

27
B(add4)
B♭°
B(add4)
full
1/2
1/2
full
1/2
T
A
B
A
T
A
B

*steel guitar using same chords but with reverse tape until bar 35

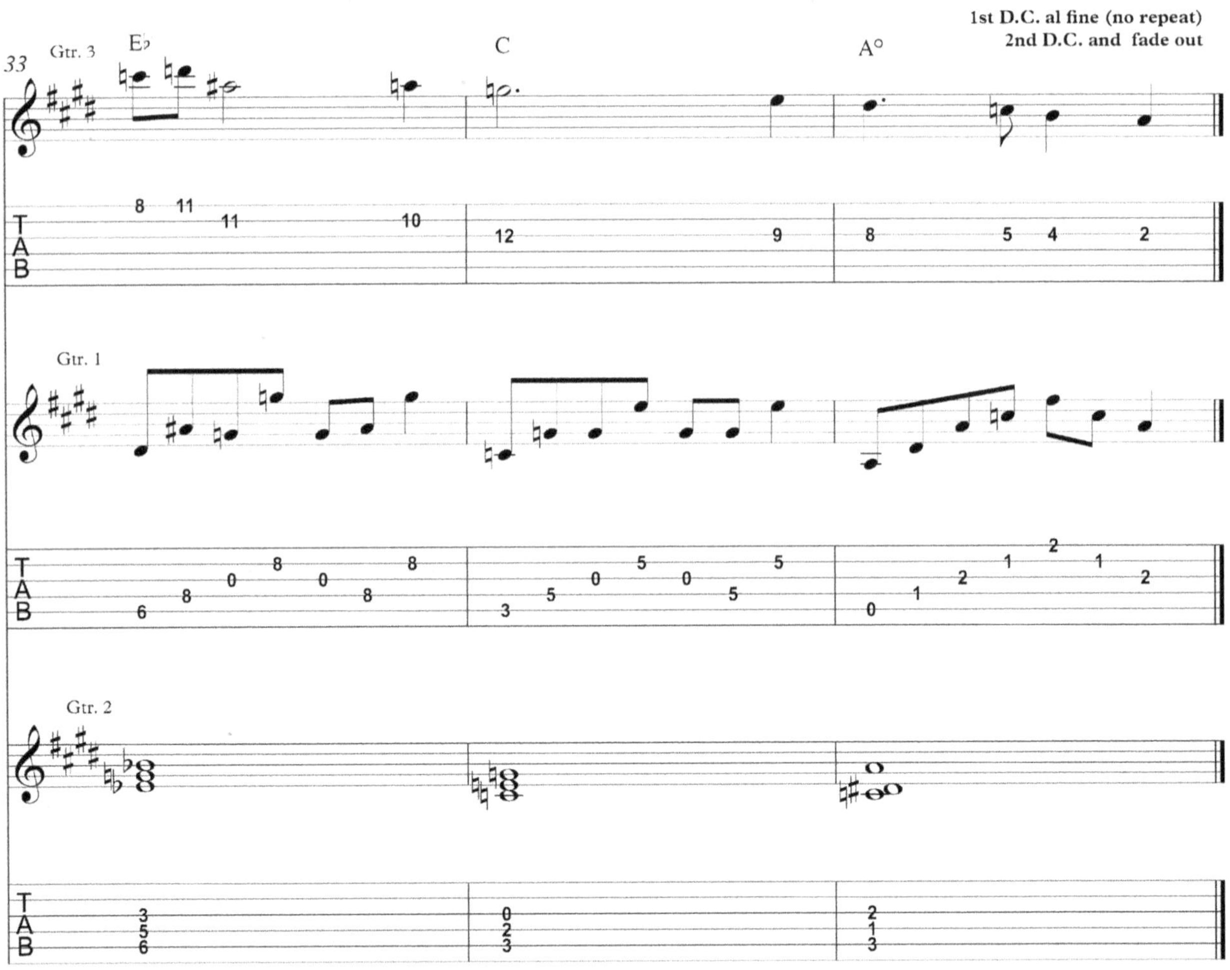
1st D.C. al fine (no repeat)
2nd D.C. and fade out
33
Gtr. 3
E♭
C
A°
Gtr. 1
Gtr. 2

A TOWER STRUCK DOWN

Steve explained how he was inspired by the Tarot card "The Tower" in this song:

I saw the fall of the Third Reich and similar repressive régimes in the Tower Card.   It also provided a direct contrast to the Priestess. Demonic peace and beauty.

He used the Synthi Hi-fli guitar synth, Tonebender, Echoplex and Octavider.

Steve recorded all the guitar strings separately.

He chose Percy Jones to play bass because Phil Collins had worked with Percy in the band *Brand X* and recommended him, Steve enjoyed Percy's wild style of playing. Percy played fretless bass not actually playing a particular rhythm: he just improvised around the instrument.

Steve knew Nigel Warren-Green, the cello player, as he went to school with his brother John, Mike Rutherford played Vox bass pedals put through a tone-bender fuzz box. Mike didn't use the Taurus bass pedals until the album *A Trick of the Tail*.

Steve explained the sound effects used in this song:

In the film that my friend Steve Tobin made, which I believe was called "Six Months from Putney", he had a section of compressed close-edit events. John Acock and I edited these down further into the most arresting moments and the result is what you hear during "A Tower". I wanted the effect of the song to be angular and disturbing like the card itself. I liked the sound effect that he have, one thing after another in the way of sampling that was used in the future like many years later Yes used in the "Owner of the Lonely Heart", it was not so much what was on it. It was a series of random moments not really related on each other.

Players/Instruments:

Steve Hackett: Gibson Les Paul Gold Top 1957, EMS Synthi HiFli, Mellotron, Danelectro baritone guitar (on the end)

John Hackett: Flute, Arp

Mike Rutherford: Vox bass pedals

Percy Jones: Fretless Bass

Phil Collins: Drums, Percussion

Nigel Warren-Green: Cello

The End of *A Tower Struck Down*

Photo 29 : Steve showing the shape he used in the end of "A Tower Struck Down", which he recorded on a Danelectro Baritone. Photo by Paulo De Carvalho, 2017

Studio Gears : A Tower Struck Down - Voyage of the Acolyte

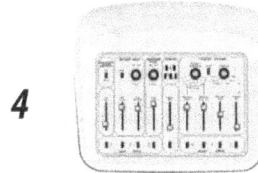

1

2

3

4

Pedal Board built by Pete Cornish

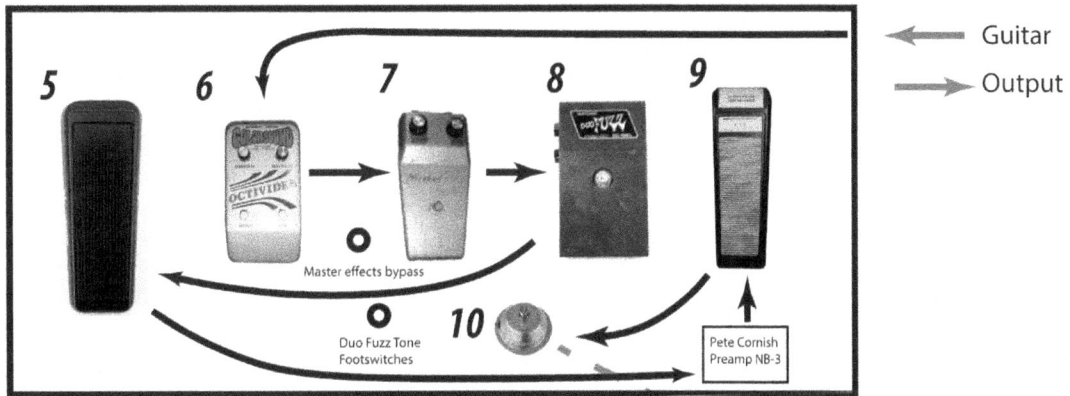

5

6

7

8

9

← Guitar

→ Output

Master effects bypass

Duo Fuzz Tone
Footswitches

10

Pete Cornish
Preamp NB-3

1 - Gibson Les Paul Gold Top 1957
2 - Danelectro Baritone Guitar
3 - Mellotron
4 - EMS Synthi Hi-Fli
5 - Cry Baby Wah-Wah
6 - Colorsound Octivider
7 - Marshall Supa Fuzz
8 - Shaftesbury Duo Fuzz
9 - Schaller Volume Pedal F121
10 -Pedal Switch for Echoplex EP-3
11 - Echoplex EP-3 Tape Echo
12 - HH 100w IC100
13 - Hlwatt 150w 4x12 Cabinets SE 4123
14 - Coloursound Tonebender (Fuzz)

12

13

11

14

Signal Routing:

Gtr1 → Octivider → Supa Fuzz → Duo Fuzz → Cry Baby → . (Preamp) Peter Cornish NB-3 → Schaller F121 Volume Pedal → Echo Send/Return (Echoplex EP-3 → Output

from Steve Hackett - *Voyage of The Acolyte*

A Tower Struck Down

by Steve Hackett, John Hackett

Transcribed by Paulo De Carvalho

* Gibson Les Paul Golden Top 1957

*** Vox Bass Pedal (Mike Rutherford) arr. for gtr.
** Chords symbols reflect overall harmony

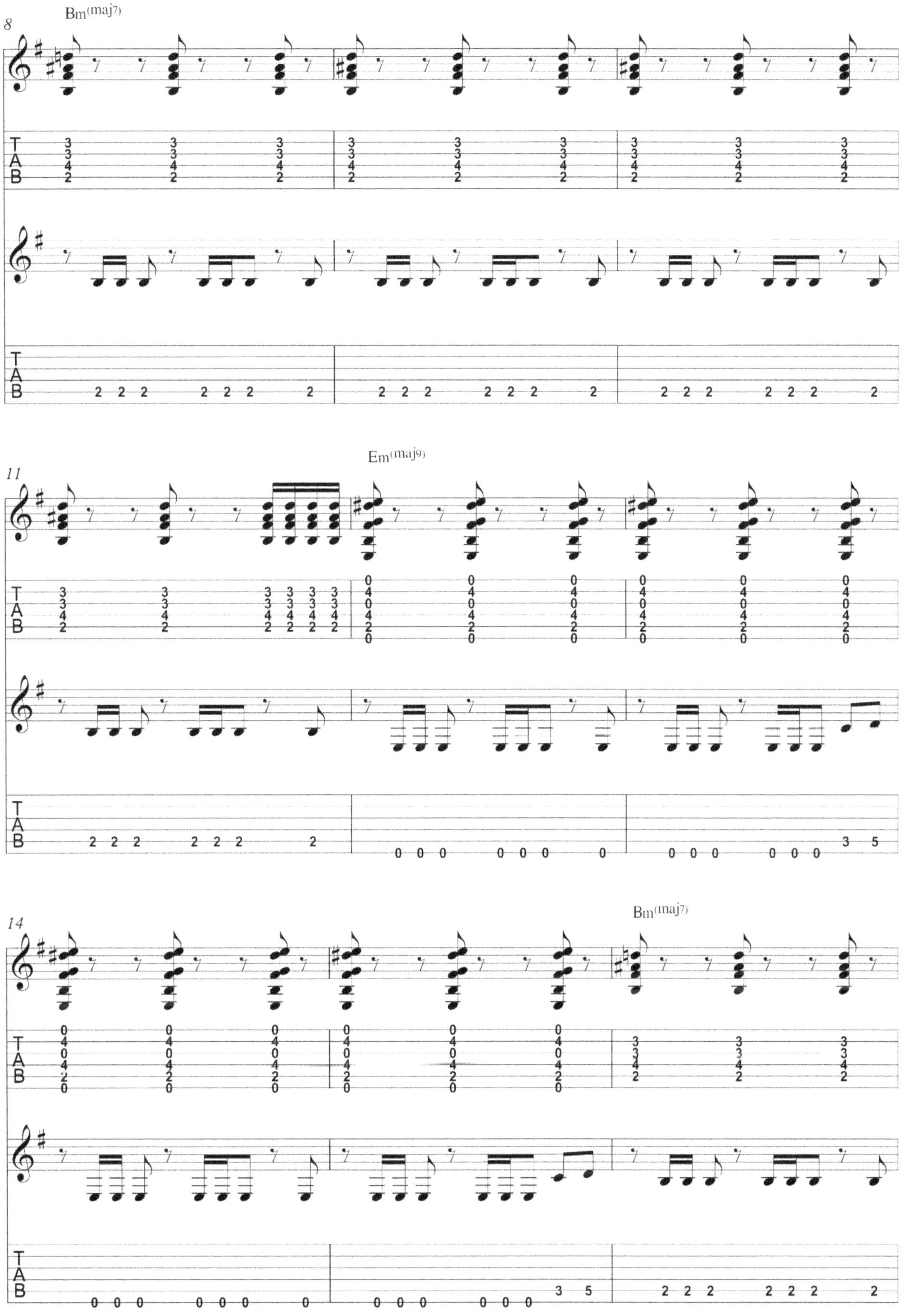
8
Bm(maj7)
11
Em(maj9)
14
Bm(maj7)

17

20
Am(maj7)
**Gtr. 4
Recorded in reverse tape
** Gibson Les Paul Golden Top 1957
Gtr. 1
*Gtr. 3
* Gibson Les Paul Golden Top 1957
Gtr. 2

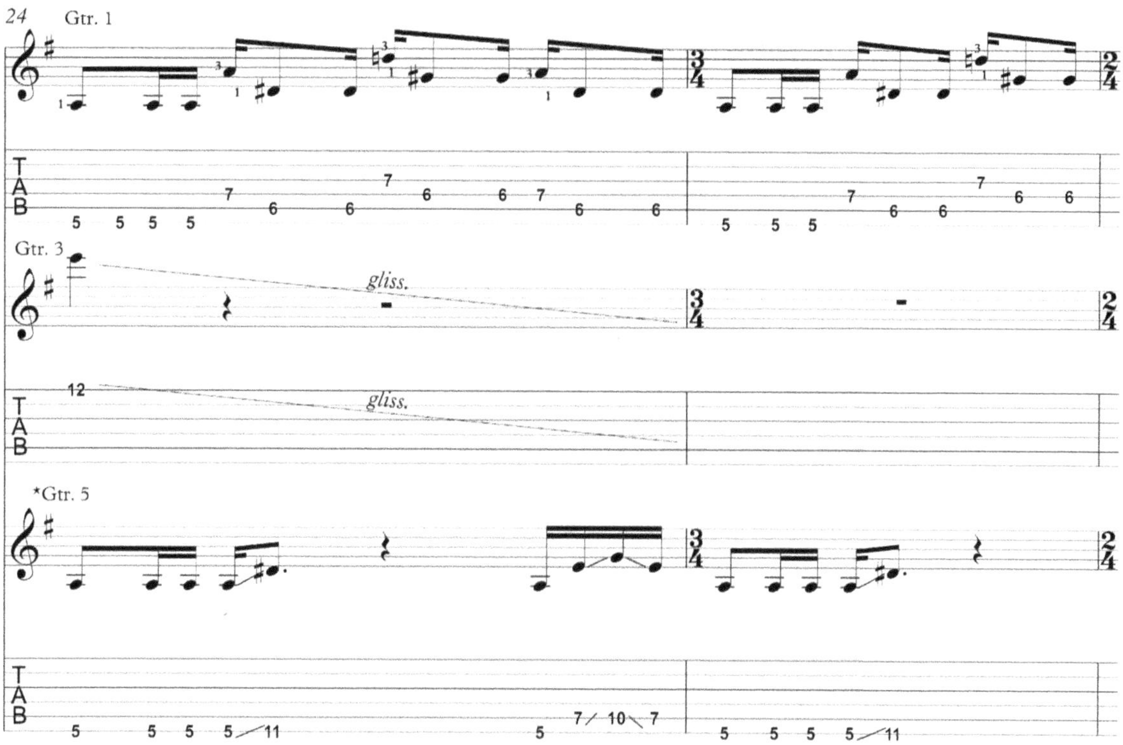

*Cello arr. for gtr.

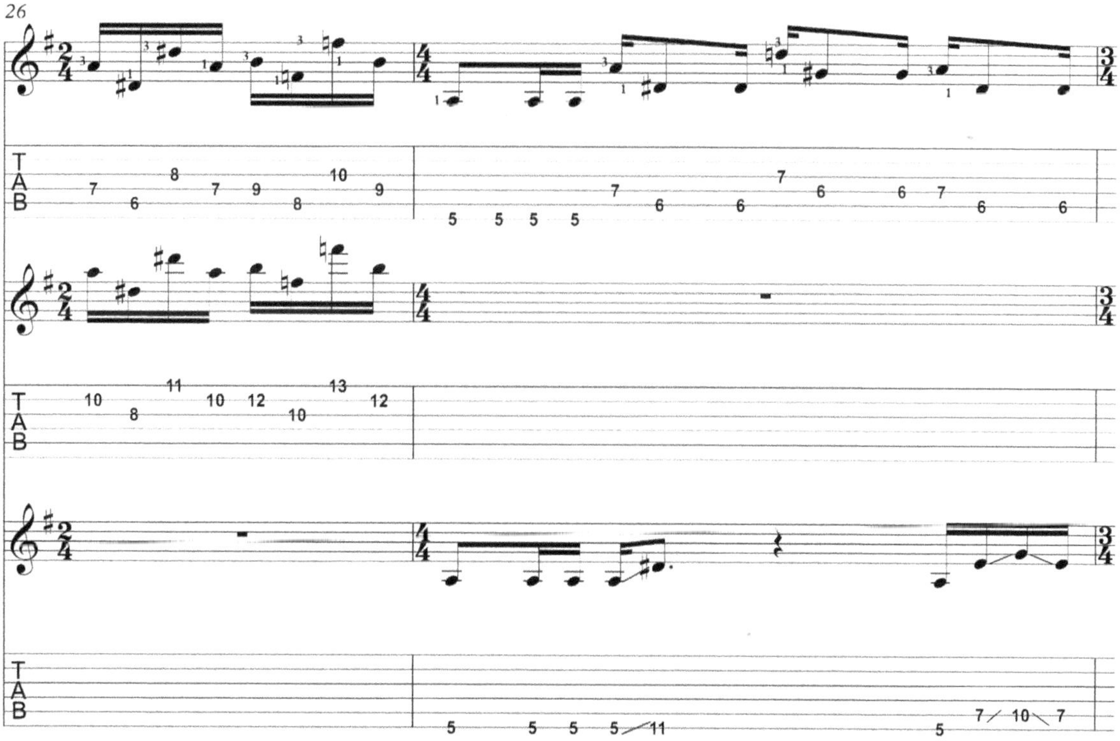

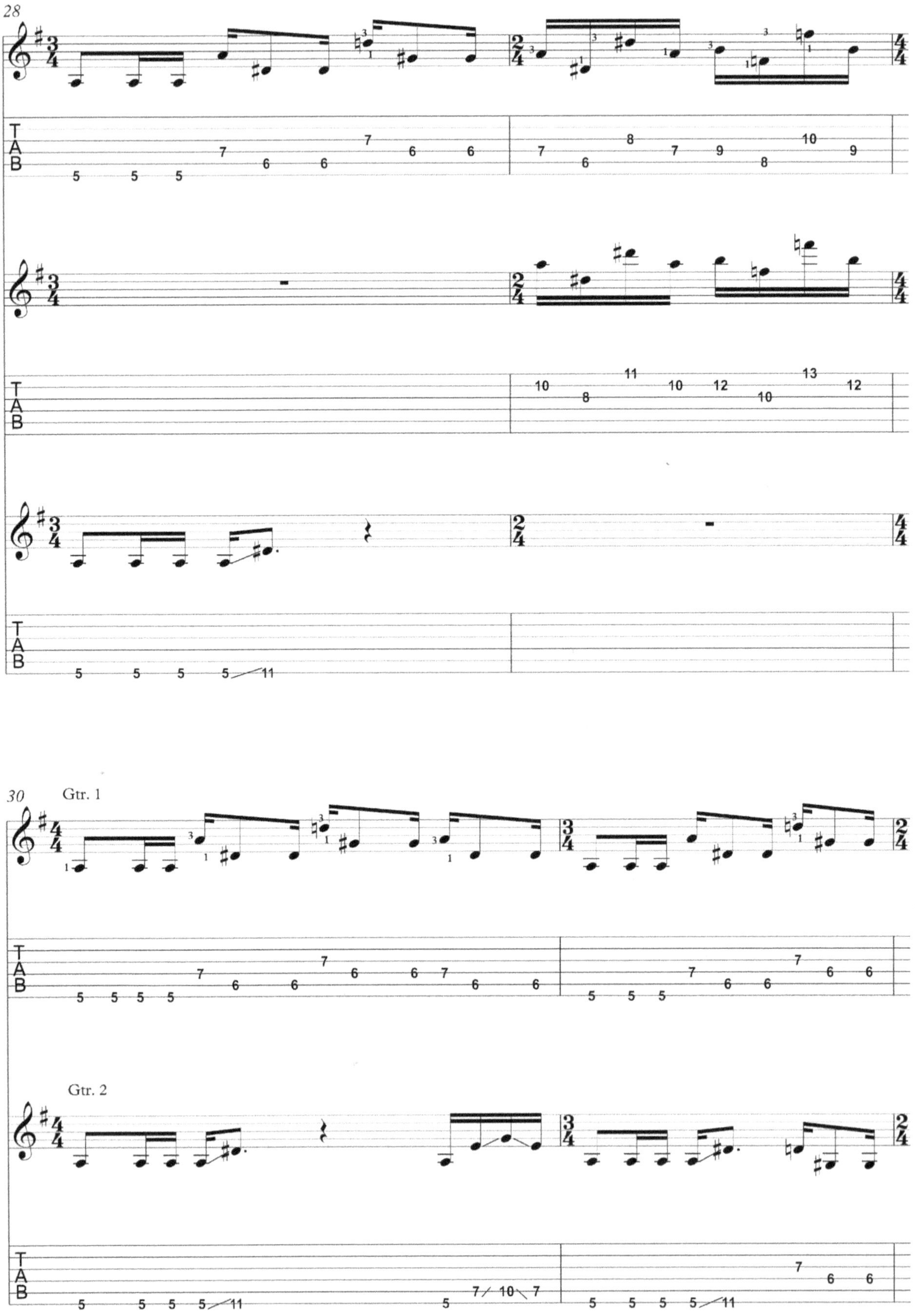
28
30
Gtr. 1
Gtr. 2

*Arp Odyssey (John Hackett) arr. for gtr.

*Mellotron arr. for gtr.

**Flute Yamaha (John Hackett) arr. for gtr.
Musical Notation for fl. but tab notation transposte for gtr.*s* (Music note for the guitar is written an octave higher)

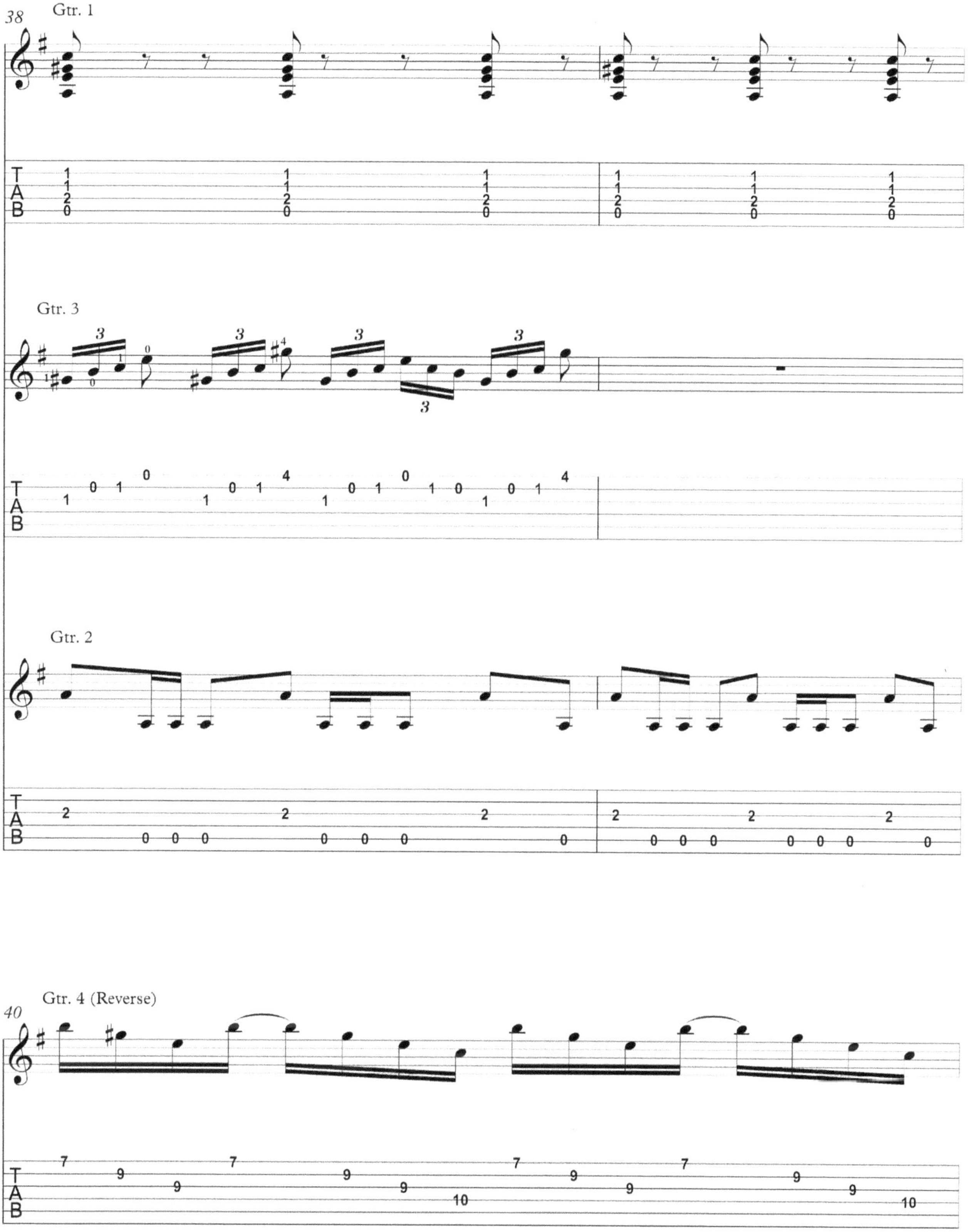
38
Gtr. 1
Gtr. 3
Gtr. 2
40
Gtr. 4 (Reverse)

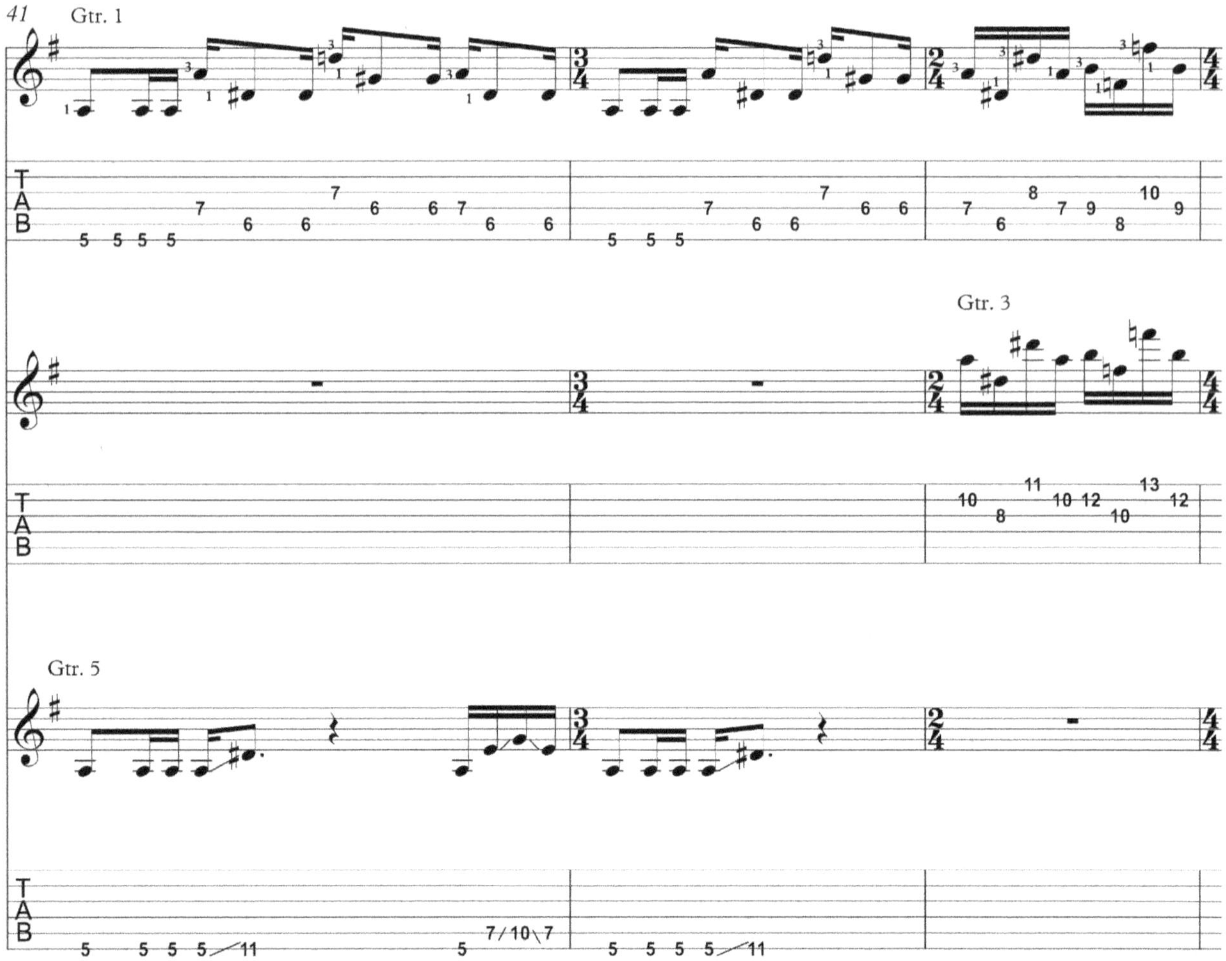
41
Gtr. 1
Gtr. 3
Gtr. 5

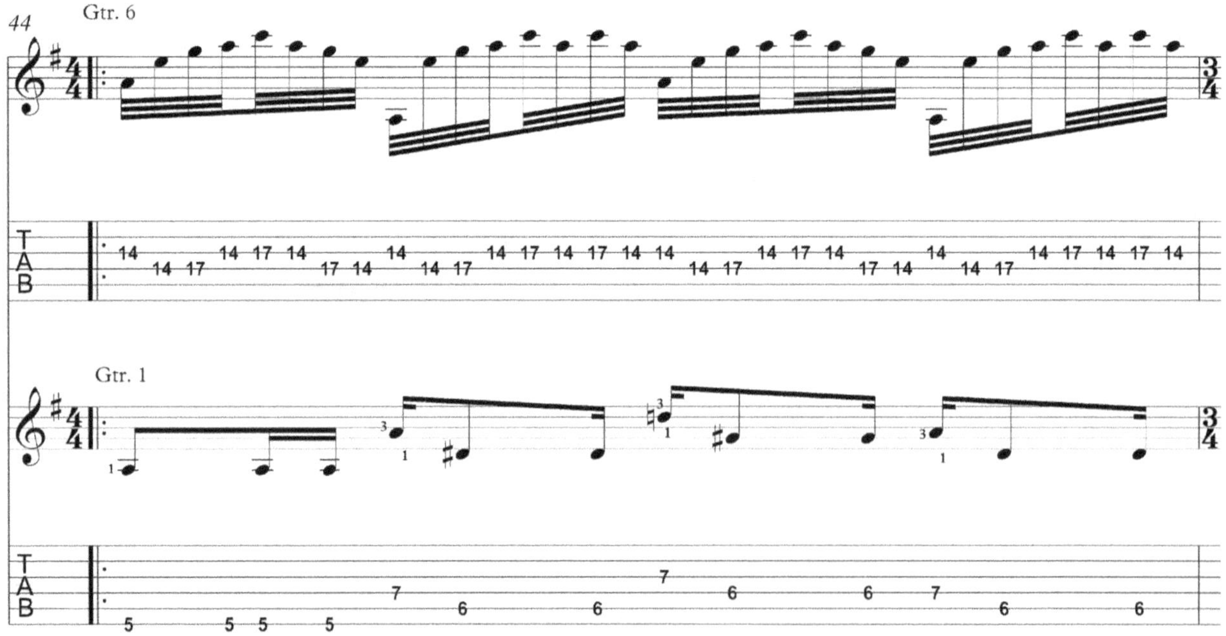
44
Gtr. 6
Gtr. 1

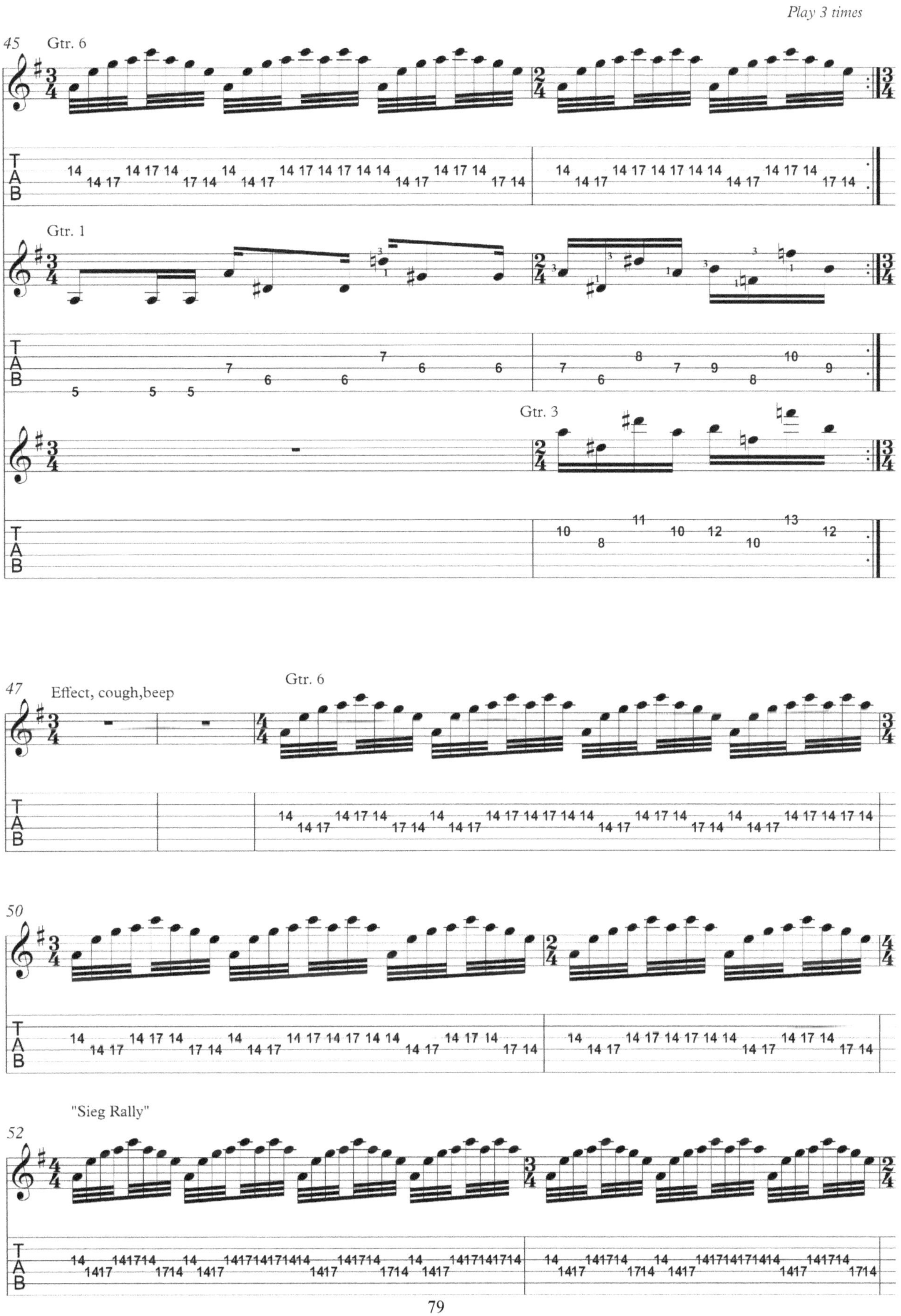
Play 3 times
45
Gtr. 6
Gtr. 1
Gtr. 3
47
Effect, cough,beep
Gtr. 6
50
52
"Sieg Rally"

*Baritone Guitar

HANDS OF THE PRIESTESS PART II

After the track *A Tower Struck Down,* comes *Hands of the Priestess Part II*, as Steve explained:

Because the music was very visual and I felt I was editing an imaginary film. The calm before the storm and then the resolution of peace after the Tower Struck Down. I was also already influence by classical music, and the approach to repetition of themes.

On this track, Steve used his Les Paul in the solo, altogether with the Fender Champ, Echoplex and Tone Bender. The guitar was double tracked.

Players/Instruments:

Steve Hackett: Zemaitis Custom 12-string, Yairi Nylon, Steel 6-string Yamaha acoustic, Gibson Les Paul Gold Top 1957, Mellotron

John Hackett: Flute

Robin Miller: Oboe

Hands of the Priestess Part II: details

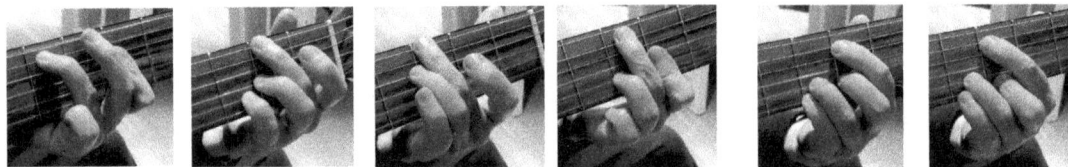

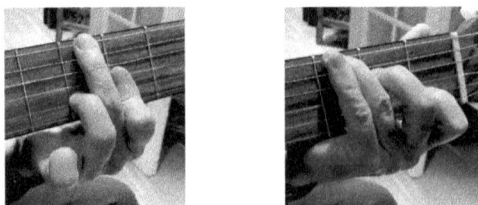

Photos 30-37: Steve showing the shape of the chords in Hands of the Priestess Part II. Photos by Paulo De Carvalho, 2017

Studio Gears : Hands of The Priestess Part II - Voyage of the Acolyte

1

2

3

4

5

6

1 - Zemaitis Custom 12 String
2 - Steel 6 String Yamaha Acoustic
3 - Gibson Les Paul Gold Top 1957
4 - Yairi Nylon
5 - Echoplex EP-3 Tape Echo
6 - Coloursound Tonebender (Fuzz)
7 - Mellotron
8 - Fender Champ

7

from Steve Hackett - *Voyage of the Acolyte*
Hands of Priestess Part II
by Steve Hackett

Transcribed by Paulo De Carvalho

*Flute arr. for gtr.

**Yairi nylon

** Chords symbols reflect overall harmony

6
*Gtr. 3
E
B11/A
E
*Oboe arr. for gtr
**Gtr. 4
** Zamaitis Custom 12 strings
9
B11/A
E
B11/A
12
E
B11/A
A/C♯

* Steel 6 string Yamaha acoustic

* Steel 6 string Yamaha acoustic

* Mellotron arr. for gtr.

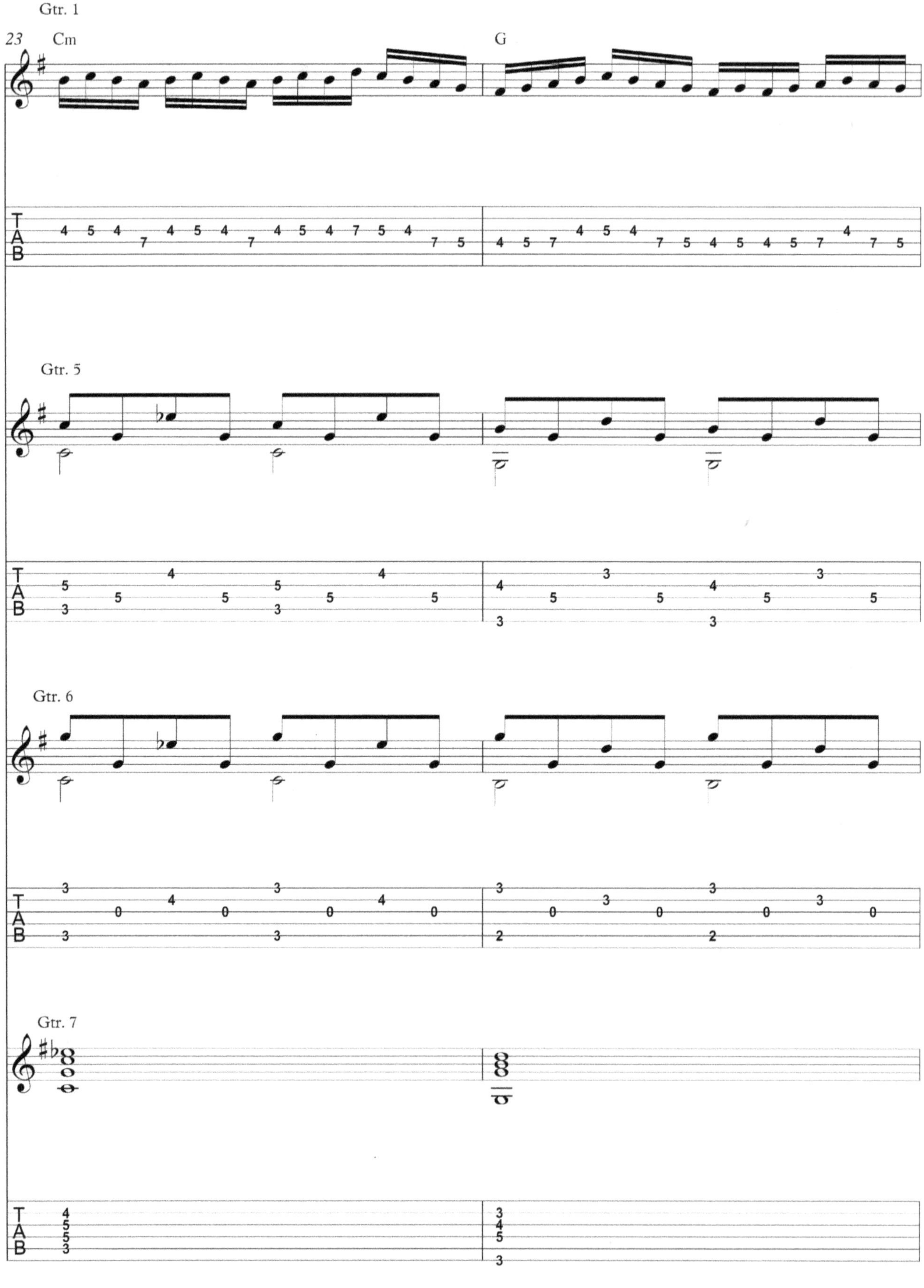
Gtr. 1
23 Cm
G
Gtr. 5
Gtr. 6
Gtr. 7

Gtr. 1

25   Cm   D/G

Gtr. 5

Gtr. 6

*Gtr. 8

* Gibson Les Paul Golden Top 1957

Gtr. 7

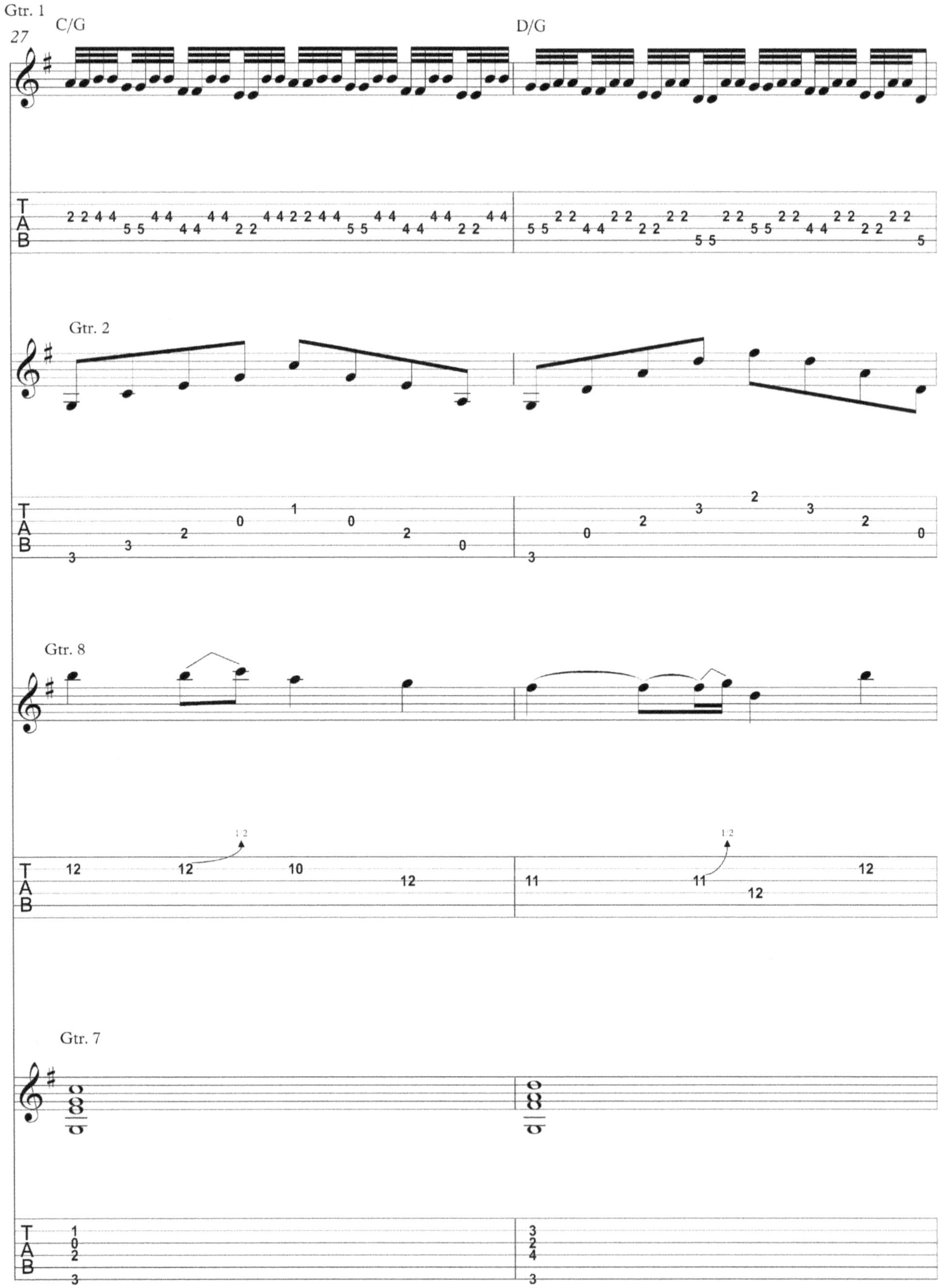
Gtr. 1
27
C/G
D/G
Gtr. 2
Gtr. 8
1/2
1/2
Gtr. 7

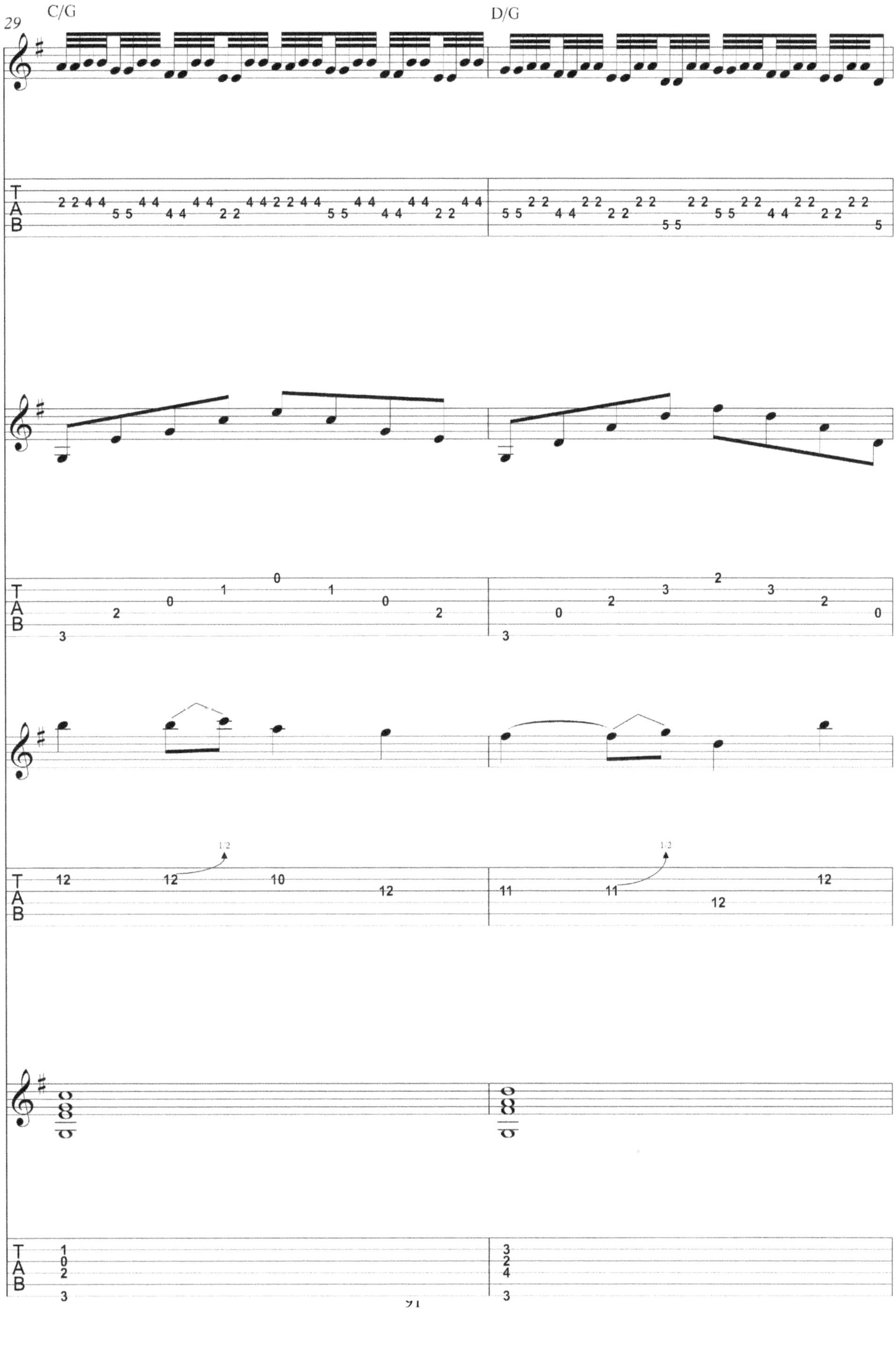
29
C/G
D/G
1/2
1/2

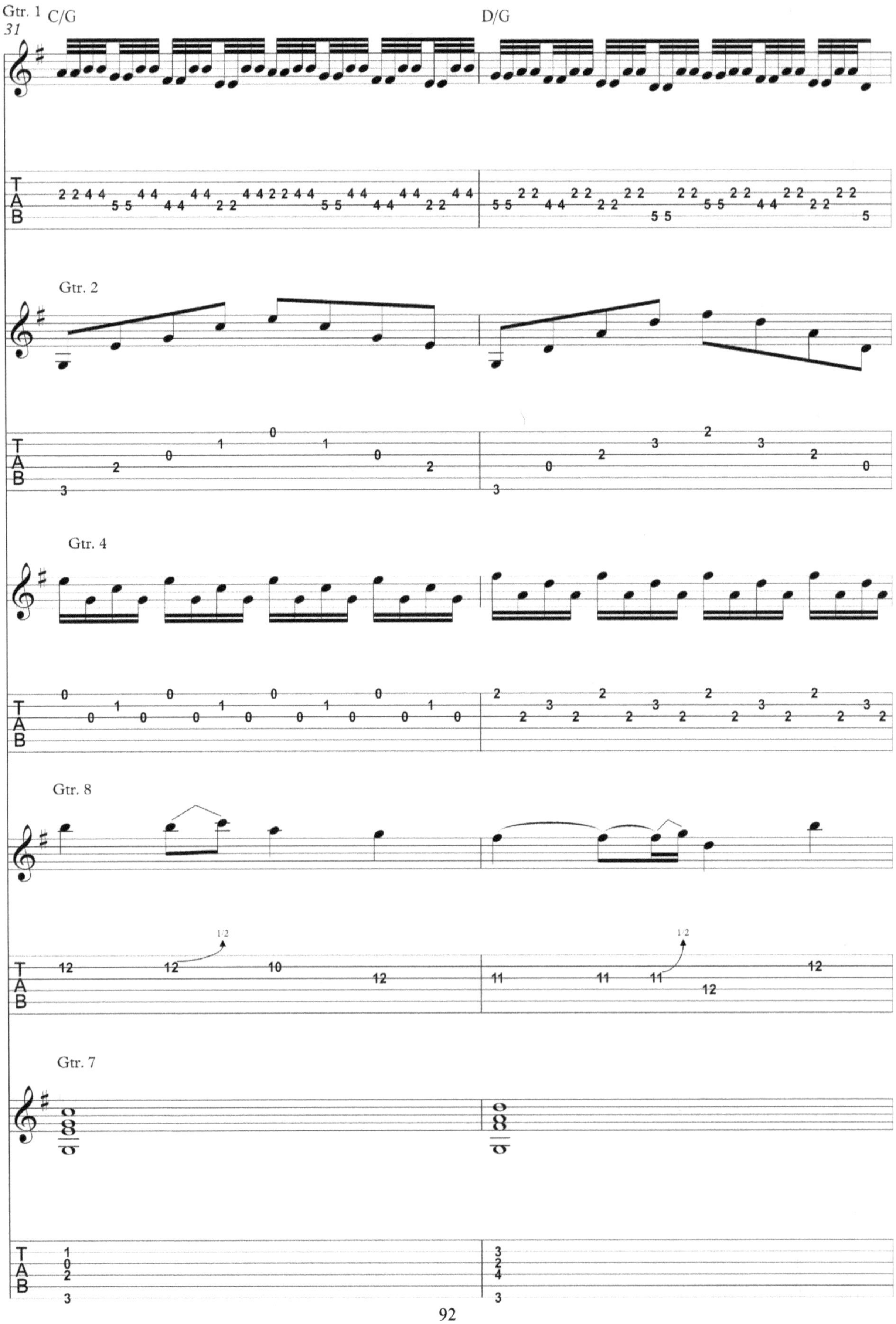
Gtr. 1
31
C/G
D/G
Gtr. 2
Gtr. 4
Gtr. 8
1/2
1/2
Gtr. 7

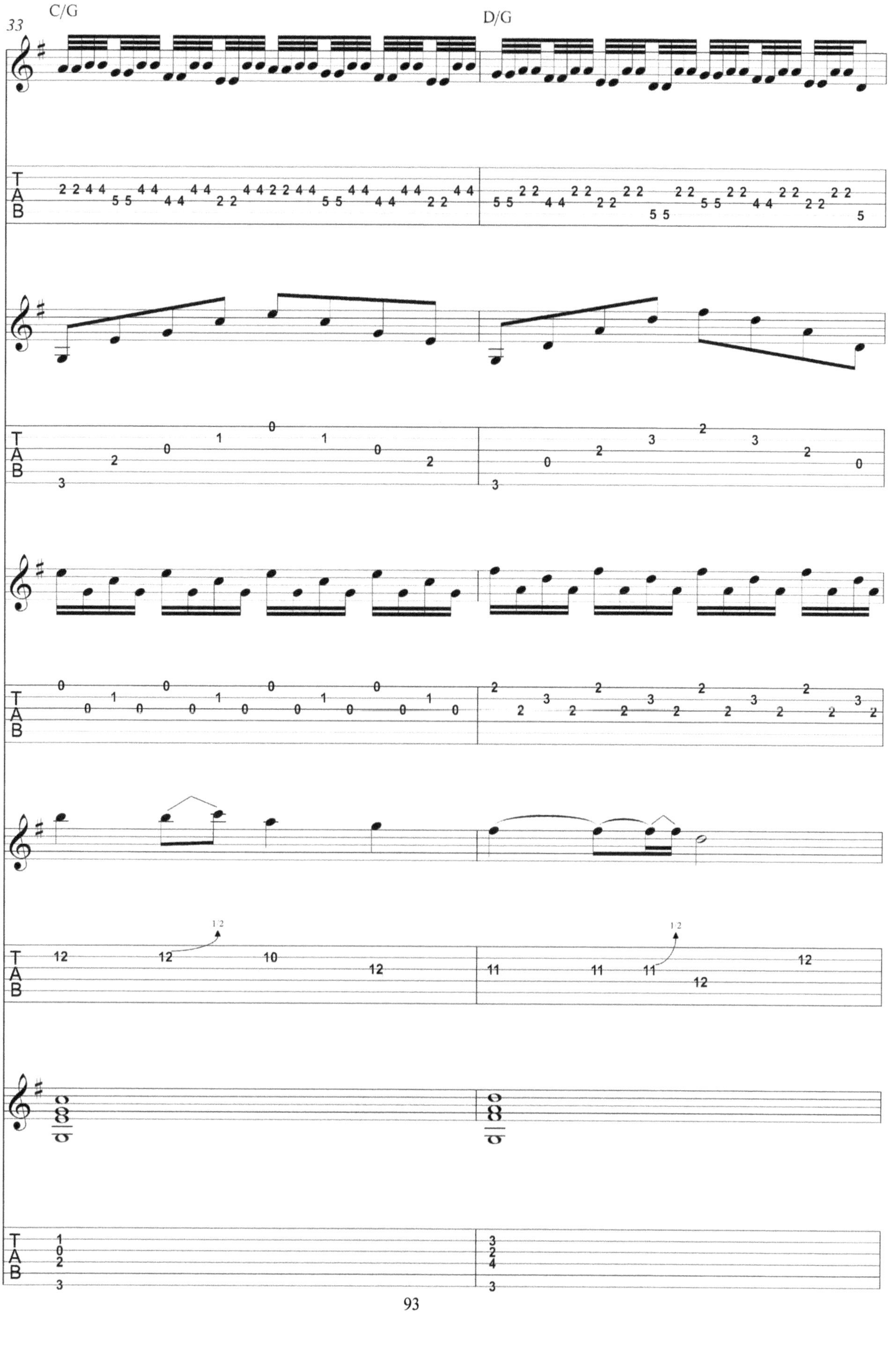
C/G
D/G

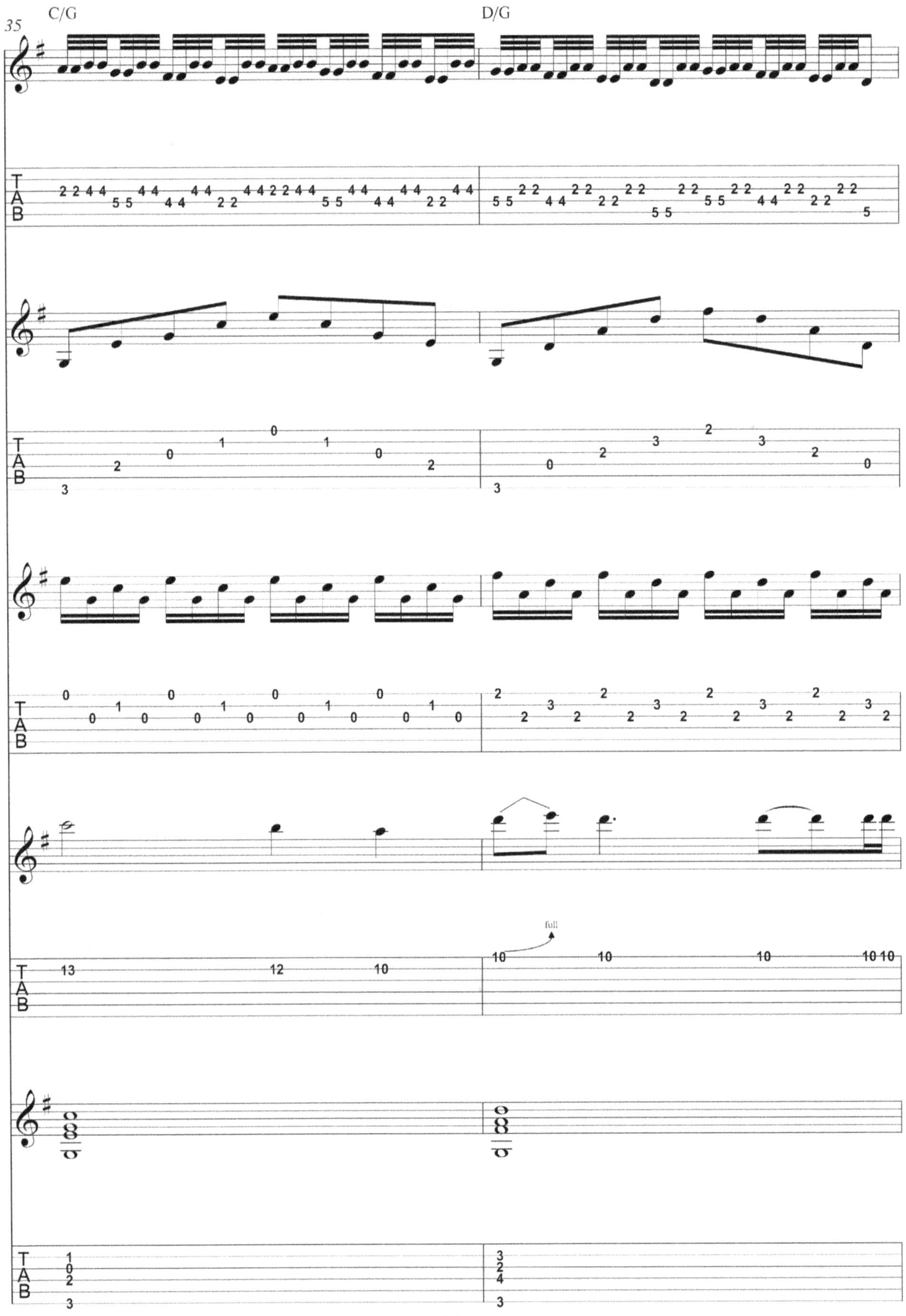
35
C/G
D/G
full

37

C/G

D/G

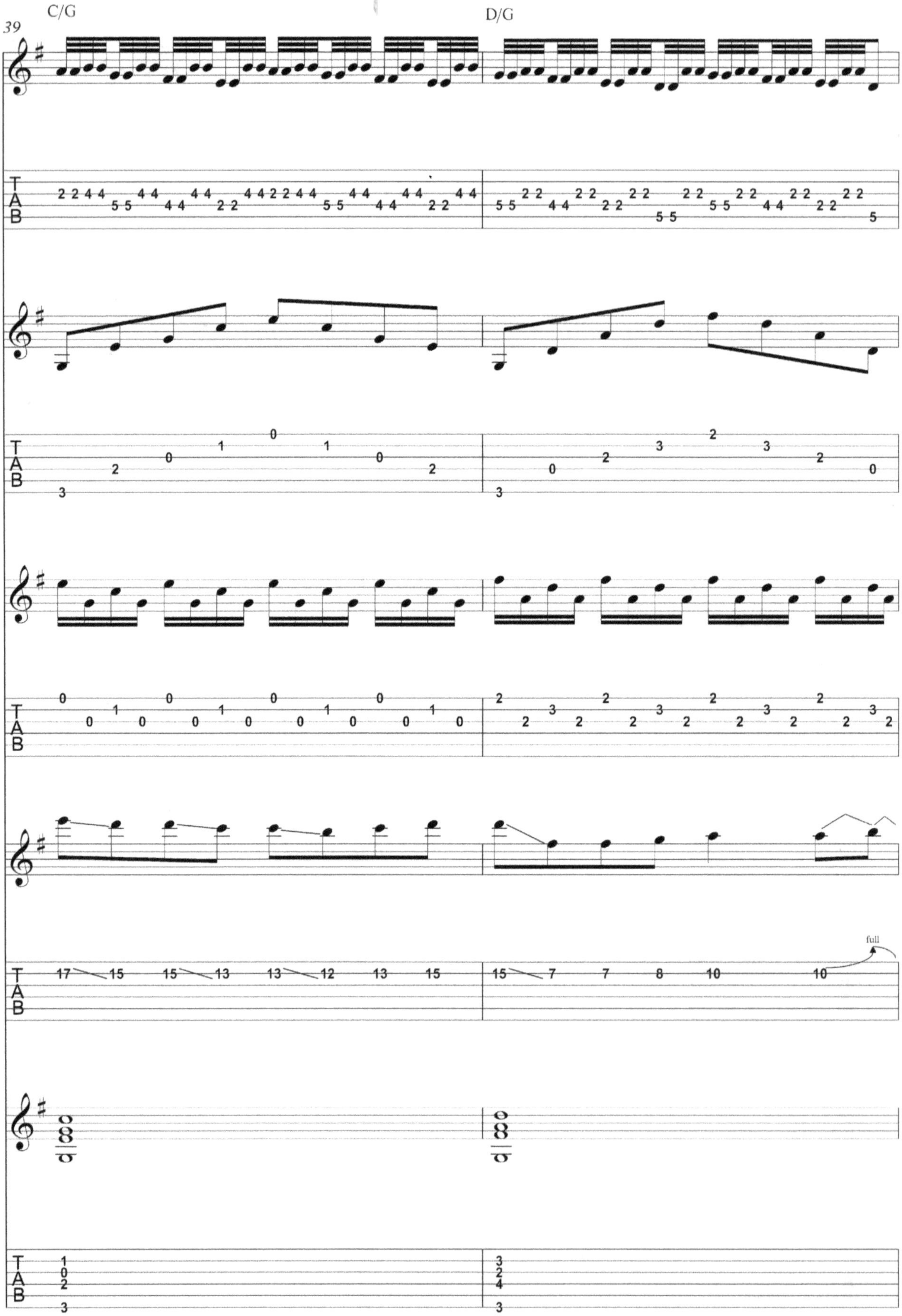
C/G
D/G
39
full

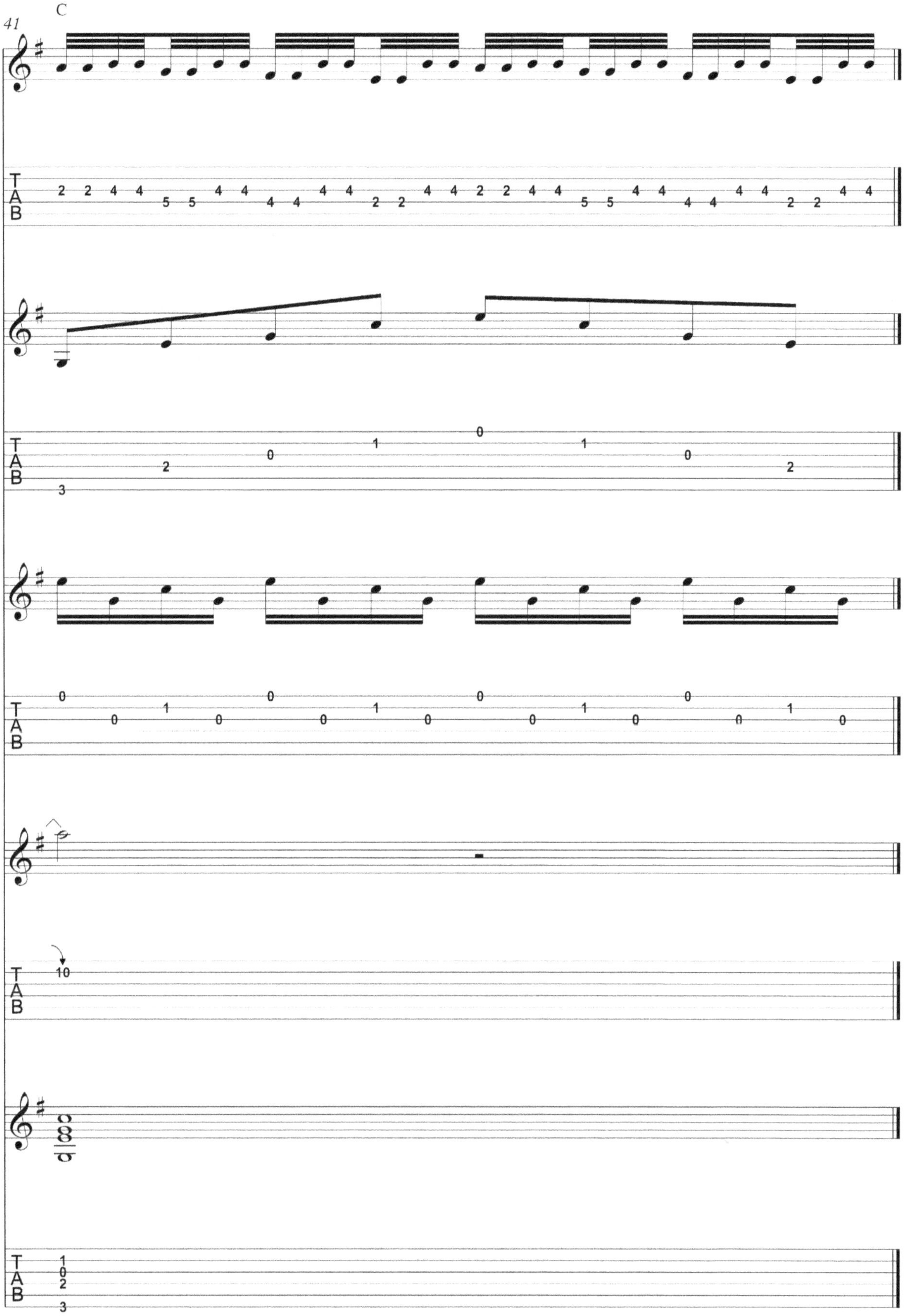
41
C

THE HERMIT

Steve explained why he chose the Tarot card "The Hermit":

Because I felt it was very much like me at the time, keeping my head down, getting in with stuff. I felt like a lone wolf having to develop myself outside the confines of the band as well within it.

He used Les Paul plugged into a MXR Phase 90, recorded through a Fender Champ. The Zemaitis twelve string and Yamaha six string were recorded with a mic.

He recorded the vocals live, in a unique room, with no added reverb. The room was like a cell with green brick walls. All vocals for *The Hermit* were recorded in this room. The reverb that you hear in the recording was the natural ambience of the room. There was no added reverb at all.

Players/Instruments:

Steve Hackett: Vocal, Zemaitis Custom 12-string, Steel 6-string Yamaha acoustic, Gibson Les Paul Gold Top 1957, Vocals

John Hackett: Flute

Robin Miller: Oboe

Nigel Warren-Green: Cello

Phil Collins: Vibraphone

Studio Gears : The Hermit - Voyage of the Acolyte

1

2

3

4

5

1 - Zemaitis Custom 12 String
2 - Steel 6 String Yamaha Acoustic
3 - Gibson Les Paul Gold Top 1957
4 - MXR phase 90
5 - Fender Champ

Intro of *The Hermit*

* Zamaitis Custom 12 strings

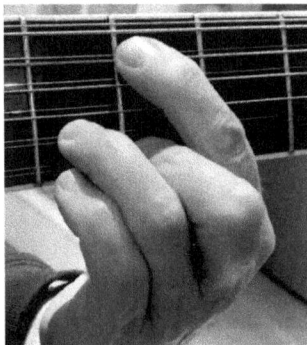

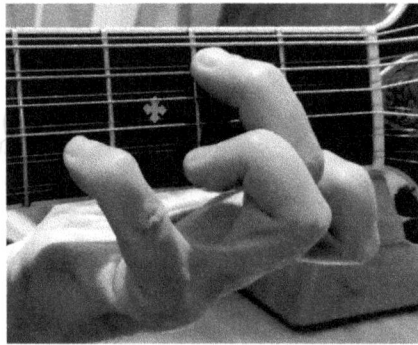

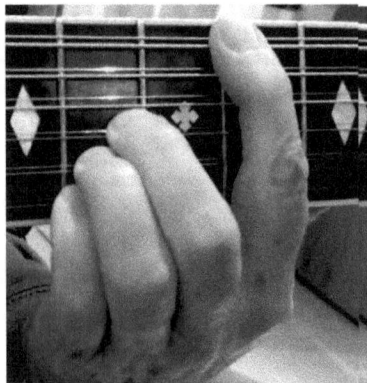

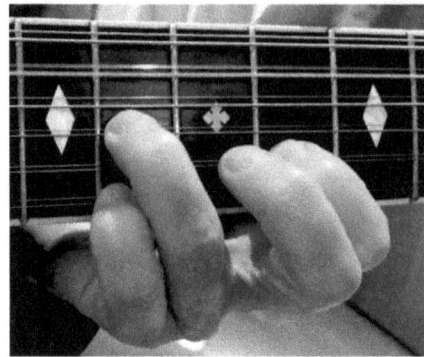

Photos 38-42: Steve showing the shape of the chords of the intro of The Hermit. Photos by Paulo De Carvalho, 2017

from Steve Hackett - *Voyage of the Acolyte*
The Hermit
by Steve Hackett

Transcribed by Paulo De Carvalho

* Zamaitis Custom 12 strings

**Chords symbols reflect overall harmony.

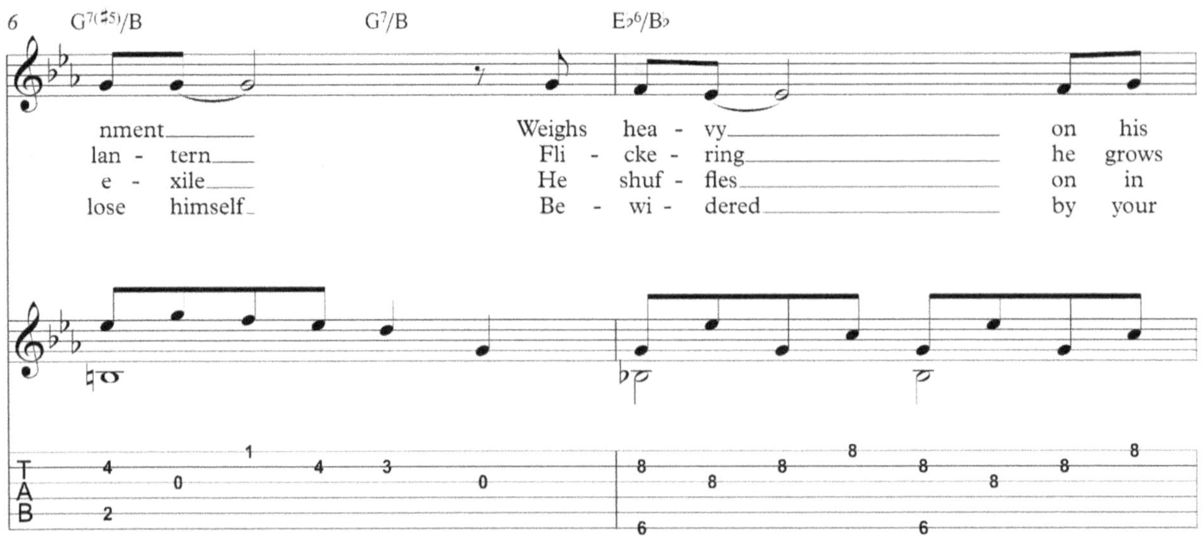
6
G7(♯5)/B
G7/B
E♭6/B♭
nment Weighs hea - vy on his
lan - tern Fli - cke - ring he grows
e - xile He shuf - fles on in
lose himself Be - wi - dered by your
TAB

8
F7/A
Repeat four times
E♭maj7/D
Cm9
shou- ders
ol - der a
blind-ness You'll
kind-ness
Gtr. 1
TAB
*Gtr. 2
TAB

*Cello arr. for gtr.

E♭maj7/D
Cm9
Am7(♭5)
B♭maj7
11
Gtr. 1
C(add2add4)
14
*Gtr. 3
* Zamaitis Custom 12 strings
Gtr. 2

* Steel 6 string Yamaha acoustic

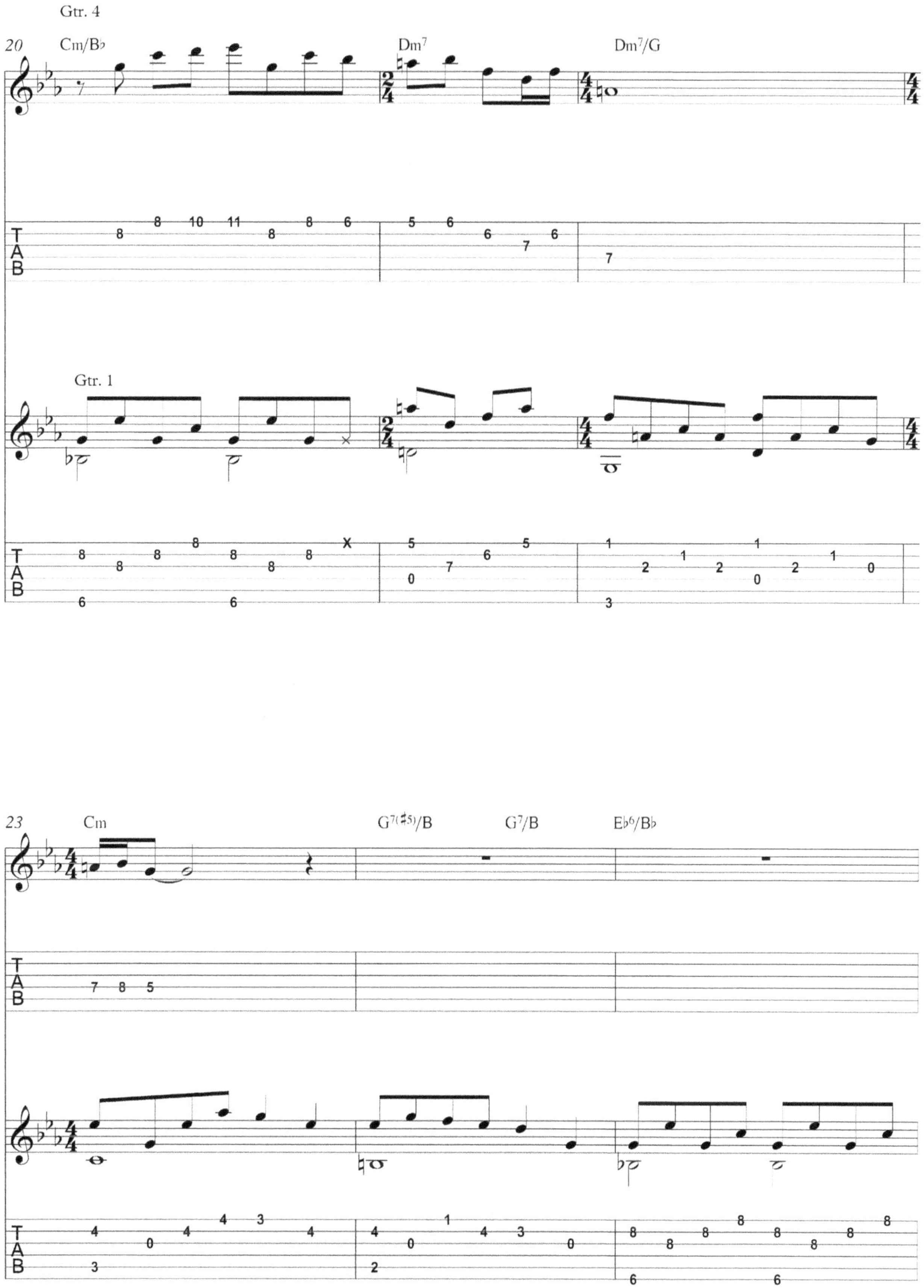
Gtr. 4
20
Cm/B♭
Dm7
Dm7/G
Gtr. 1
23
Cm
G7(♯5)/B
G7/B
E♭6/B♭

* Gibson Les Paul Golden Top 1957

* Gibson Les Paul Golden Top 1957

31
Cm
G7(♯5)/B
G7/B
E♭6/B♭
F7/A
many years of ba nishment No shel- ter from the storm To
TAB
TAB
TAB

find this slave of so-li-tude you'll know him by his star Then

*Cello arr. for gtr.

47
Am7(♭5)
B♭maj7
D(add9)/A
D
E7/A
51
*Gtr. 8
B♭maj9
C/B♭
B♭maj9
C/B♭
*Oboe arr. for gtr
Gtr. 5

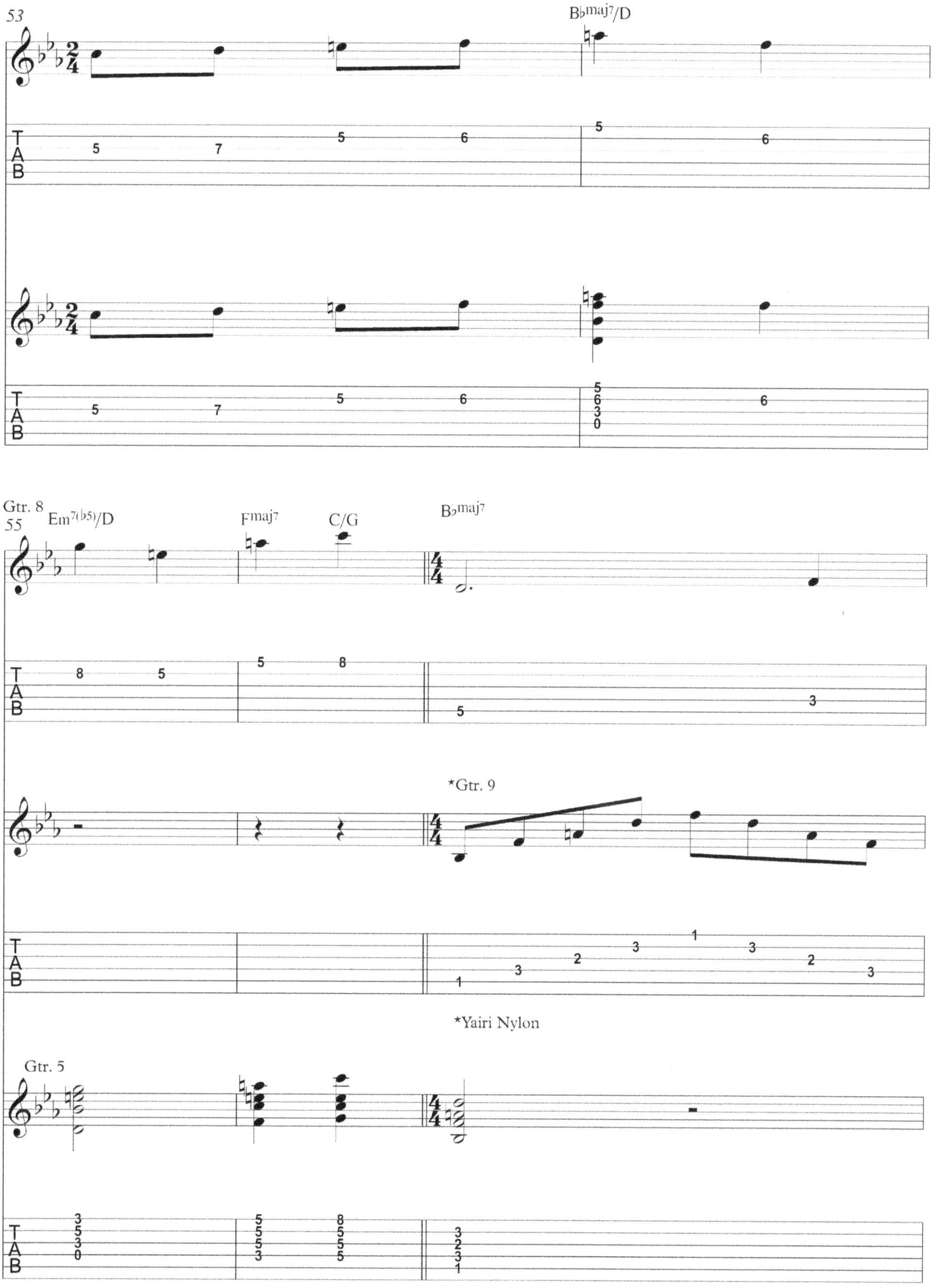
53
B♭maj7/D
Gtr. 8
55
Em7(♭5)/D
Fmaj7
C/G
B♭maj7
*Gtr. 9
*Yairi Nylon
Gtr. 5

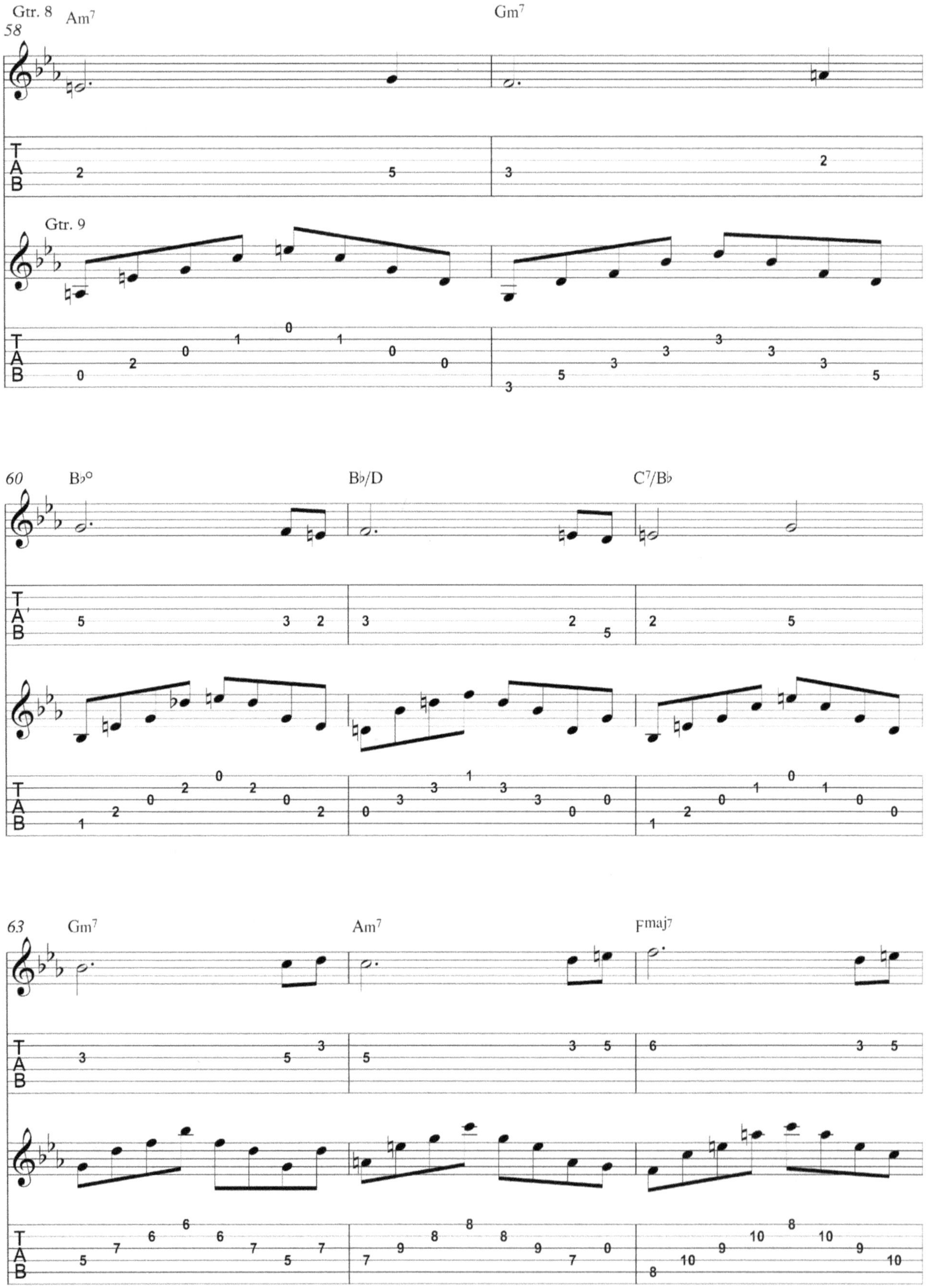
Gtr. 8
58
Am7
Gm7
Gtr. 9
60
B♭°
B♭/D
C7/B♭
63
Gm7
Am7
Fmaj7

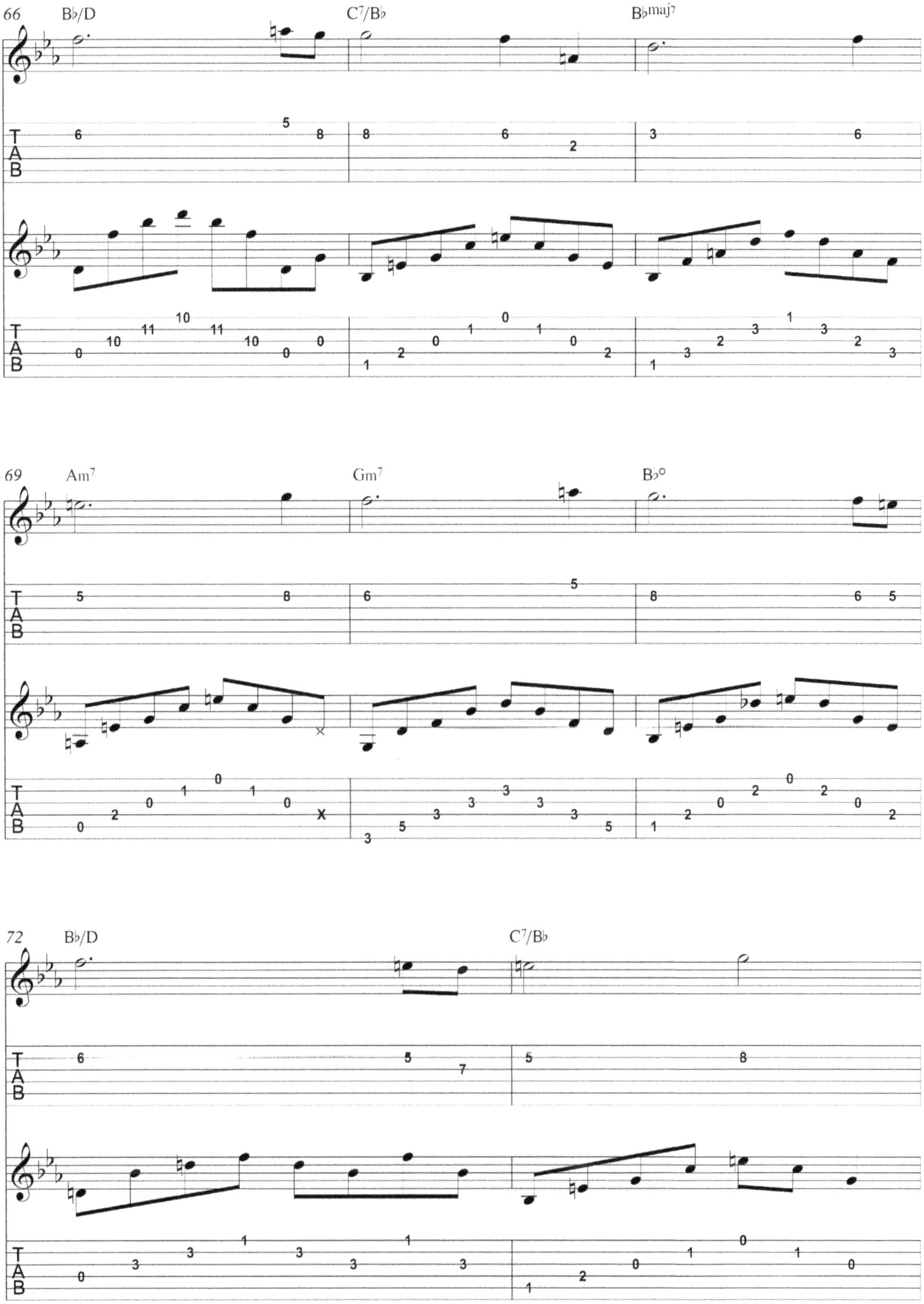
66
B♭/D
C7/B♭
B♭maj7
69
Am7
Gm7
B♭°
72
B♭/D
C7/B♭

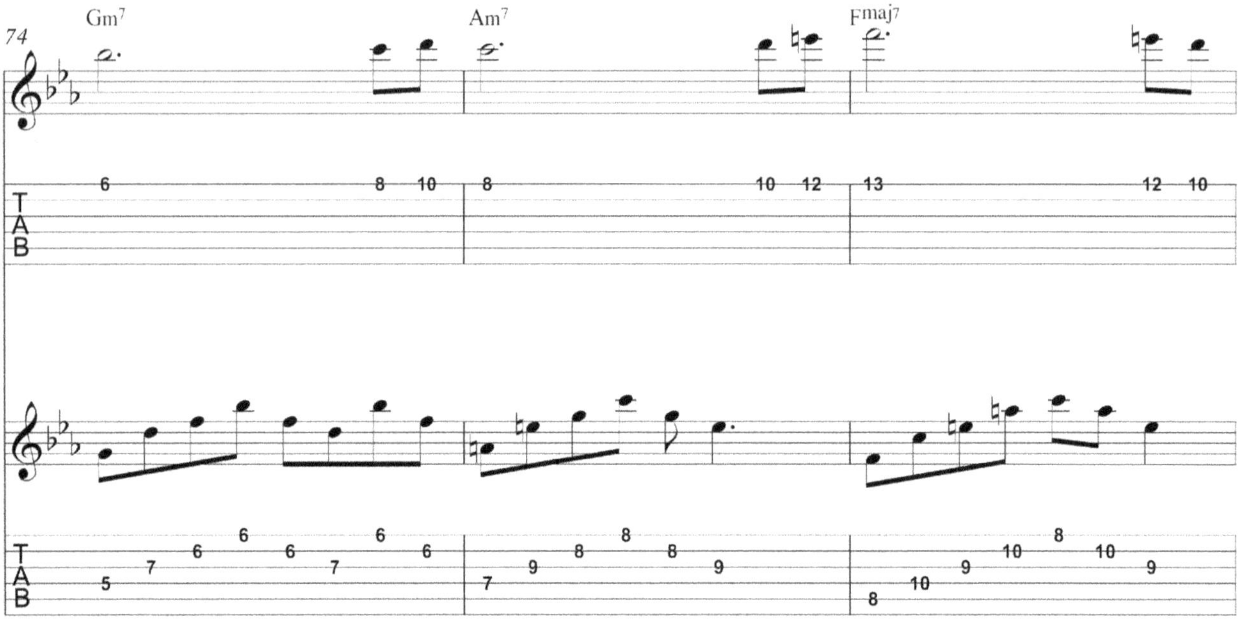
74
Gm7
Am7
Fmaj7

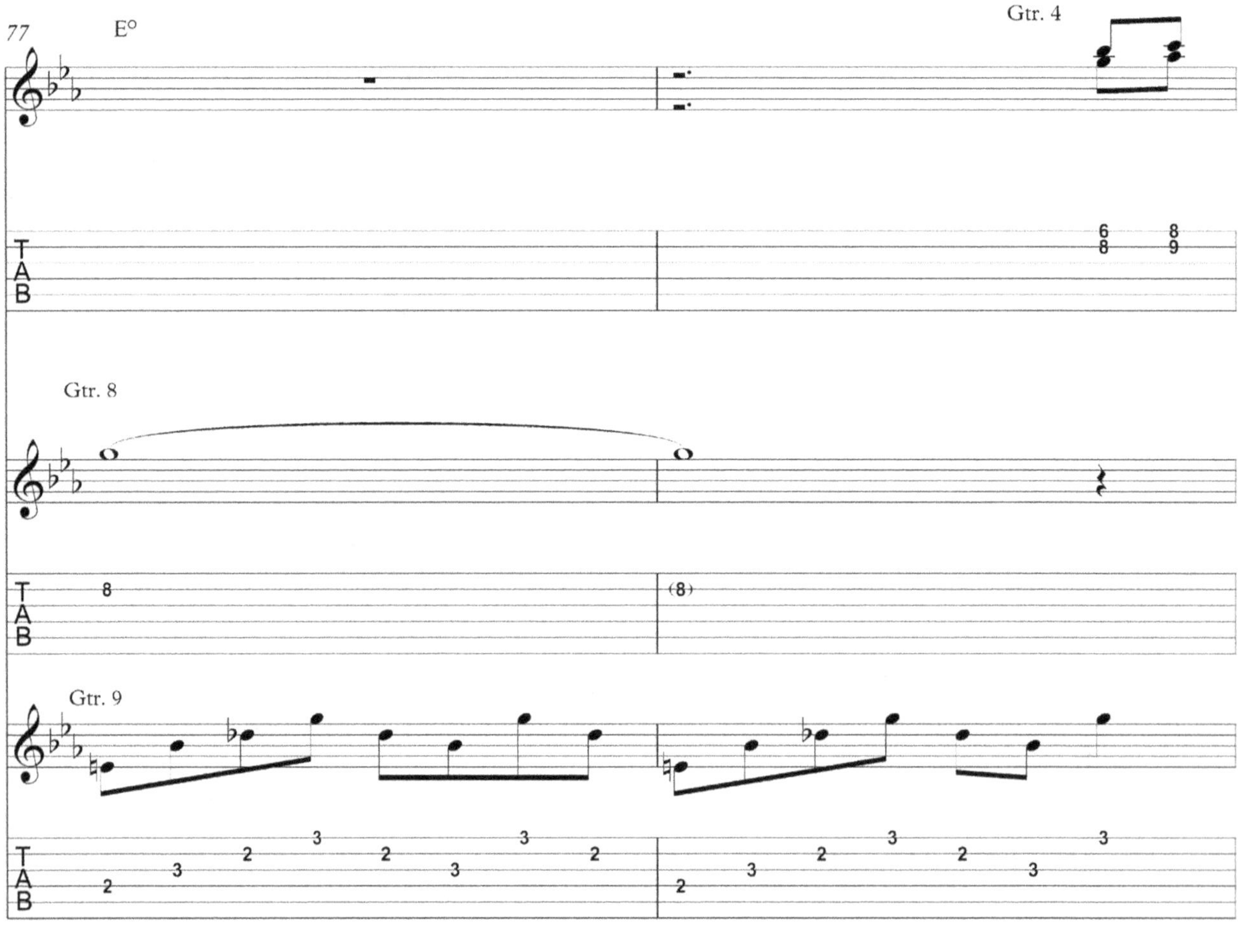
77
E°
Gtr. 4
Gtr. 8
Gtr. 9

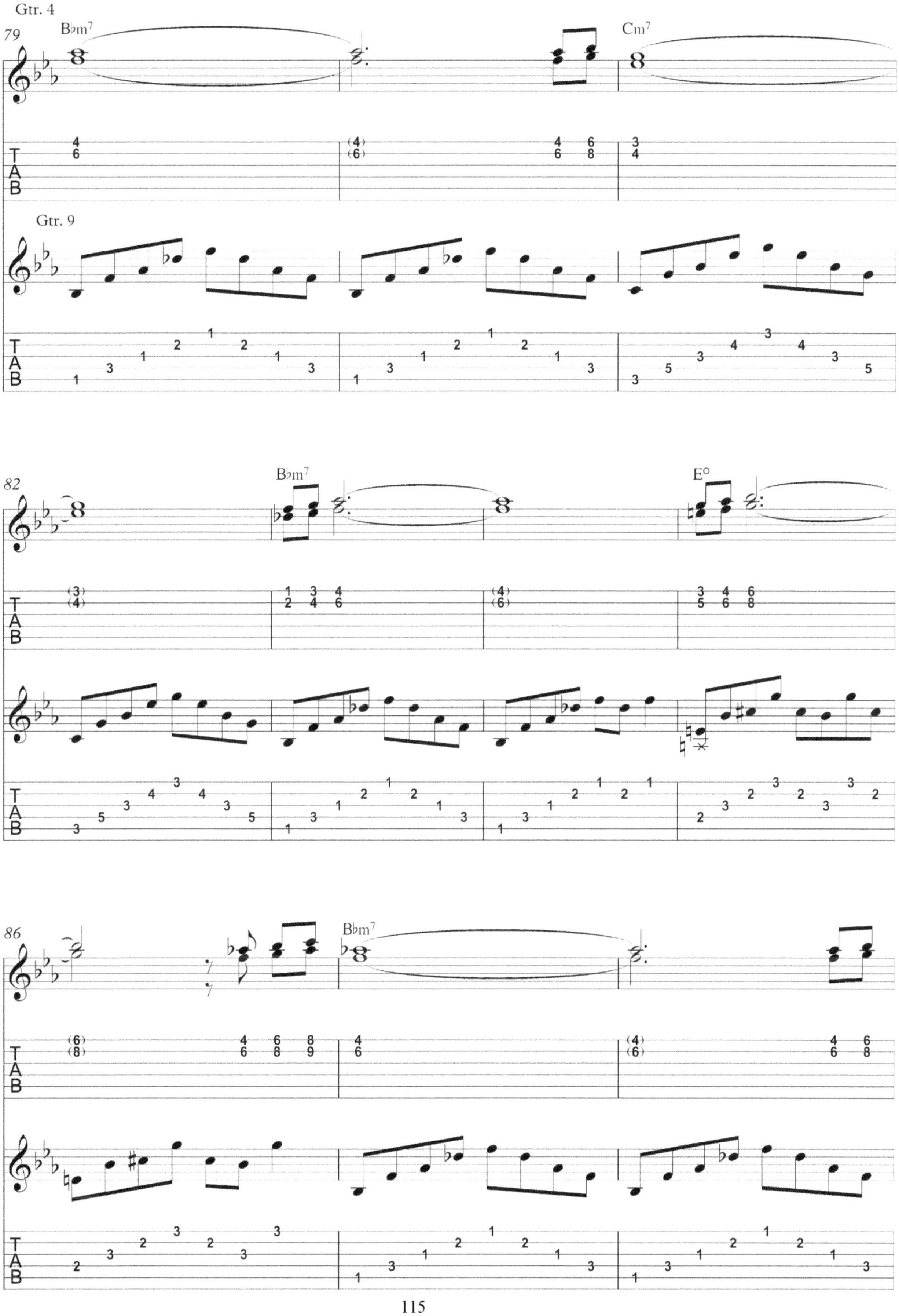
Gtr. 4
79
B♭m7
Cm7
Gtr. 9
82
B♭m7
E°
86
B♭m7

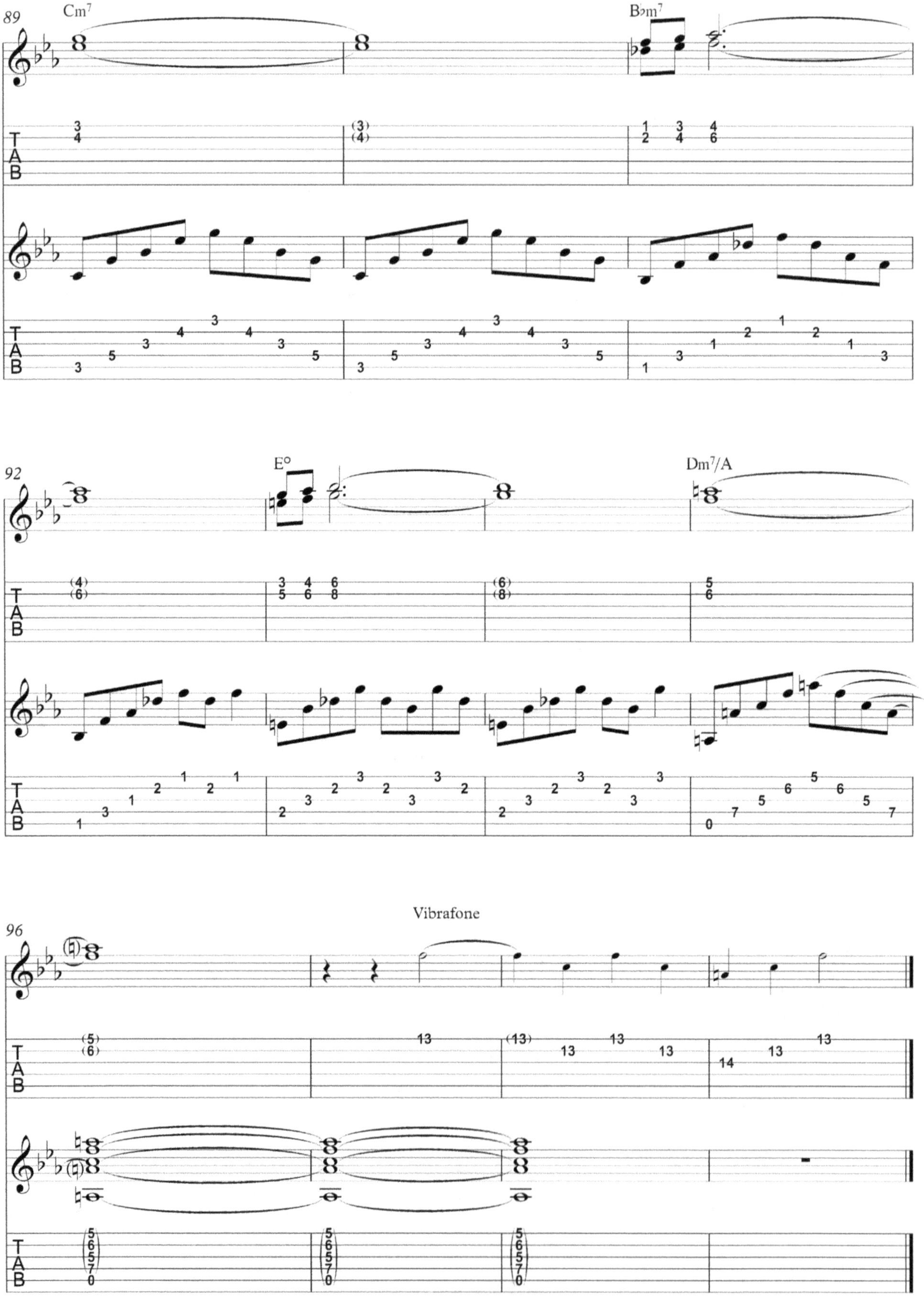
89
Cm7
B♭m7
92
E°
Dm7/A
96
Vibrafone

THE HERMIT
BY STEVE HACKETT

Intro:
|Cm |G7(5#)/B   G7/B | Eb6/Bb |F7/A |

    Cm   **G7(5#)/B**   **G7/B**
THE MANTLE OF ATTAINMENT

    Eb6/Bb   **F7/A**
WEIGHS HEAVY ON HIS SHOULDERS

Cm   **G7(5#)/B**   **G7/B**
GUIDED BY A LANTERN

Eb6/Bb   **F7/A**
FLICKERING HE GROWS OLDER

  Cm   **G7(5#)/B**   **G7/B**
A REFUGE FOUND IN EXILE

    Eb6/Bb   **F7/A**
HE SHUFFLES ON IN BLINDNESS

     Cm   **G7(5#)/B**   **G7/B**
YOU'LL TAKE HIS HAND, HE'LL LOSE HIMSELF

    Eb6/Bb   **F7/A**
BEWILDERED BY YOUR KINDNESS

|EbMaj7/D   Cm9 | | EbMaj7/D   Cm9 | |

|Am7(b5)   BbMaj7| C(add2add4) |Gm13/Bb | |

|Cm | G(add9)/B   G/B |Cm/Bb   Dm7 |Dm7/G |

| Cm | G7(5#)/B   G7 |Eb6/Bb |F7/A |

Cm   G7(5#)/B   G7/B
ENSHROUDED BY DARKNESS

Eb6/Bb   F7/A
A FIGURE SLOWLY FORMS

    Cm   G7(5#)/B   G7/B
THROUGH MANY YEARS OF BANISHMENT

Eb6/Bb   F7/A
NO SHELTER FROM THE STORM

Cm   G7(5#)/B   G7/B
TO FIND THIS SLAVE OF SOLITUDE

Eb6/Bb   F7/A
YOU'LL KNOW HIM BY HIS STAR

Cm   G7(5#)/B   G7/B
THEN TAKE HIS HAND, HE'LL LOSE HIMSELF

Eb6/Bb   F7/A
KNOWING WHO YOU ARE

|EbMaj7/D   Cm9 | |EbMaj7/D   Cm9 | |

|Am7(b5)   BbMaj7 |D(add9)/A |D | E7/A |

|Bbmaj9   C/Bb |Bbmaj9   C/Bb | |Bbmaj7/D |

|Em7(b5) | Fmaj7   C/G||

||BbMaj7 |Am7 |Gm7 |Bbdim |Bb/D |C7/Bb |

|Gm7 |Am7 |Fmaj7 |Bb/D | C7/Bb |BbMaj7 |

Am7 |Gm7 |Bbdim |Bb/D |C7/Bb |Gm7 |Am7 |

Famj7 |Edim | | Bbm7 | |Cm7 | | Bbm7 | |

|Edim |Bbm7 | | Cm7 | |Bbm7 | |Edim | |

|Dm7/A |

STAR OF SIRIUS

Steve explained why he chose "The Star" Tarot card because…

I liked the image of the Egyptian goddess Isis pouring water on the land. It gave a sense of renewal, restoration and rebirth.

Steve used a Yamaha acoustic six-string through a Leslie cabinet.

He chose Robin Miller to play the cor anglais as well as the oboe on this track. He had heard Robin playing on King Crimson's *Lizard* and he thought he sounded really well.

Players/Instruments:

Steve Hackett: Zemaitis Custom 12-string, Steel 6-string Yamaha acoustic, Gibson Les Paul Gold Top 1957, EMS Synthi Hi-Fli, Harmonium

John Hackett: Synth Arp Odyssey

John Acock: Elka-Rhapsody Synth, Mellotron

Phil Collins: Vocals, Vibes, Drums

Johnny Gustafson: Bass

Robin Miller: Oboe and Cor anglais

Studio Gears : Star of Sirius - Voyage of the Acolyte

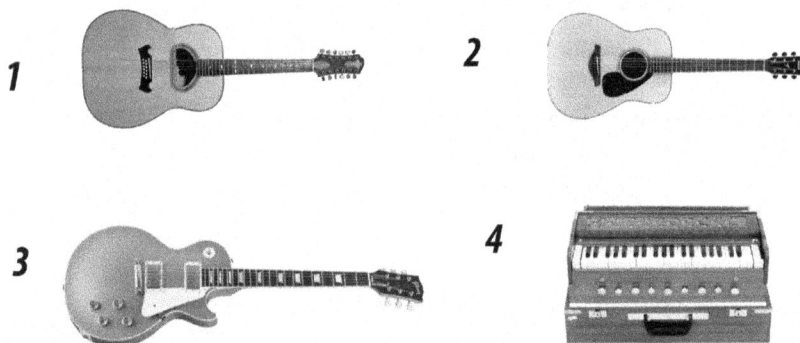

Pedal Board built by Pete Cornish

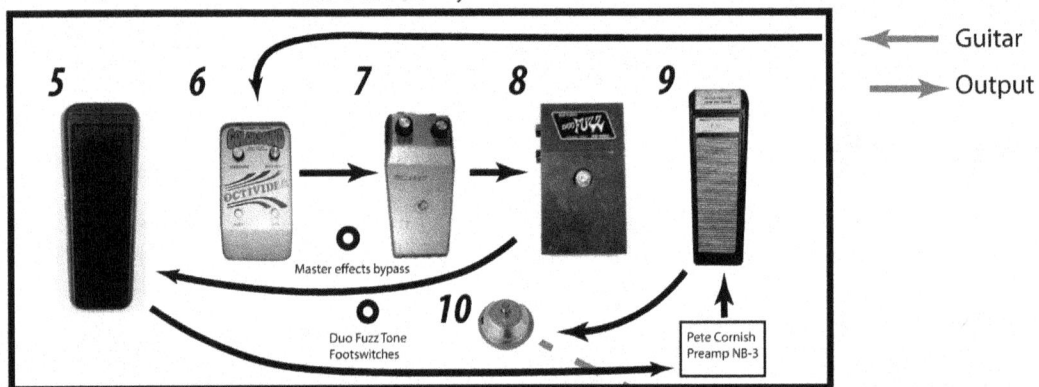

Guitar

Output

Master effects bypass

Duo Fuzz Tone
Footswitches

Pete Cornish
Preamp NB-3

1 - Zemaitis Custom 12-String
2 - Yamaha Acoustic 6-string
3 - Gibson Les Paul Gold Top 1957
4 - Harmonium
5 - Cry Baby Wah-Wah
6 - Colorsound Octivider
7 - Marshall Supa Fuzz
8 - Shaftesbury Duo Fuzz
9 - Schaller Volume Pedal F121
10 -Pedal Switch for Echoplex EP-3
11 - Echoplex EP-3 Tape Echo
12 - HH 100w IC100
13 - Hiwatt 150w 4x12 Cabinets SE 4123
14 - EMS Syth Hi-Fli
15 - Leslie Cabinet

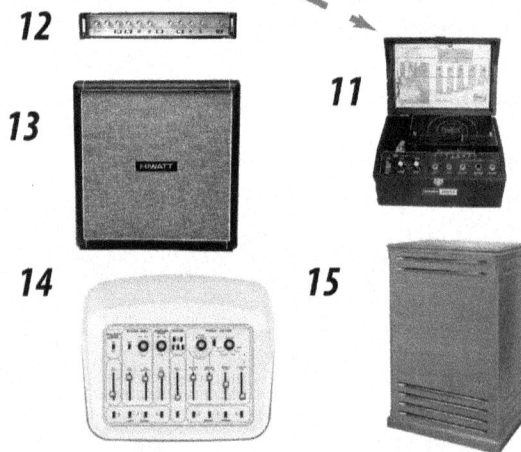

Signal Routing:

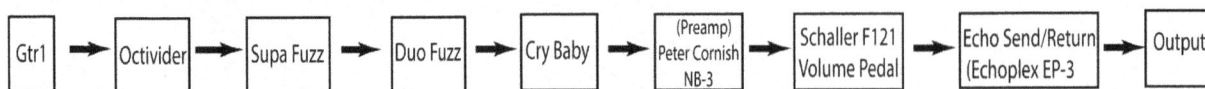

Gtr1 → Octivider → Supa Fuzz → Duo Fuzz → Cry Baby → (Preamp) Peter Cornish NB-3 → Schaller F121 Volume Pedal → Echo Send/Return (Echoplex EP-3) → Output

Star of Sirius: details

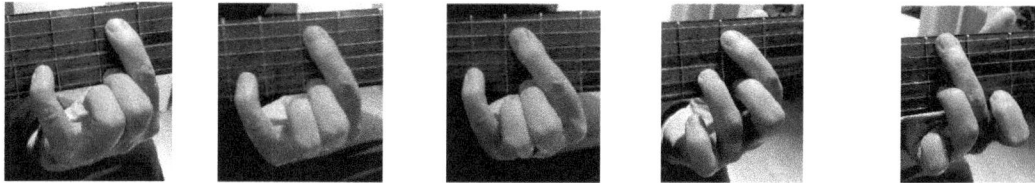

Photos 43-52: Steve showing how to play these parts in Star of Sirius

from Steve Hackett - *Voyage of the Acolyte*
Star of Sirius
by Steve Hackett

Transcribed by Paulo De Carvalho

*English Horn arr. for gtr.

* Zamaitis Custom 12 strings
**Chords symbols reflect overall harmony.

lock   the   door   of   night   Ne - bu - lous

*Gtr. 3   Arp (John)

*Synth Arp Odyssey (John Hacket) arr. for gtr.

Gtr. 1

Dm⁷/G   C⁹⁽ˢᵘˢ⁴⁾

bright

A - gain re - newed___ by the ves - sels of I - sis
Al-though the jour - ney is still___ far from en - ded

Lyrics:
You're rea - dy to fly
You gave at the___
sky___
A - - - bo - ce cloud - less night
Ne - bu - lous bright___

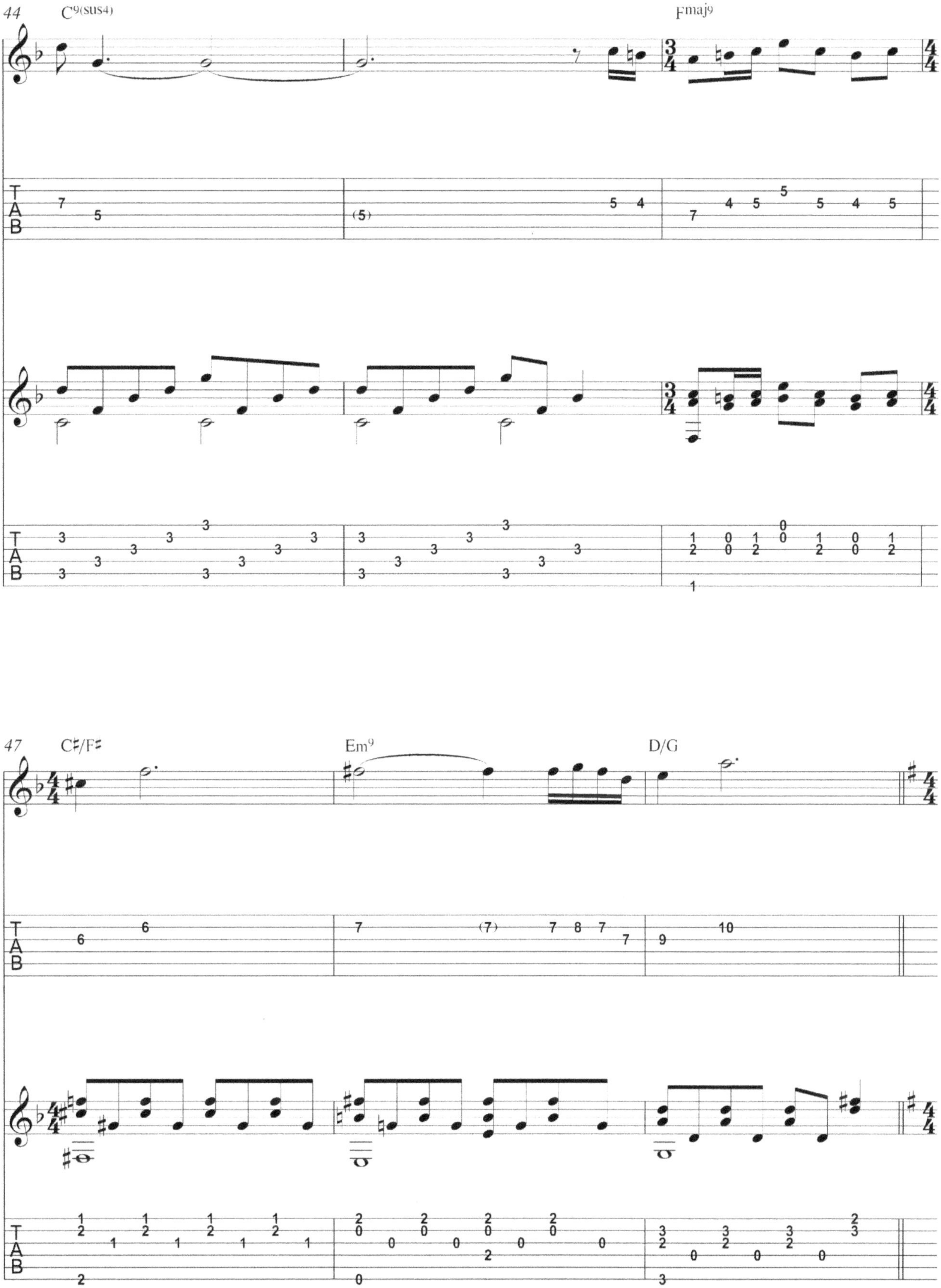
44
C9(sus4)
Fmaj9
47
C♯/F♯
Em9
D/G

*Vibes arr. for gtr.

*Mellotron arr. for gtr.

He who knows love

*Steel 6 strings Yamaha acoustic

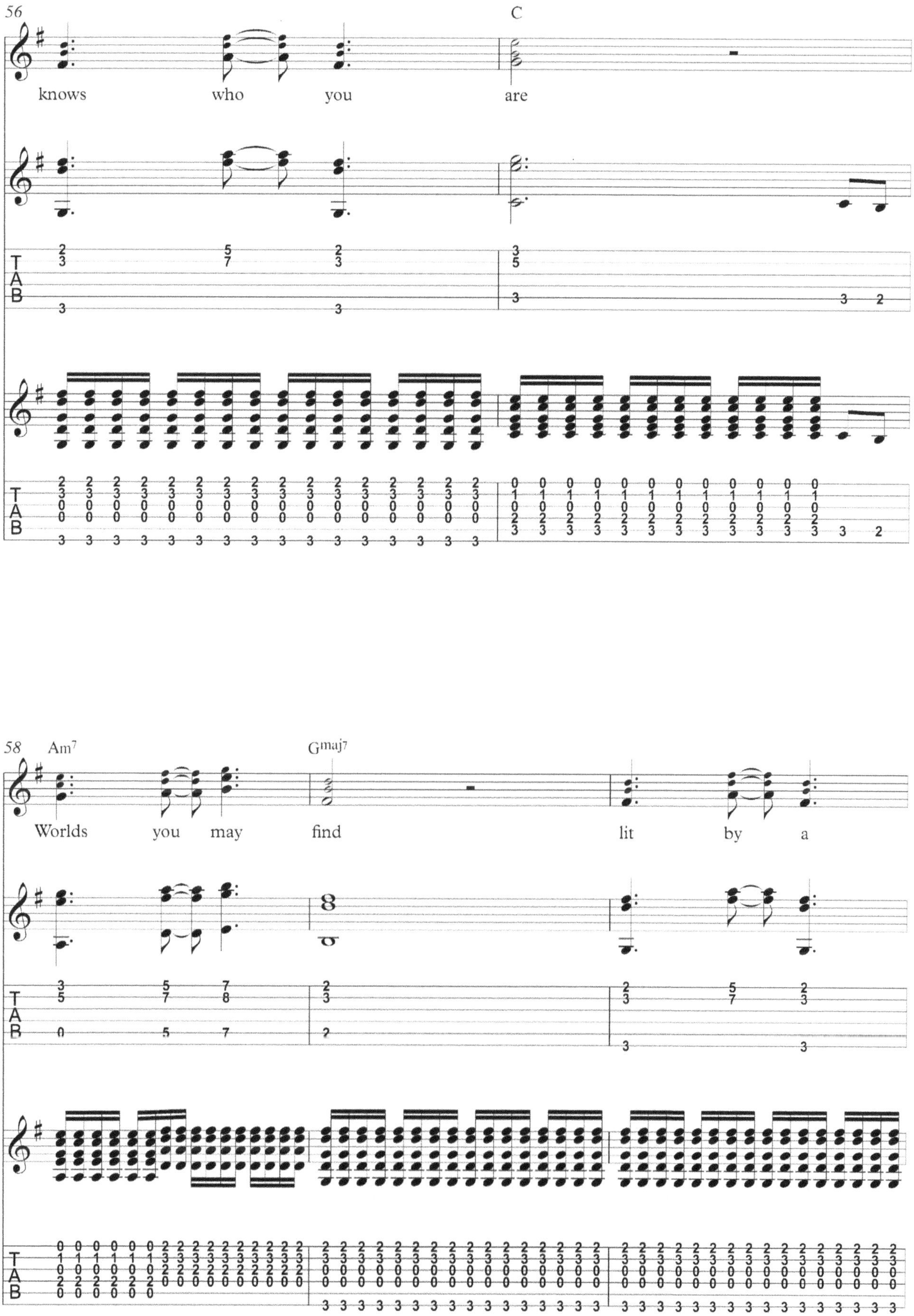
56
C
knows who you are
58 Am7
Gmaj7
Worlds you may find
lit by a

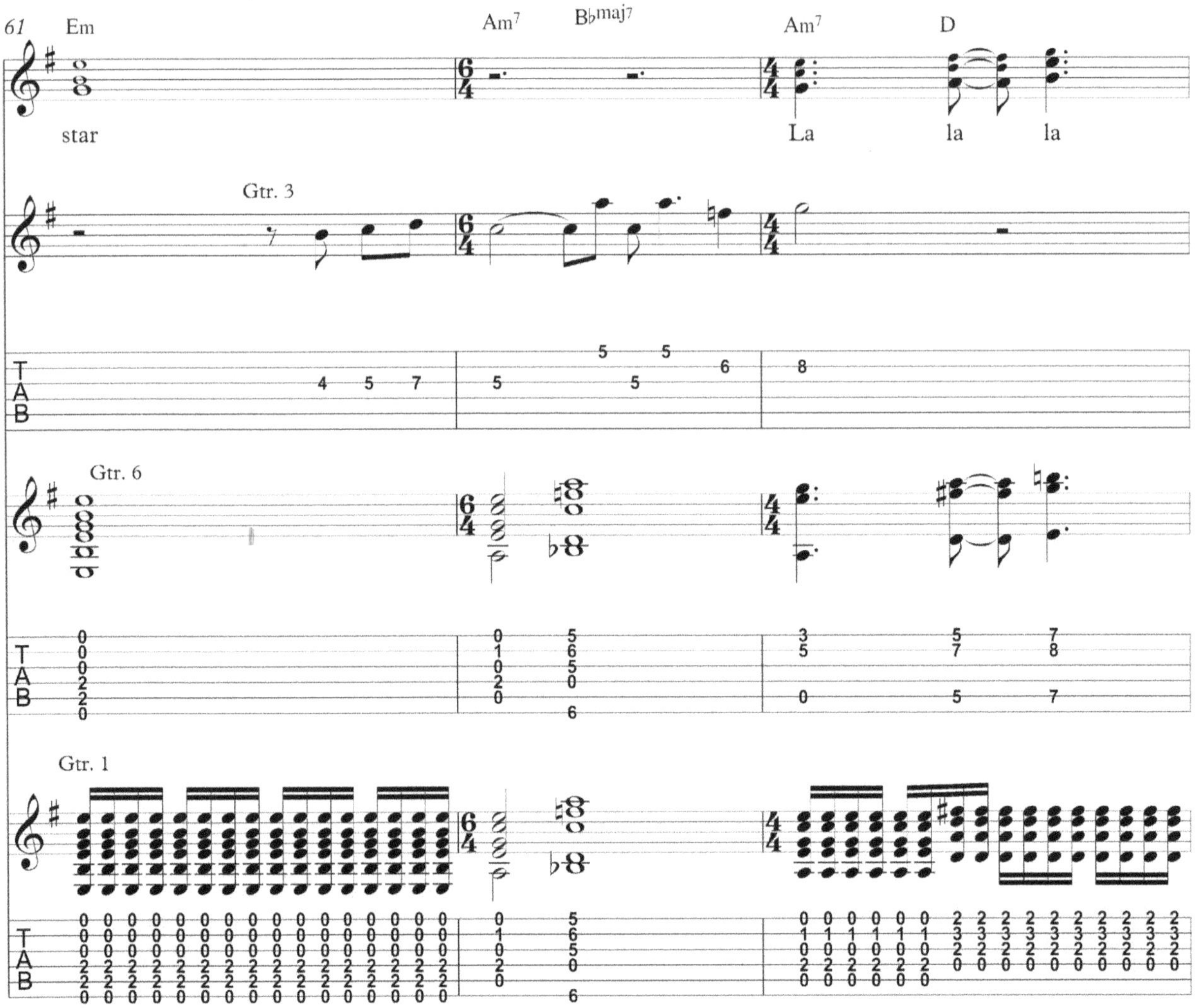
61
Em
Am7
B♭maj7
Am7
D
star
La
la
la
Gtr. 3
Gtr. 6
Gtr. 1

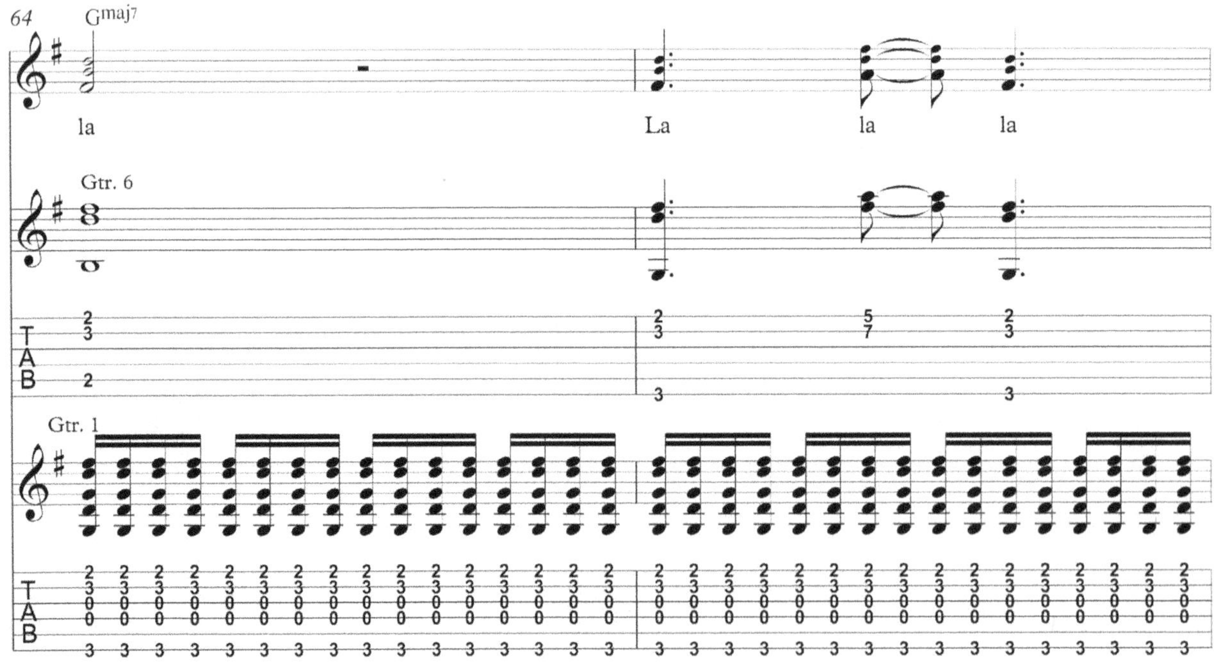
64
Gmaj7
la
La
la
la
Gtr. 6
Gtr. 1

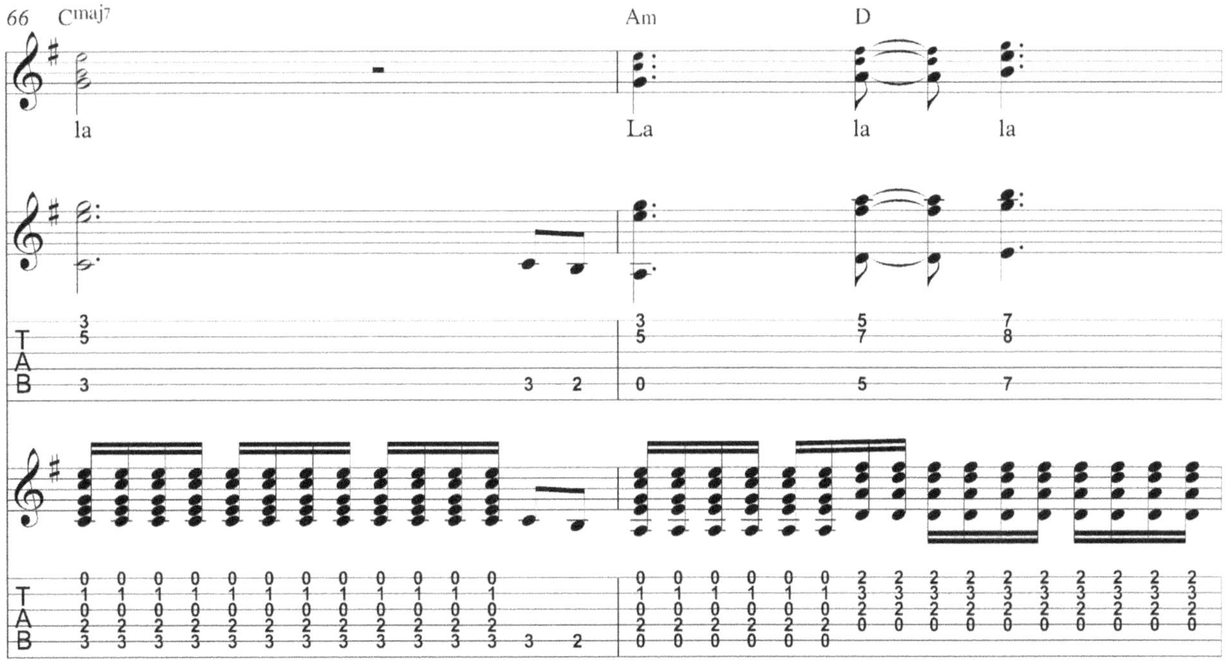
66
Cmaj7
Am
D
la
La
la
la

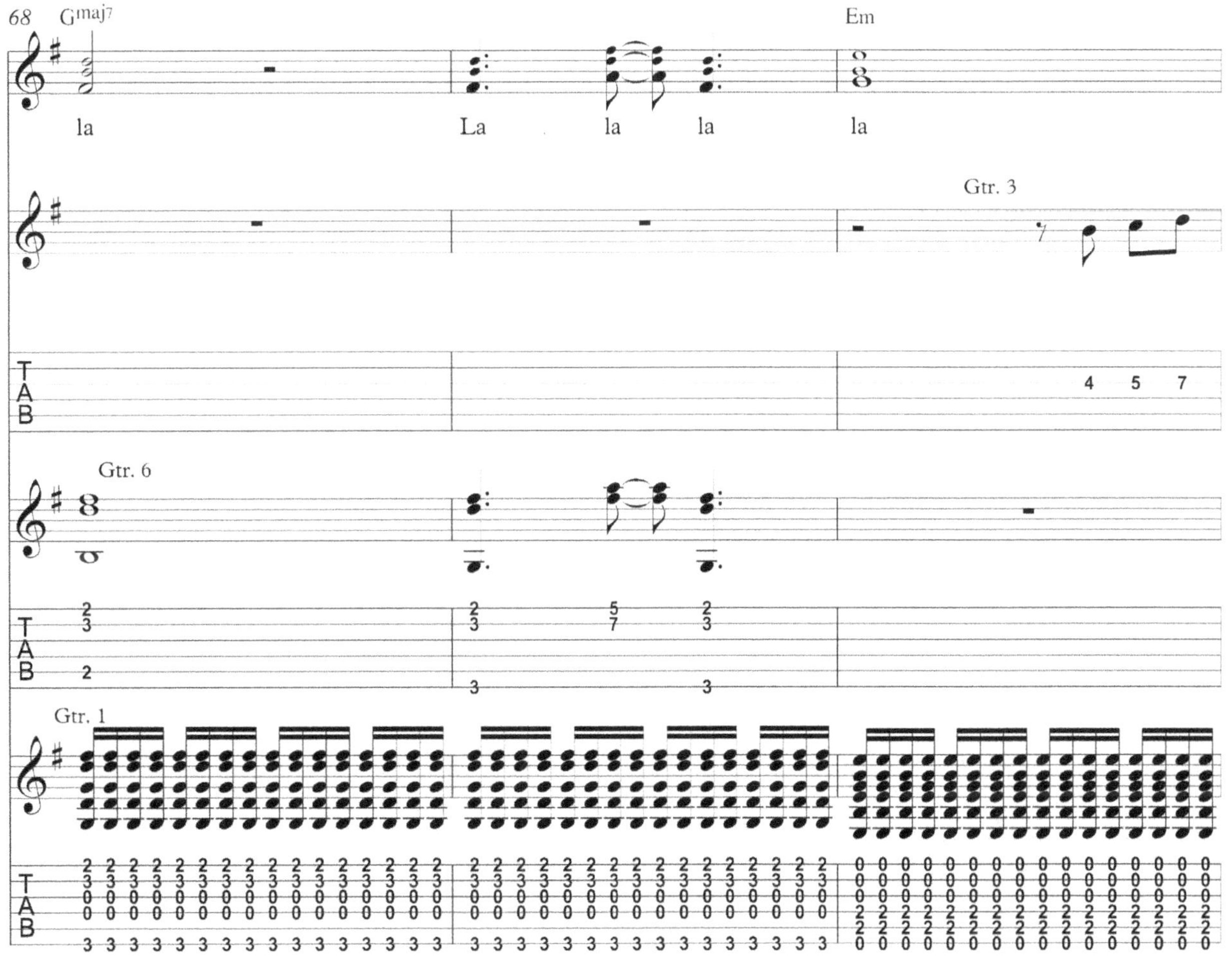
68
Gmaj7
Em
la
La
la
la
la
Gtr. 3
Gtr. 6
Gtr. 1

Gtr. 3
71
Em
Am7
B♭maj7
C(add4)
C
C(add4)
Gtr. 1
74
G
Am
G/B
G/B
C/E
G/F
76
Dm/C
F/B♭

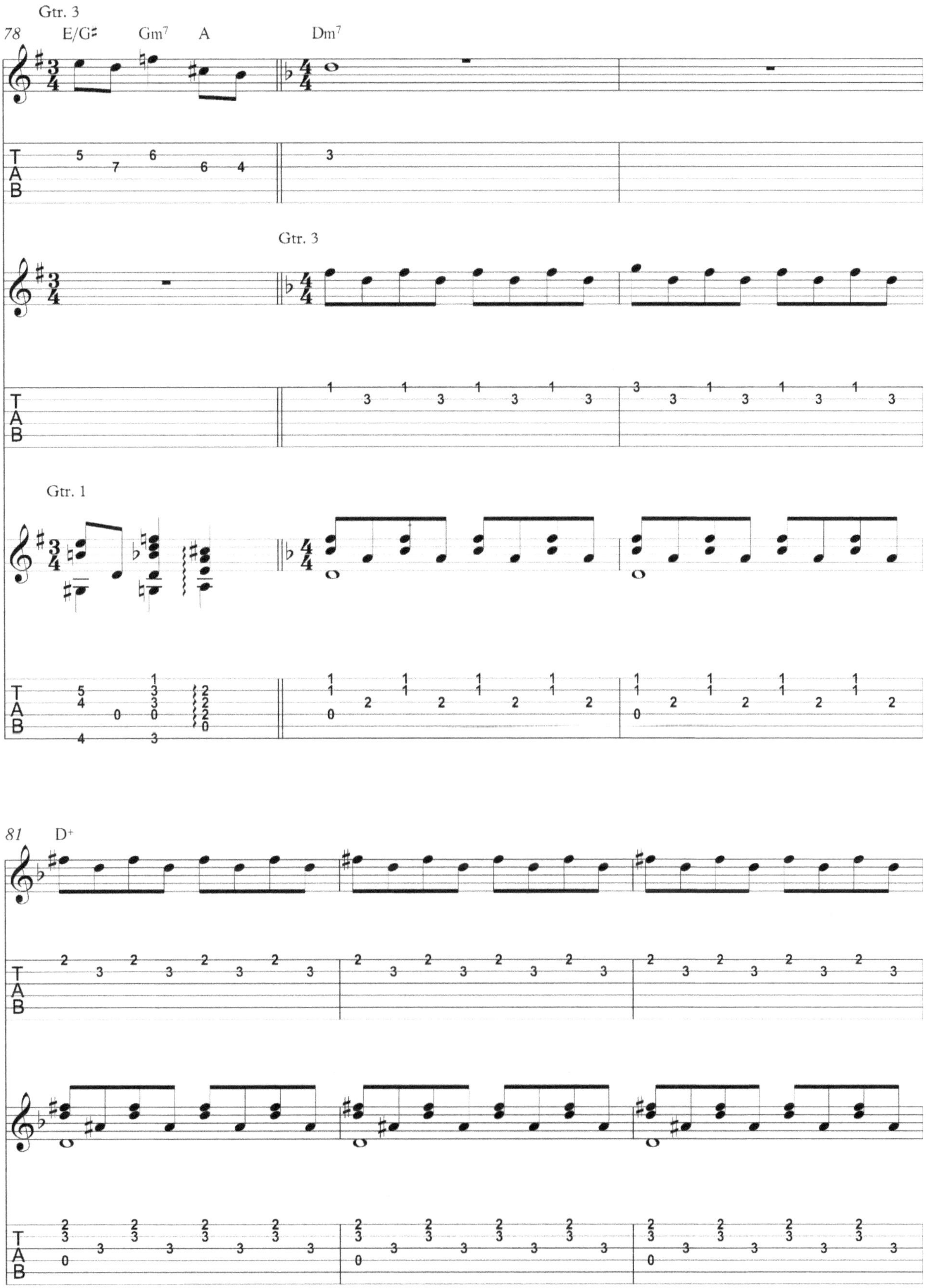
Gtr. 3
78
E/G♯
Gm7
A
Dm7
Gtr. 3
Gtr. 1
81
D+

84
D♯(♯5)
B7(♯5)
B
Gtr. 3
87
E
B7(add4)/A
E
B7(add4)/A
*Gtr. 7
*Flute arr. for gtr.
Gtr. 6

*Gtr. 8
89
E
B7(add4)/A
E
*Oboe arr. for gtr.
Gtr. 7
Gtr. 6
91
Gtr. 8
A6
B/A
E
B7(add4)/A
Gtr. 6

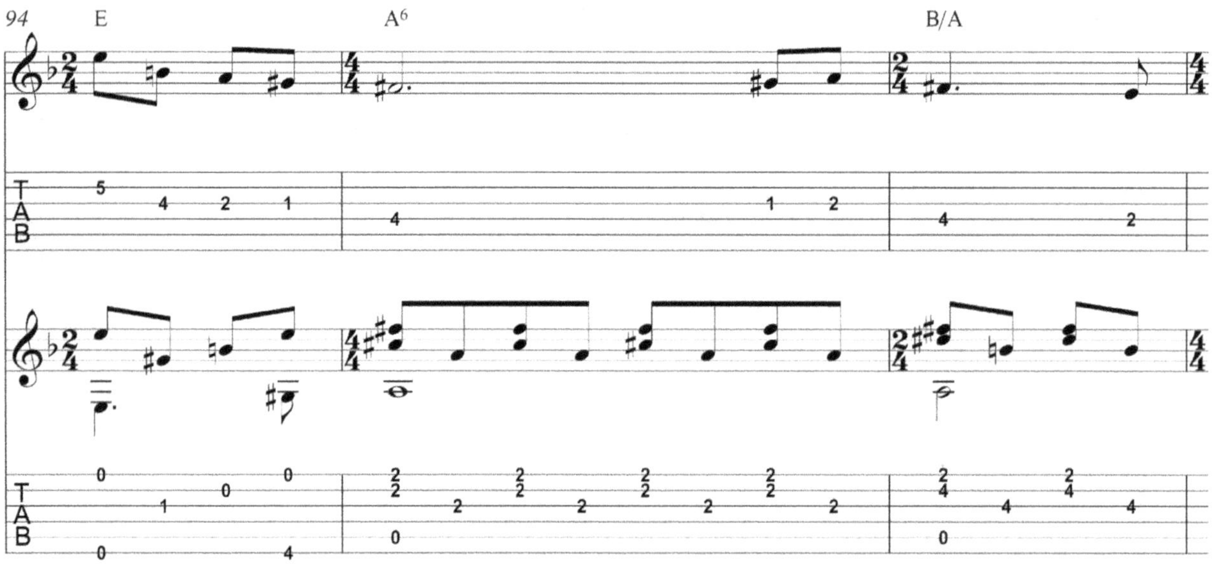
94
E
A6
B/A

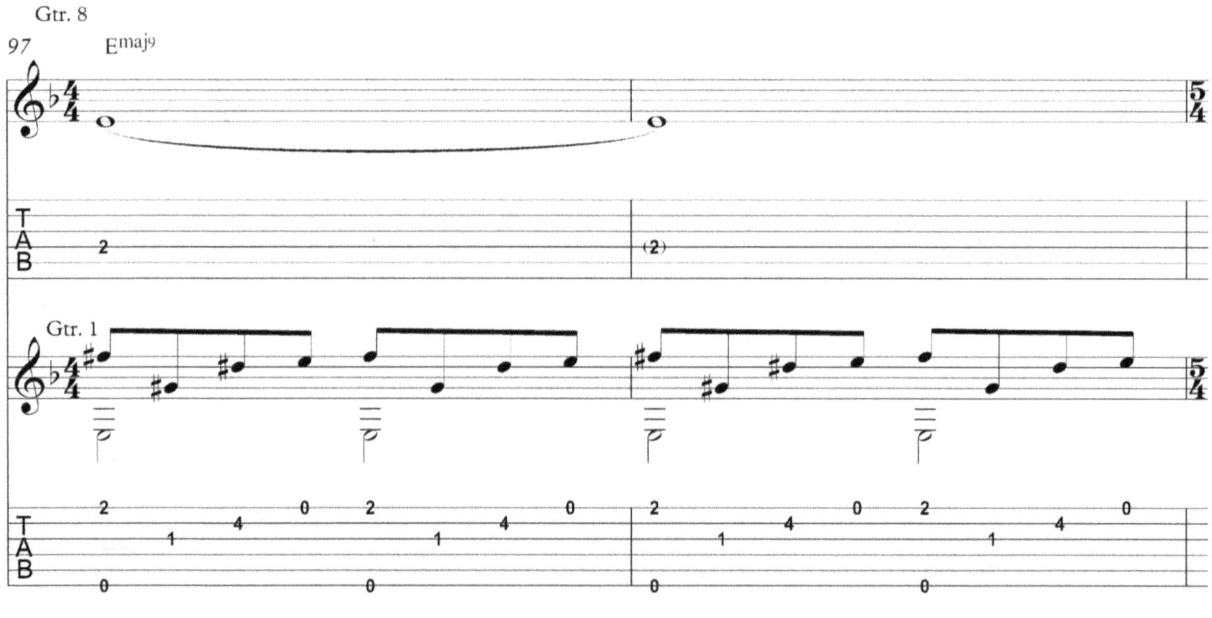
Gtr. 8
97
Emaj9
Gtr. 1

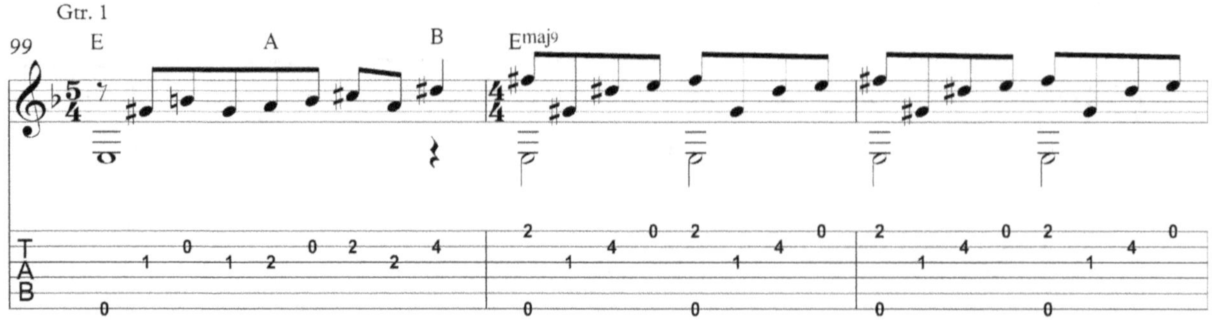
Gtr. 1
99
E
A
B
Emaj9

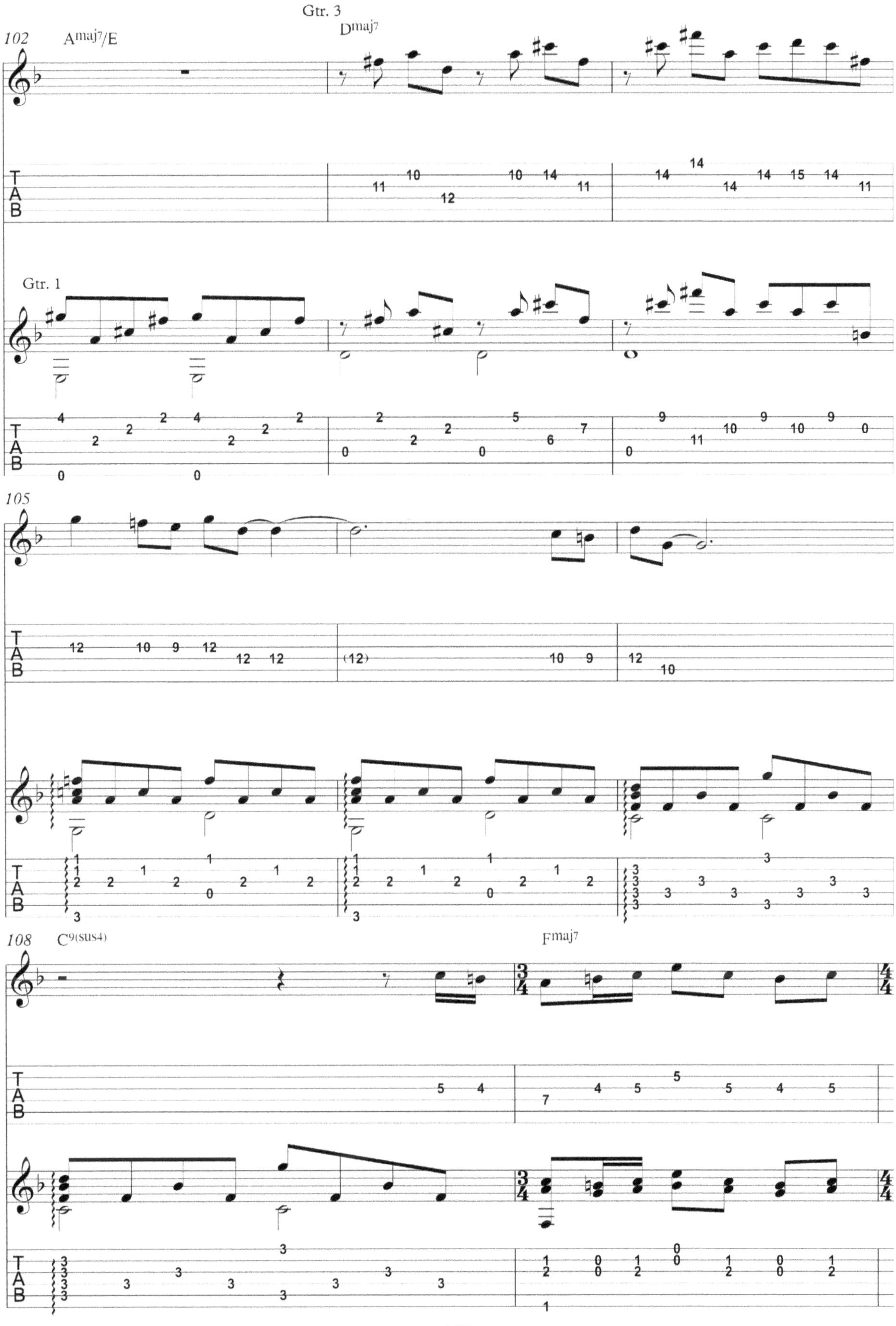
102
Amaj7/E
Gtr. 3
Dmaj7
Gtr. 1
105
108
C9(sus4)
Fmaj7

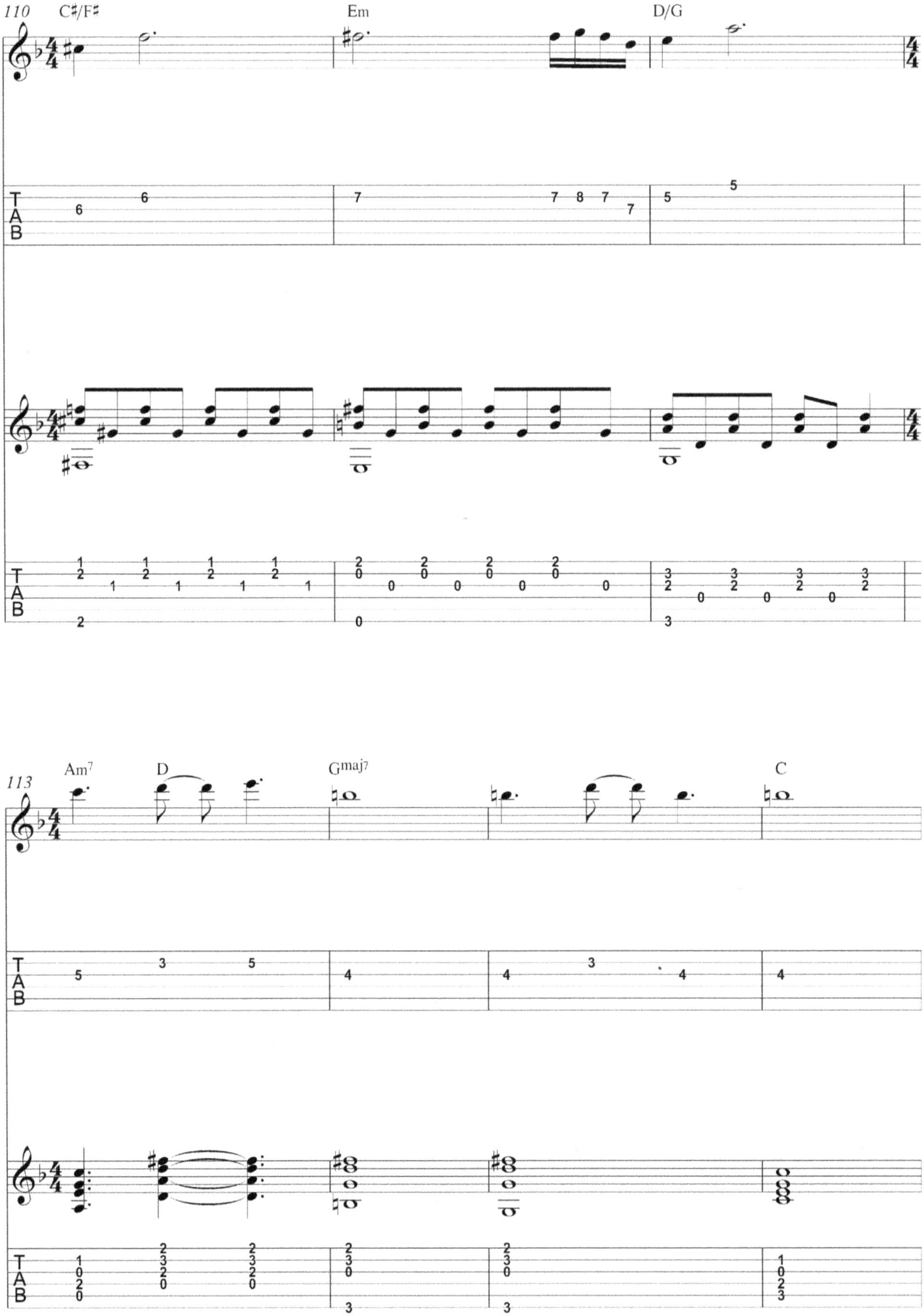
110
C♯/F♯
Em
D/G
113
Am7
D
Gmaj7
C

He who knows love

knows who you

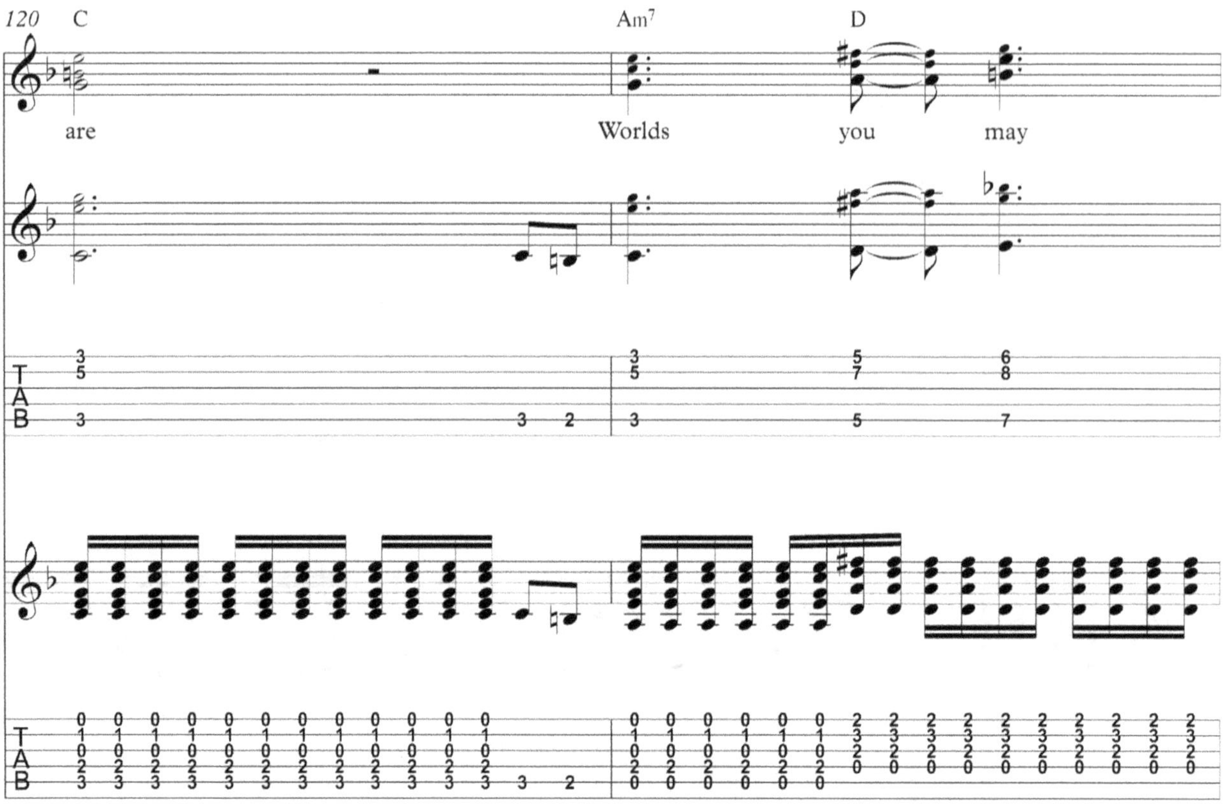
120
C
Am7
D
are
Worlds
you
may

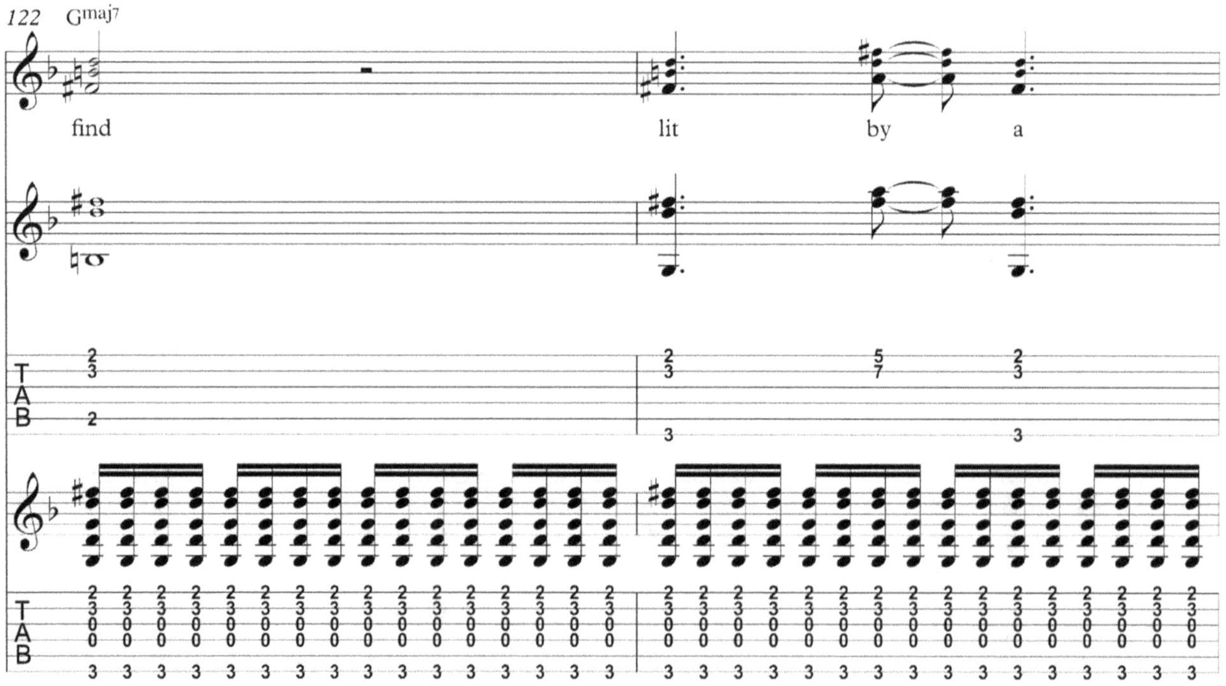
122
Gmaj7
find
lit
by
a

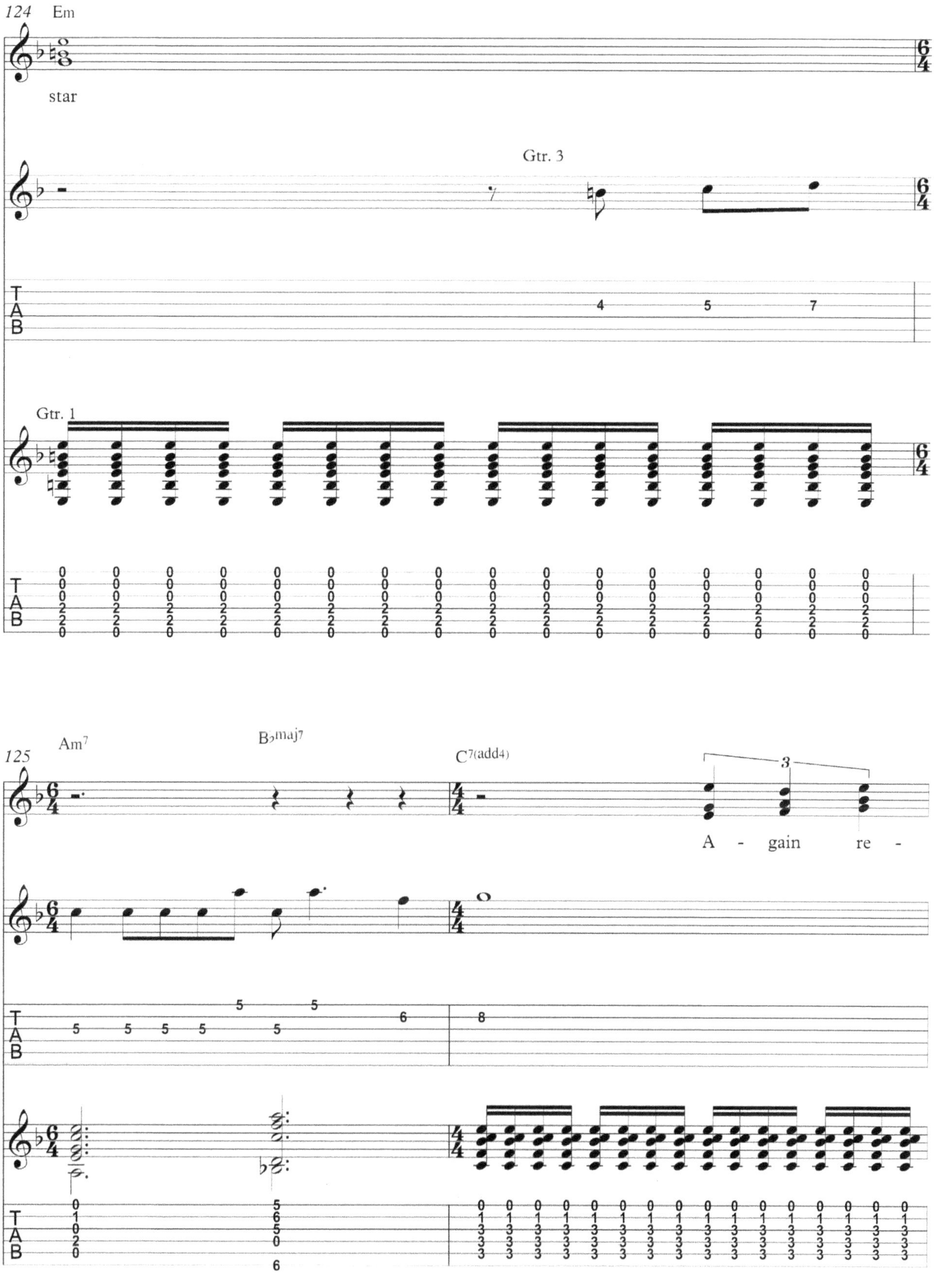
124
Em
star
Gtr. 3
Gtr. 1
125
Am7
B♭maj7
C7(add4)
A - gain re -

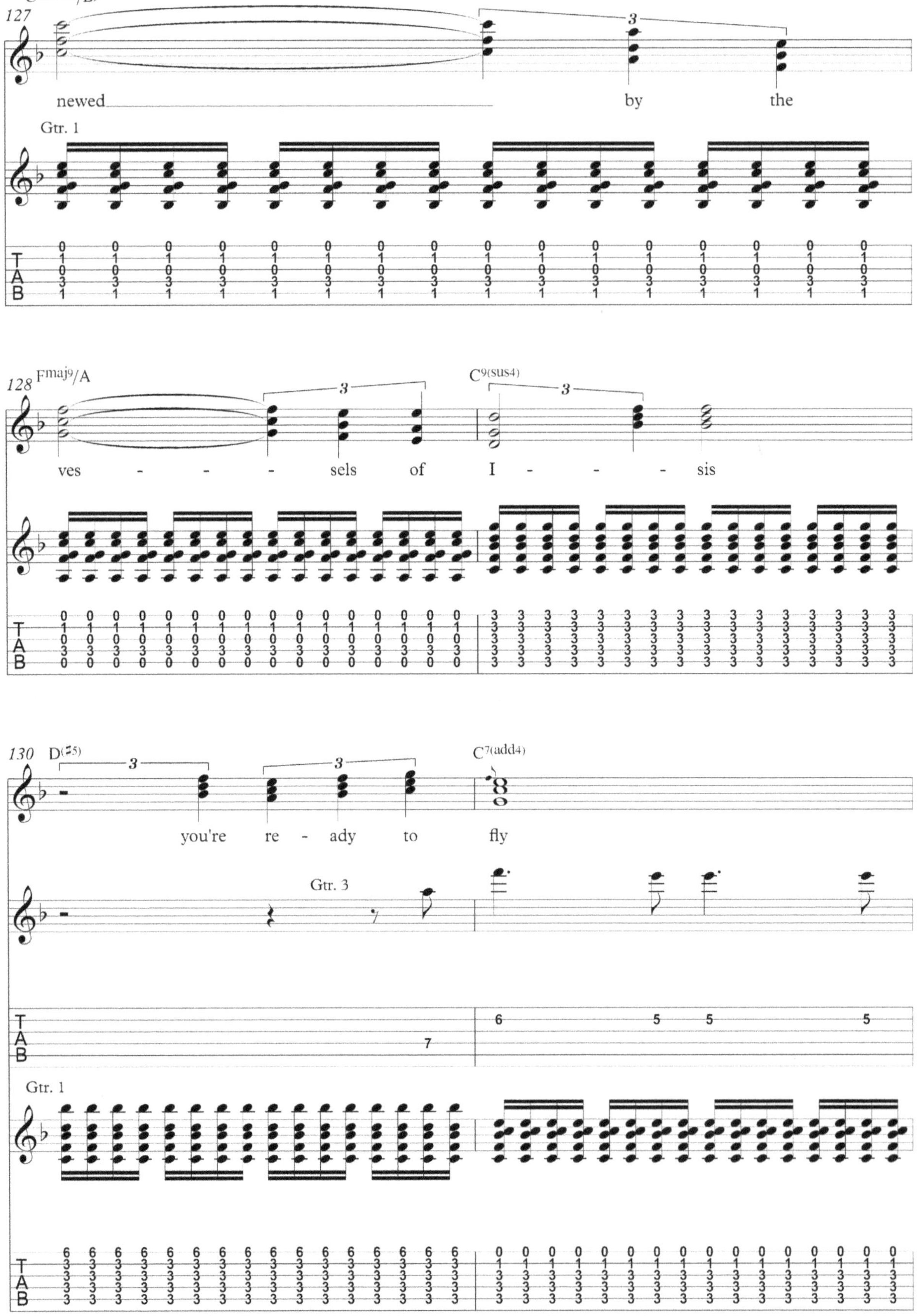
127 C7(add4)/B♭
newed by the
Gtr. 1
128 Fmaj9/A
C9(sus4)
ves - - - sels of I - - - sis
130 D(♯5)
C7(add4)
you're re - ady to fly
Gtr. 3
Gtr. 1

Gtr. 3

C⁷⁽ᵃᵈᵈ⁴⁾/B♭

Fᵐᵃʲ⁹/A

Gtr. 1

C⁹⁽ˢᵘˢ⁴⁾

136
D/G
Am7
D
He
who
knows
Gtr. 3
Gtr. 6
Gtr. 1
138
Gmaj7
love
knows
who
you
Gtr. 6
Gtr. 1

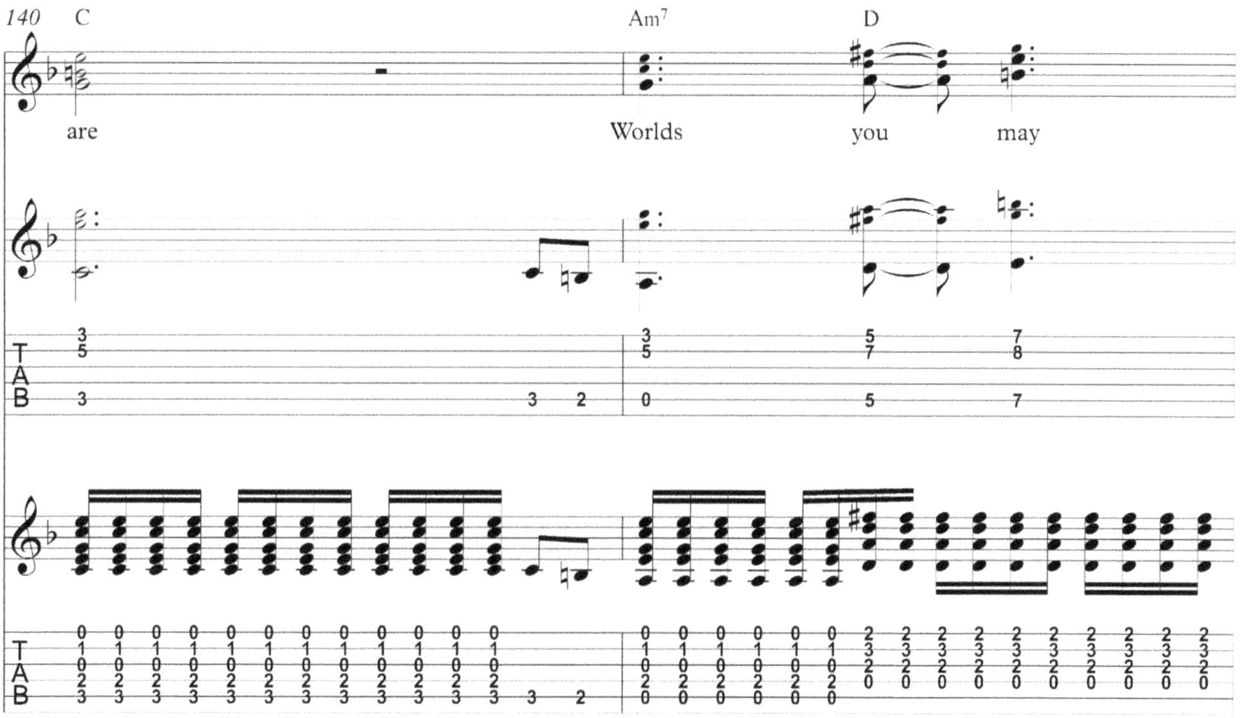
140
C
Am7
D
are
Worlds
you
may
TAB

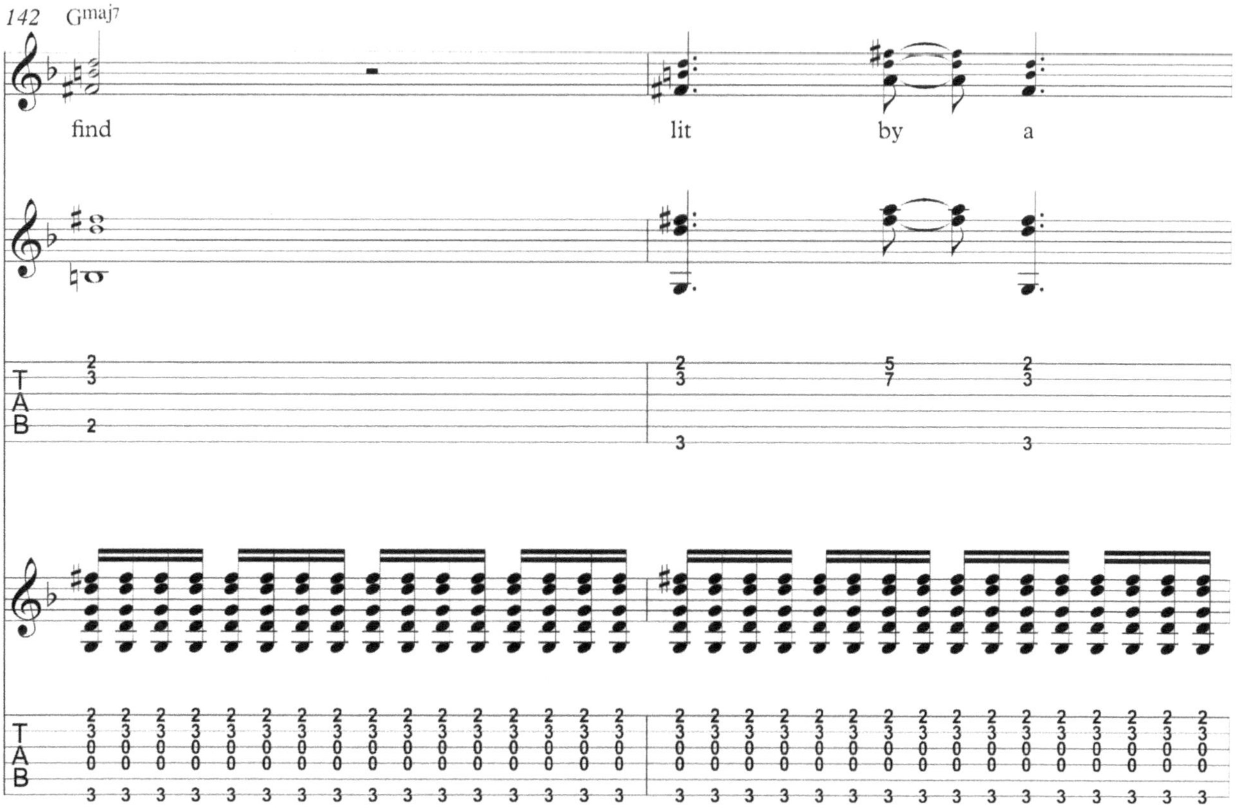
142
Gmaj7
find
lit
by
a
TAB

*Gibson Les Paul Golden Top 1957

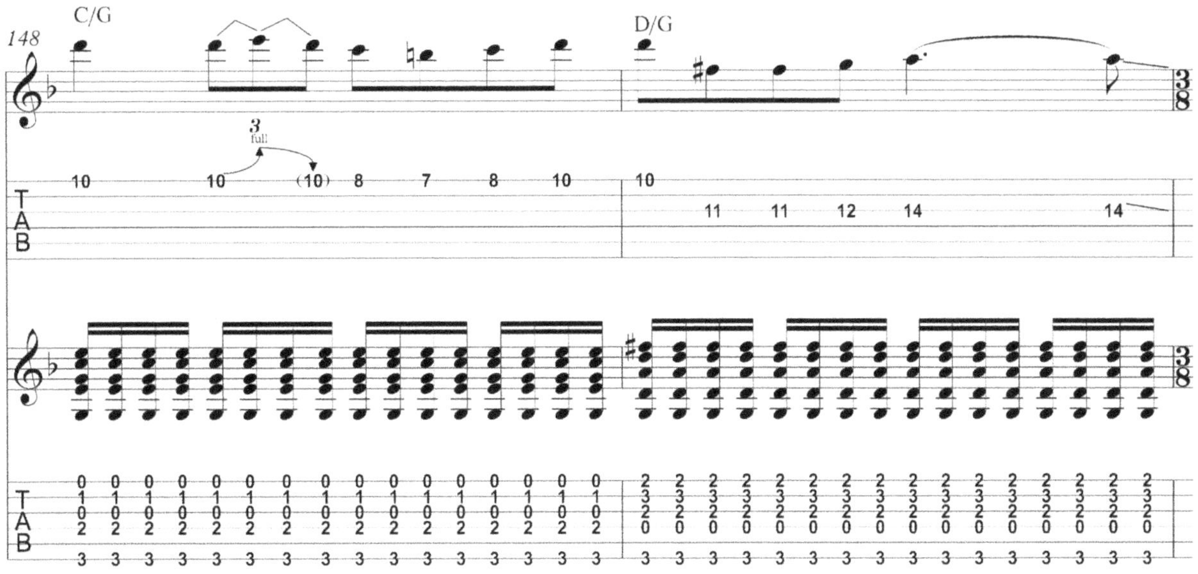

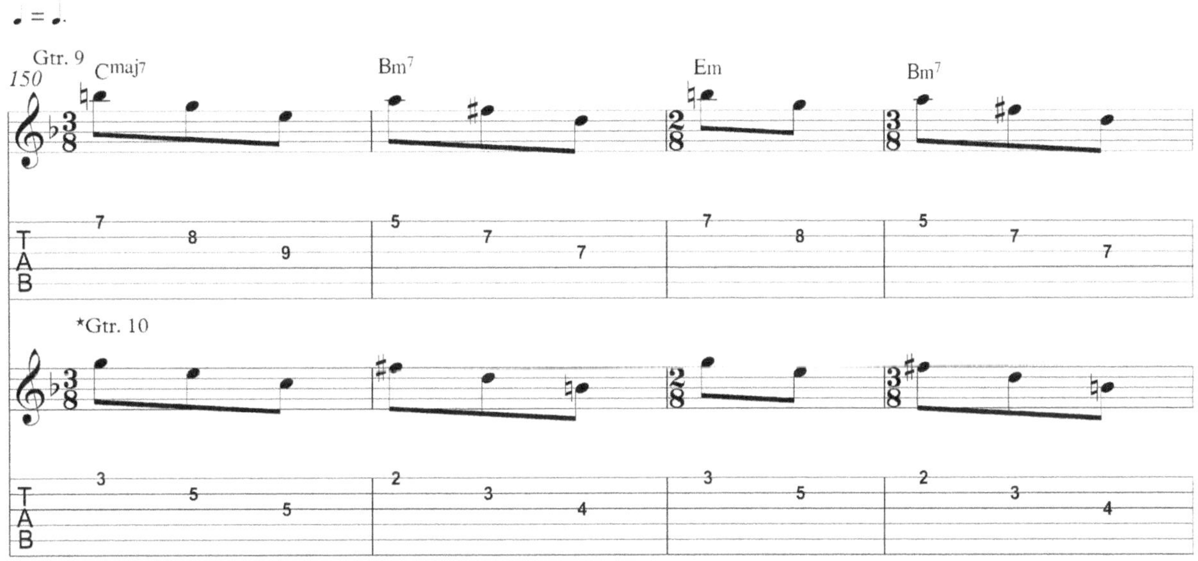

* Gibson Les Paul Golden Top 1957

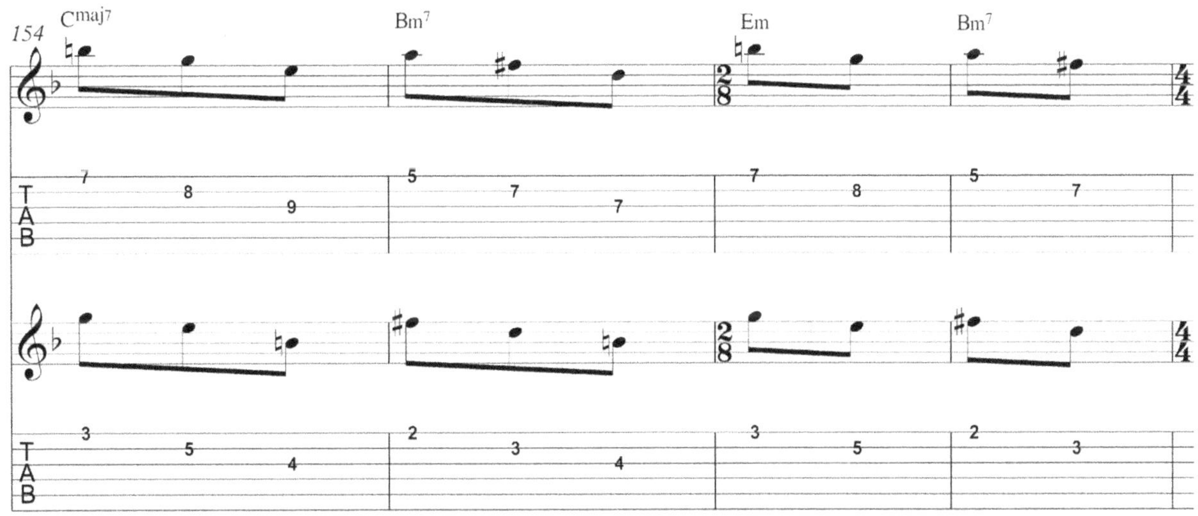

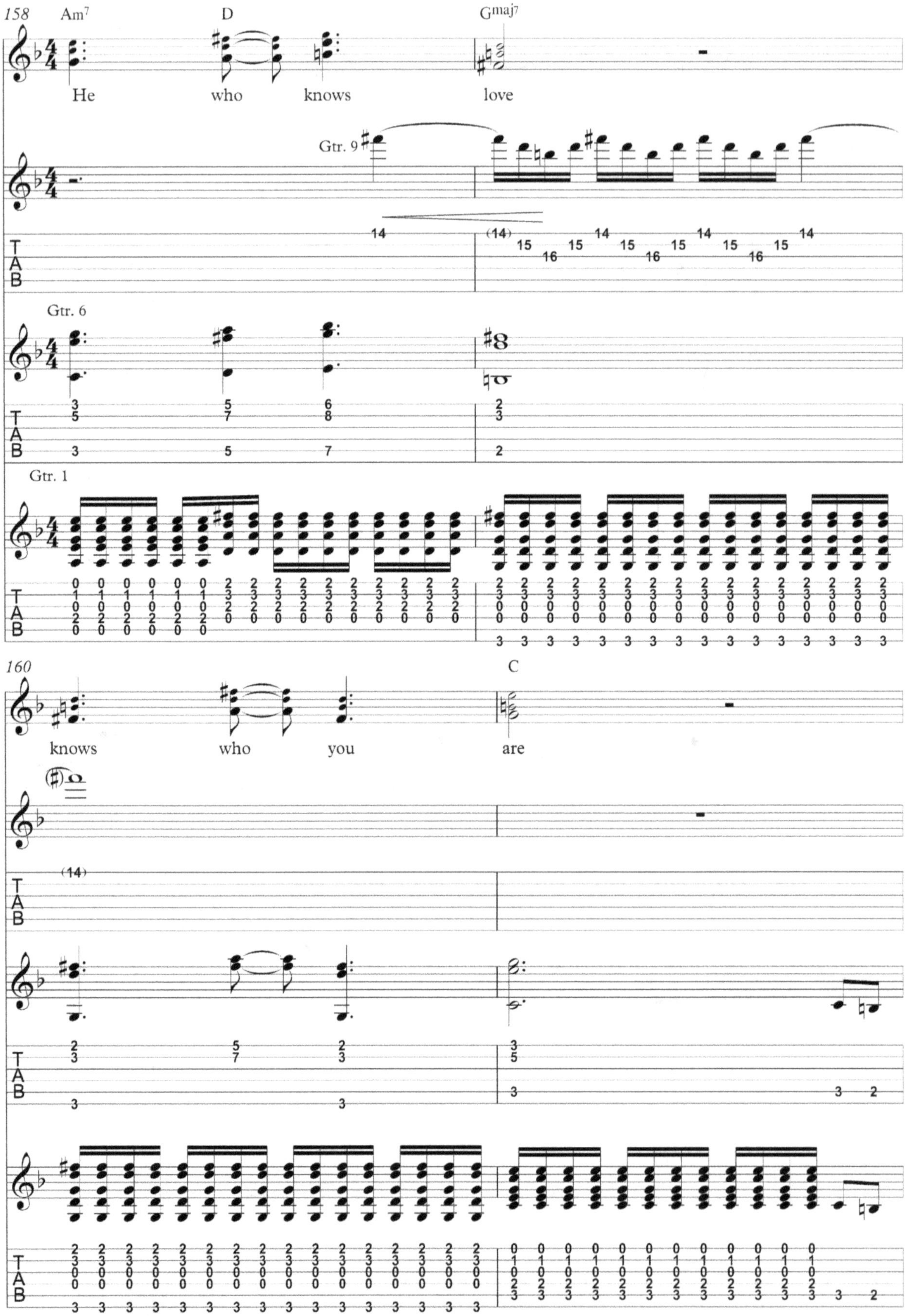
158
Am7
D
Gmaj7
He
who
knows
love
Gtr. 9
Gtr. 6
Gtr. 1
160
C
knows
who
you
are

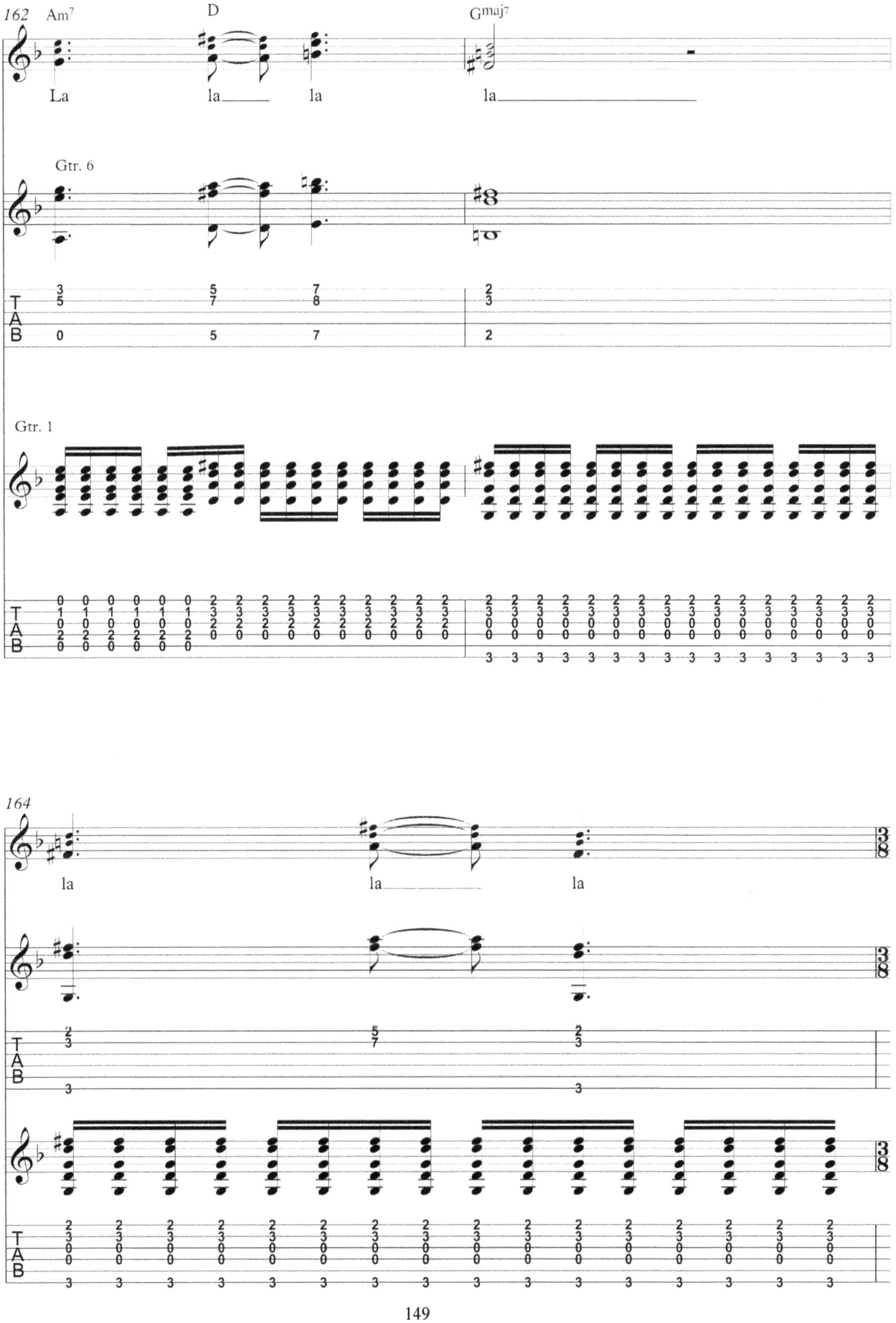
162
Am7
D
Gmaj7
La la la la
Gtr. 6
Gtr. 1
164
la la la

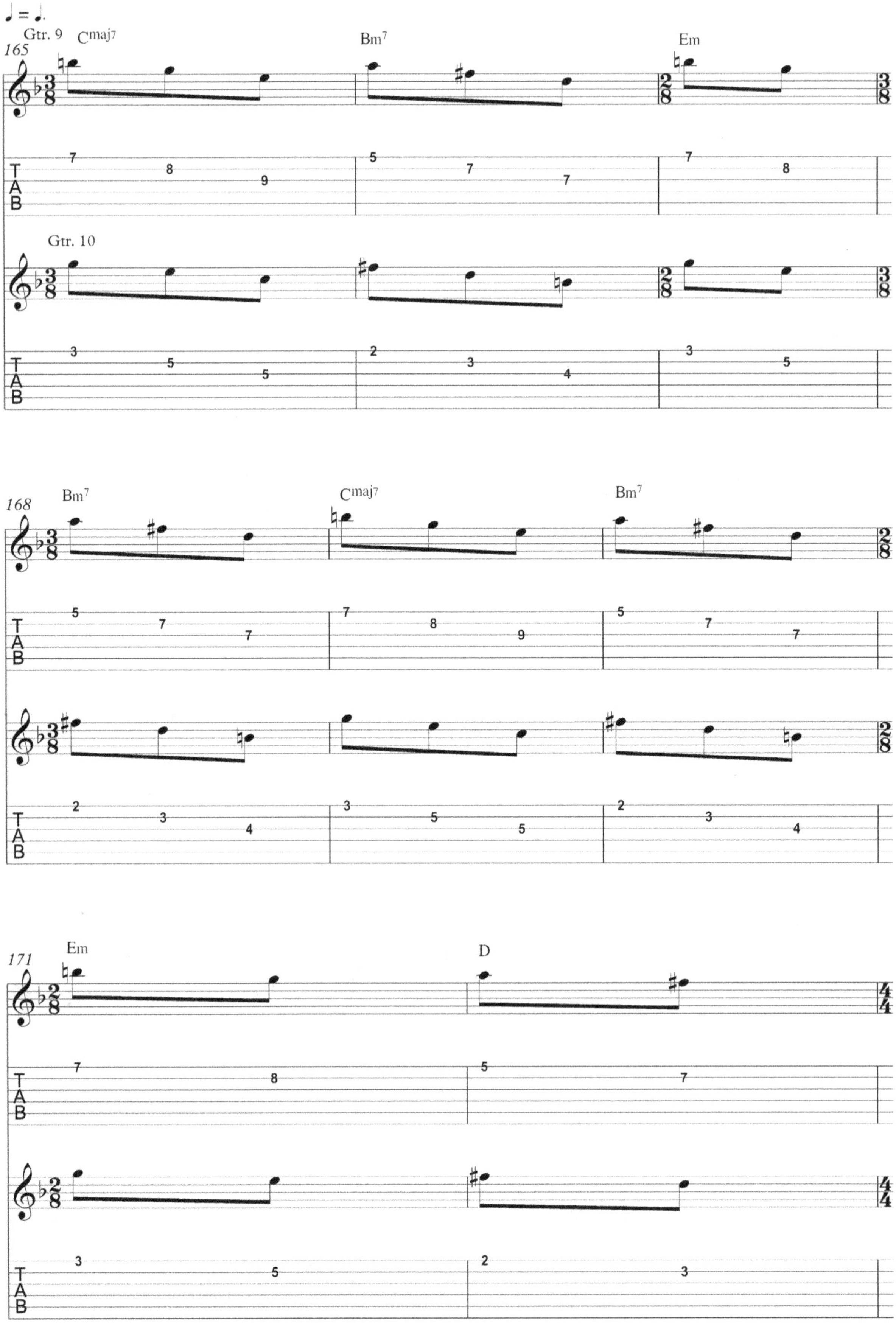
Gtr. 9
165
Cmaj7
Bm7
Em
Gtr. 10
168
Bm7
Cmaj7
Bm7
171
Em
D

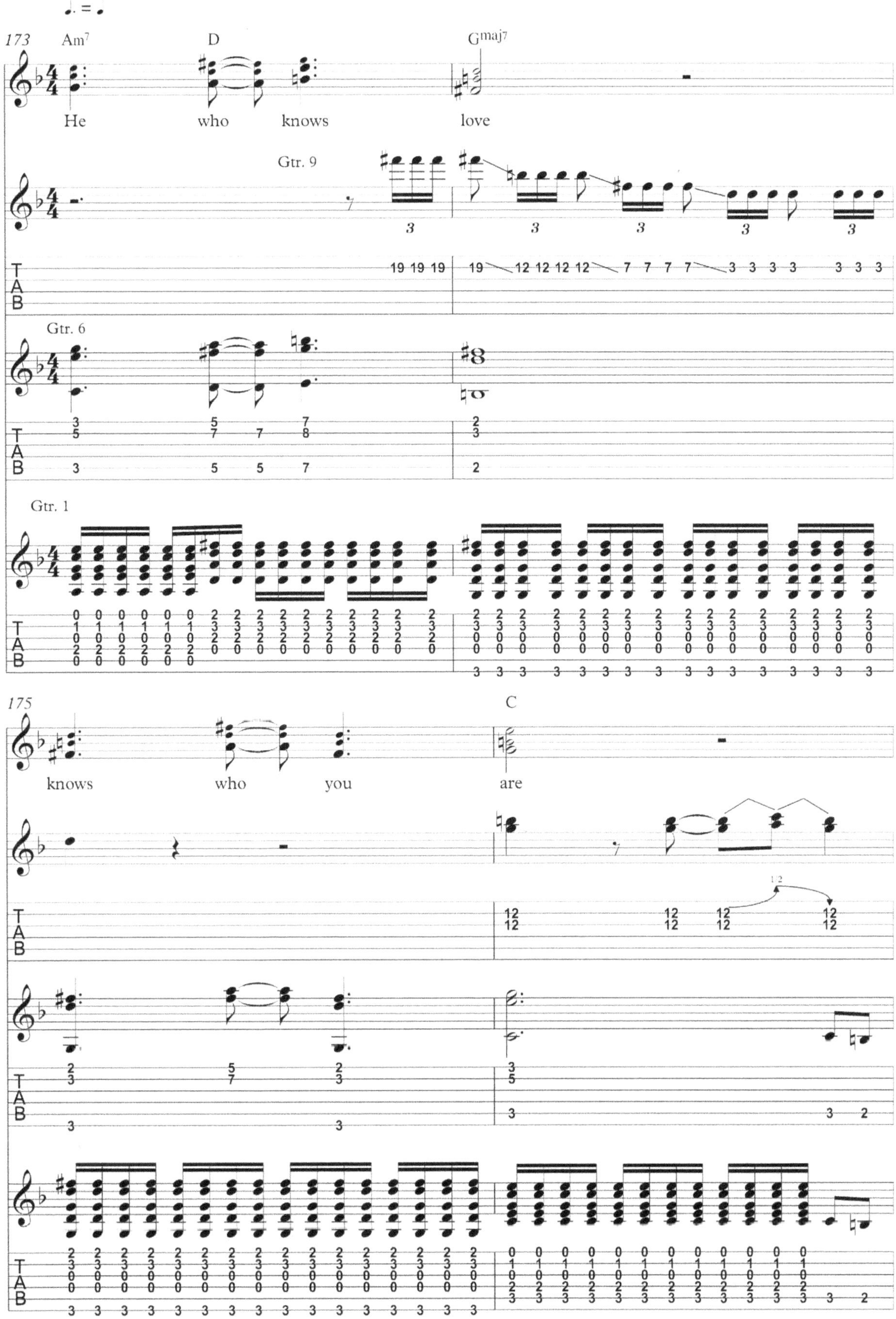
173
Am7
D
Gmaj7
He
who
knows
love
Gtr. 9
Gtr. 6
Gtr. 1
175
C
knows
who
you
are
1/2

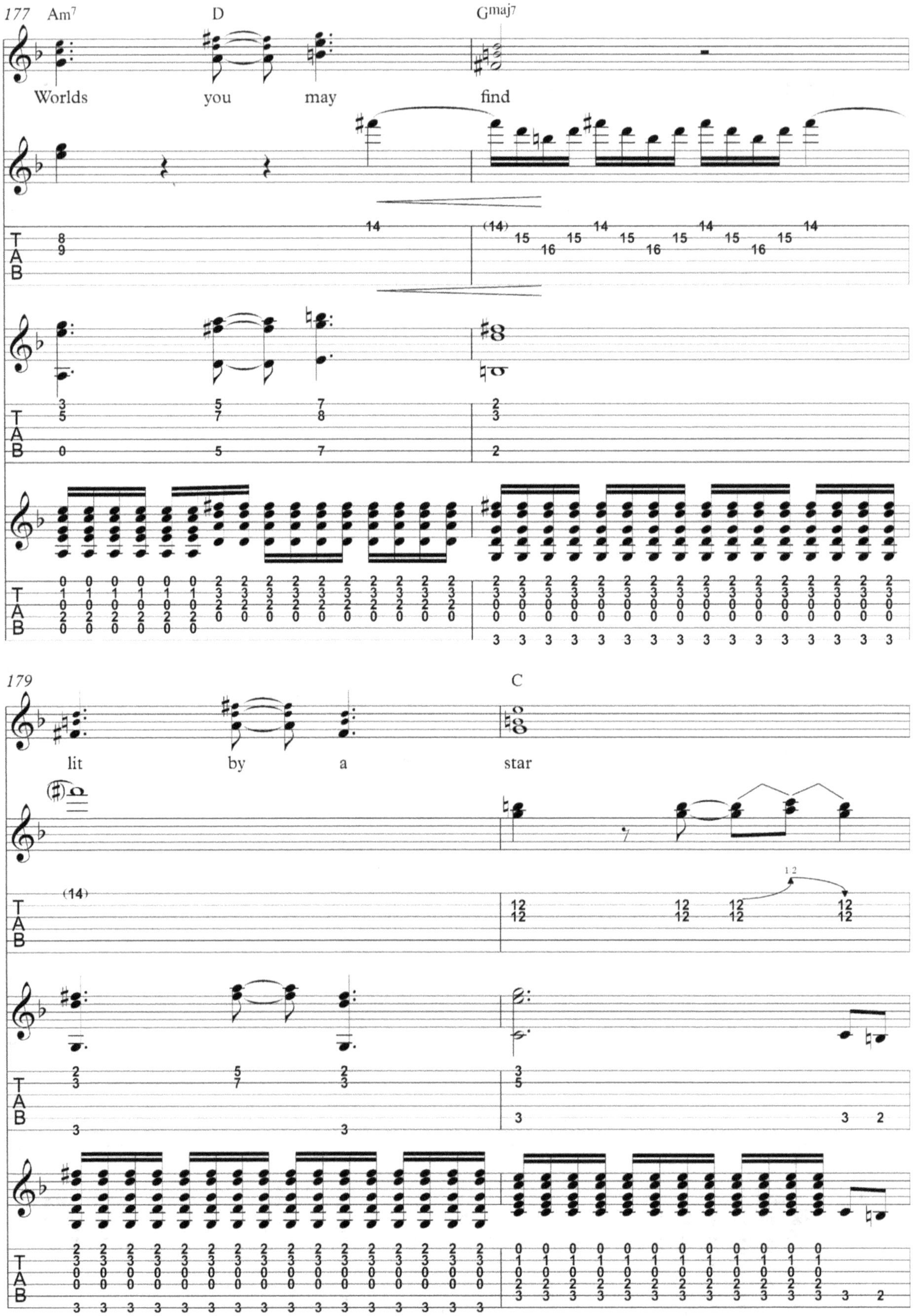
177
Am7
D
Gmaj7
Worlds
you
may
find
179
C
lit
by
a
star

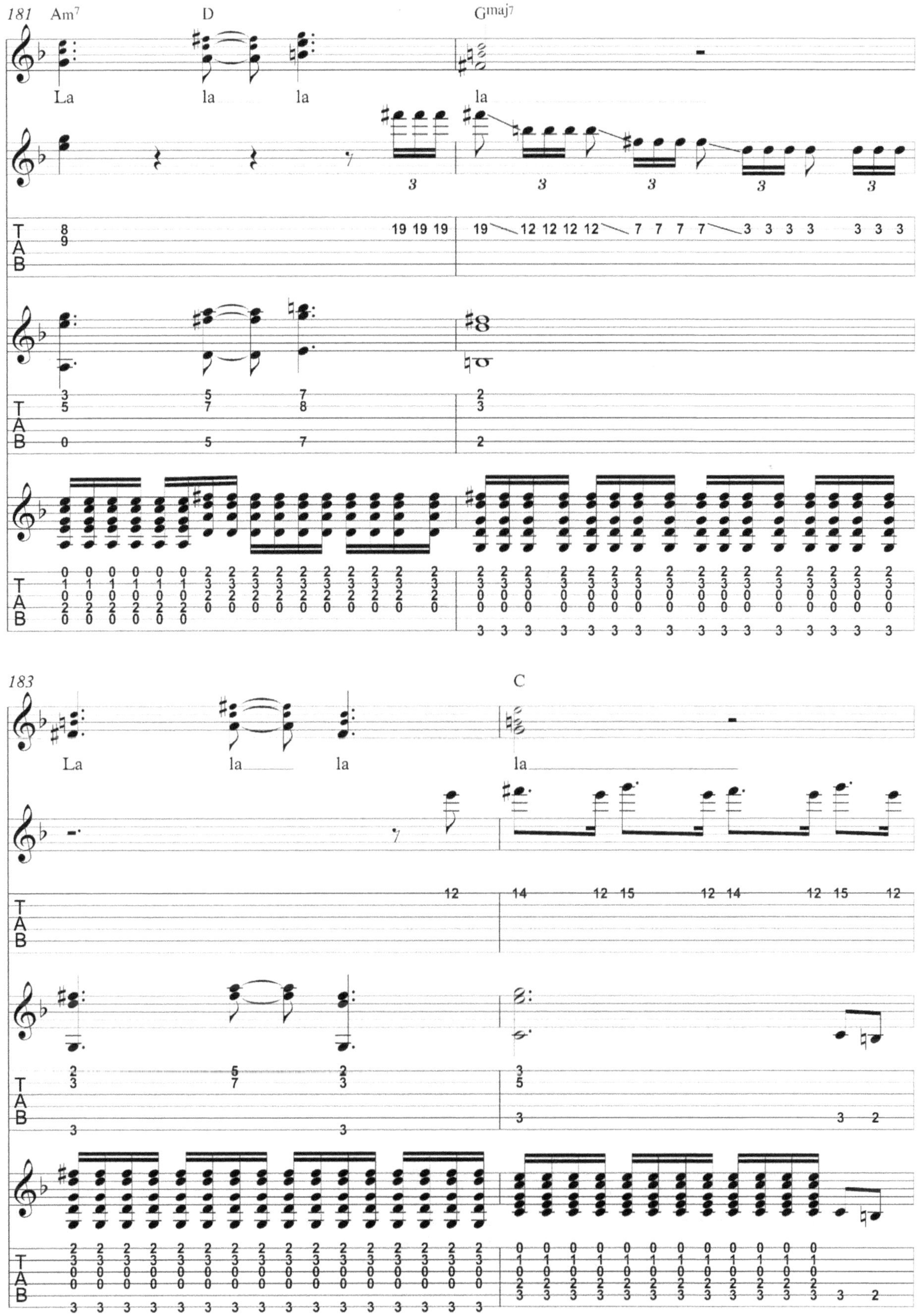
181
Am7
D
Gmaj7
La
la
la
la
183
C
La
la
la
la

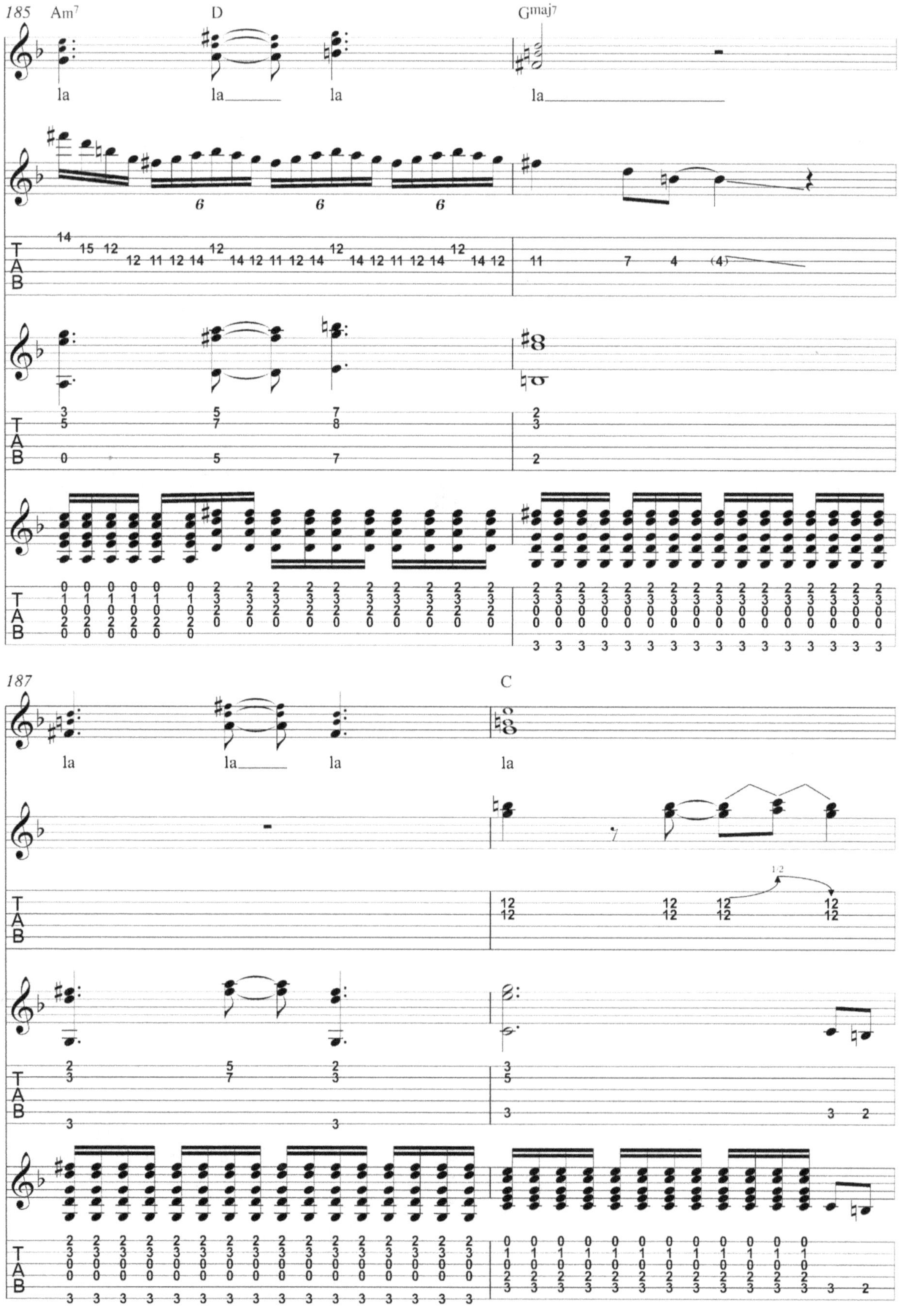
185
Am7
D
Gmaj7
la
la
la
la
187
C
la
la
la
la

Fade out till the end

Worlds you may find lit by a star

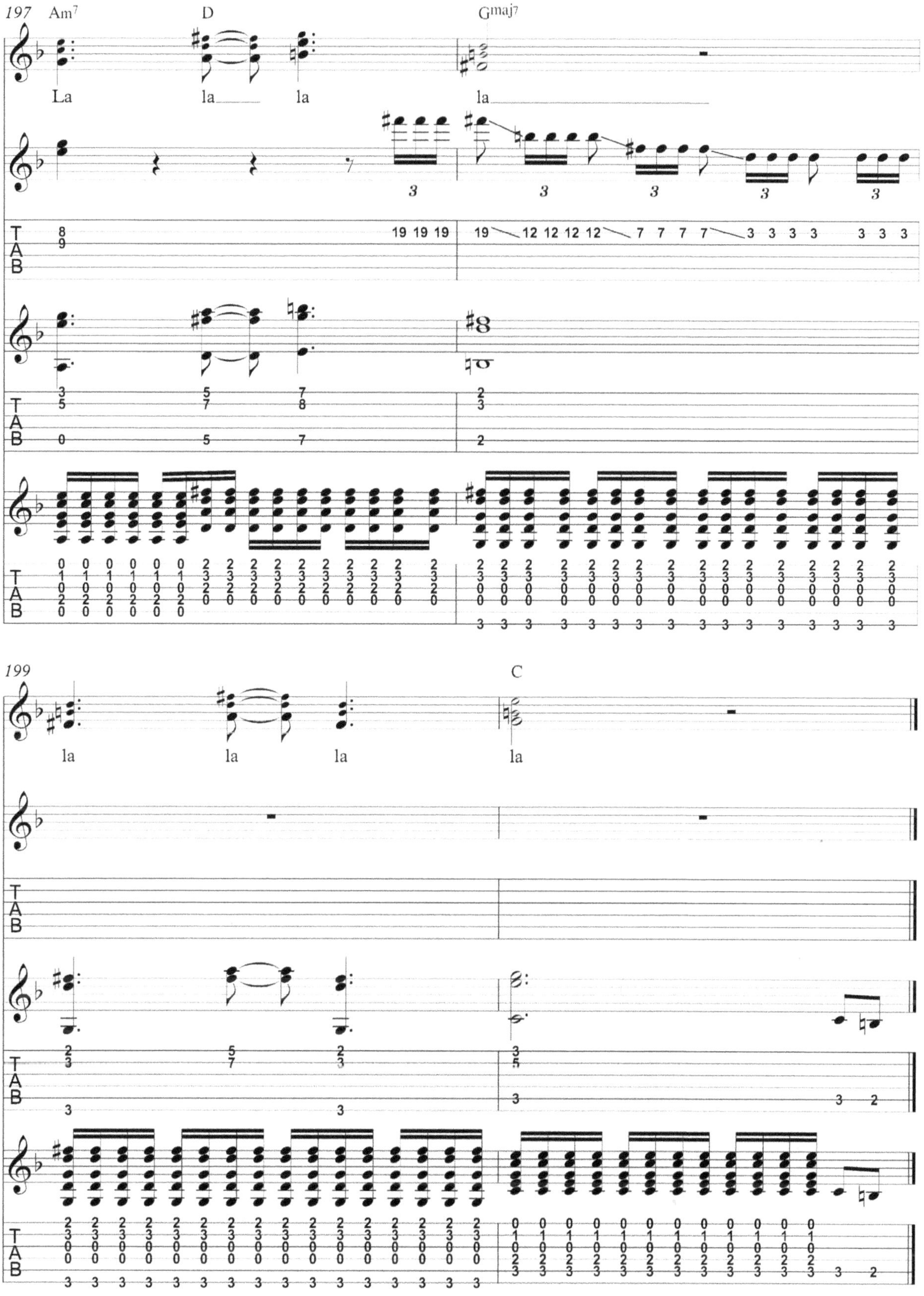
197
Am7
D
Gmaj7
La
la
la
la
199
C
la
la
la
la

STAR OF SIRIUS
BY STEVE HACKETT

Intro:
|C7(add4) | |C7(add4)/Bb |Fm9/A |C9(sus4) |
     |C7(add4) |

C7(add4) C7(add4)/Bb Fmaj9/A   C9(sus4)
ABOVE THE COLOUR   OF AMBER STAINED EVENING

      D(#5)   C7(add4)
AN AUDIENCE DANCED

        C7(add4)/Bb Fmaj9/A   C9(sus4)
LED BY A SHOWERING HAND THAT BRINGS WATER

     D(#5)   G/C
TO BOTH SEA AND LAND

        FMaj9/A
UNLOCK THE DOOR OF NIGHT

        Dm7/G
NEBULOUS BRIGHT

C9(sus4) | |Fmaj9 |C#/F# |Em9 |D/G |

C9(Sus4) |C7(add4) |

C7(add4) C7(add4)/Bb Fmaj9/A   C9(sus4)
AGAIN RENEWED BY THE VESSELS OF ISIS

      D(#5)   C7(add4)
YOU'RE READY TO FLY

        C7(add4)/Bb Fmaj9/A   C9(sus4)
ALTHOUGH THE JOURNEY IS STILL FAR FROM ENDED

     D(#5)   G/C
YOU GAZE AT THE SKY

      Fmaj9/A
ABOVE THE CLOUDLESS NIGHT

        Dm7/G
NEBULOUS BRIGHT

C9(sus4) | |Fmaj9 |C#/F# |Em9 |D/G |

Am7   D |Gmaj7 | |C |

Am7 D   Gmaj7   C
HE   WHO KNOWS LOVE KNOWS WHO YOU ARE

Am7   D   Gmaj7   Em   Am7 BbMaj7
WORLDS YOU MAY FIND LIT BY A STAR

Am7 D   Gmaj7   C
LA LA LA LA..   LA   LA LA LA LA

Am7 D   Gmaj7   Em   Am7   Bmaj7
LA LA LA LA..   LA   LA LA LA LA

|

| C(add4) C C(add4) | G/B C/E G/F| G Am G/B|
Dm/C |F/Bb | E/G# Gm7 A | Dm7 | |
Daug			D#(#5)	B7(5#) B
E B7(add4)/A	E B7(add4)/A	E B7(add4)/A
E	A6	B/A	E B7(add4)	E
A6	B/A	Emaj7		E A B
Emaj7	Amaj7/E	Dmaj7	
C9(sus4)	Fmaj7	C#/F#	Em
D/G	Am7 D	Gmaj7	
C

Am7   D   Gmaj7   C
HE   WHO KNOWS LOVE KNOWS WHO YOU ARE

Am7   D   Gmaj7   Em   Am7 BbMaj7
WORLDS YOU MAY FIND LIT BY A STAR

C7(add4)   C7(add4)/Bb Fmaj9/A C9(sus4)   D(#5)
  AGAIN RENEWED BY THE VESSELS OF ISIS

           C7(add4)
YOU'RE READY TO FLY

```
|C7(add4)/Bb      |Fmaj9/A      |C9(sus4)   |        |D/G      |
```

```
Am7  D                Gmaj7                           C
HE    WHO KNOWS LOVE KNOWS WHO YOU ARE
```

```
Am7       D          Gmaj7       C/G
WORLDS YOU MAY FIND LIT BY A STAR
```

```
|D/G       |C/G      |D/G      |C/G      |D/G      |
```

```
|Cmaj7  |Bm7  |Em  |Bm7  |
```

```
|Cmaj7  |Bm7  |Em  |Bm7  |
```

```
Am7  D                Gmaj7                   C
HE     WHO KNOWS LOVE KNOWS WHO YOU ARE
```

```
Am7  D            Gmaj7
LA LA LA LA..   LA     LA LA LA
```

```
|Cmaj7  |Bm7  |Em  |Bm7  |
```

```
|Cmaj7  |Bm7  |Em  |Bm7  |
```

```
Am7  D                Gmaj7                        C
HE     WHO KNOWS LOVE KNOWS WHO YOU ARE
```

```
Am7       D          Gmaj7       C
WORLDS YOU MAY FIND LIT BY A STAR
```

```
Am7  D          Gmaj7            C
LA LA LA LA..   LA      LA LA LA LA
```

```
Am7  D          Gmaj7            C
LA LA LA LA..   LA      LA LA LA LA
```

```
Am7  D                Gmaj7                        C
HE     WHO KNOWS LOVE KNOWS WHO YOU ARE
```

```
Am7       D          Gmaj7       C
WORLDS YOU MAY FIND LIT BY A STAR
```

```
Am7  D          Gmaj7            C
LA LA LA LA..   LA      LA LA LA LA
```

```
Am7  D          Gmaj7            C     (Fade out)
LA LA LA LA..   LA      LA LA LA LA
```

THE LOVERS

Steve composed this music based on a melody that his brother John used to play with him. Steve felt the piece worked as a pallet cleanser between *Sirius* and *Hierophant*. He recorded his guitar through a mic.

Steve explained the choice of "The Lovers" card:

I'd already chosen to do the Hermit and this was an opposite card – oboe melody from The Hermit played backwards and also major arcana. It was also romantic and mysterious.

He chose *The Hermit* to be in reverse at the end of the guitar solo part because he thought the melody was as interesting backwards as it was forwards.

Players/Instruments:

Steve Hackett: Yairi Nylon, Steel 6-string Yamaha acoustic (in reversed tape effect)

John Hackett: Flute (in reversed tape effect)

Studio Gears : The Lovers - Voyage of the Acolyte

1

2

1 - Yairi Nylon
2 - Steel 6 String Yamaha Acoustic

Intro of *The Lovers*

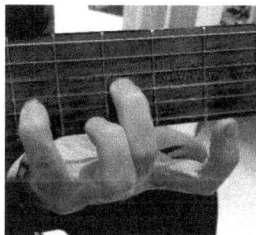

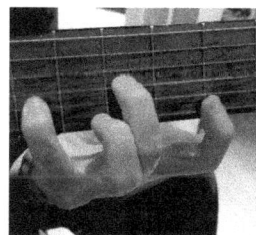

Figure 54-55: Steve showing the intro of The Lovers. Photo by Paulo De Carvalho

from Steve Hackett - *Voyage of the Acolyte*

The Lovers

by Steve Hackett

Transcribed by Paulo De Carvalho

♩ = 94

*Yairi Nylon

*Flute arr. for gtr.

**Yamaha Acoustic

* This is the original take that was used as reverse tape effect (from the Hermit song)

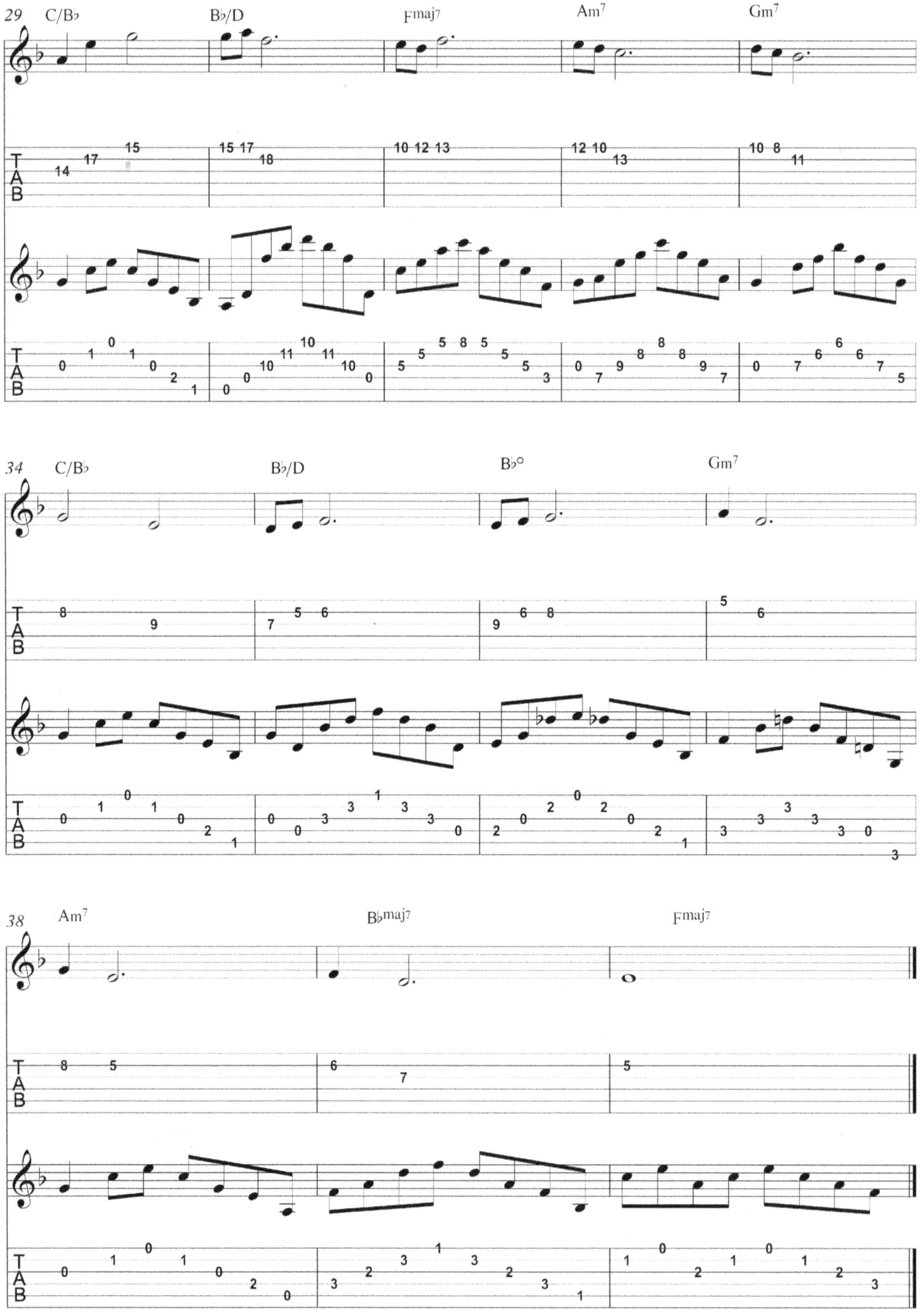
29
C/B♭
B♭/D
Fmaj7
Am7
Gm7
34
C/B♭
B♭/D
B♭°
Gm7
38
Am7
B♭maj7
Fmaj7

SHADOW OF THE HIEROPHANT

Steve explained why he chose "The Hierophant" Tarot card in the last track of *Voyage of the Acolyte*:

I was interested in exploring the negative impact of religion when it becomes dogma. Too much faith in any one particular religion can lead to prejudice and religion can corrupt. For me, the second half of the song embraces both the tragedy and power of humanity marching through space and time, moving through religion but beyond it to the point of pure spirit. In recent years, Amanda Lehmann has been taking on the singing role for live shows. You can hear her beautiful vocal on recent live albums.

Steve used a Tone Bender with Echoplex for the beginning of the song with a volume pedal, and slide on his little finger for the guitar part. For the taping on the latter part of the song he used the Tone Bender and Duo fuzz together, with the Echoplex and MXR Phase 90 on a slow setting. He used this setup for the remainder of the song.

Steve played the Mellotron for the verses and John played it at the ending part of the song.

Mike played Vox bass pedals put through a Tone Bender fuzz box.

Steve chose Sally Oldfield to sing because he heard her singing on the duo The Sallyangie. He thought her voice was beautiful, similar to the young Marianne Faithful who she had befriended at school.

They used the click track in the first part of the song because of the gaps in which the drums didn't play, as there were a lot of bars where nothing happened for Phil Collins. That was the first time that Phil played with a click track. Later on Steve re-recorded this song on *Genesis Revisited II* and it was a little bit faster.

While still on Genesis, Steve had already drafted, along with Mike Rutherford, the last part of *Shadow of the Hierophant*, about the same time of the recording of *Foxtrot*, in 1972.

Players/Instruments:

Steve Hackett: Gibson Les Paul Gold Top 1957, Zemaitis Custom 12-string, Yairi Nylon, Autoharp, Mellotron, Tubular bells

Sally Oldfield: Vocals

Mike Rutherford: Bass, Vox bass pedals through a Tone Bender fuzz box and MXR Phase 90, fuzz 12-string guitar

John Acock: Elka-Rhapsody Synth, Mellotron

John Hackett: Flute, Mellotron

Phil Collins: Drums, Vibraphone

Studio Gears : Shadow of he Hierophant - Voyage of the Acolyte

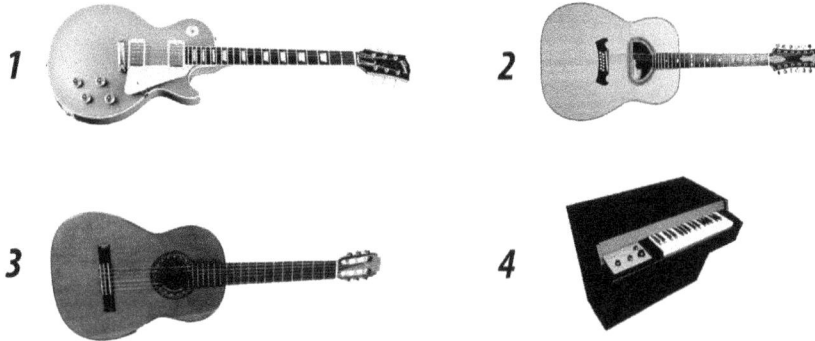

Pedal Board built by Pete Cornish

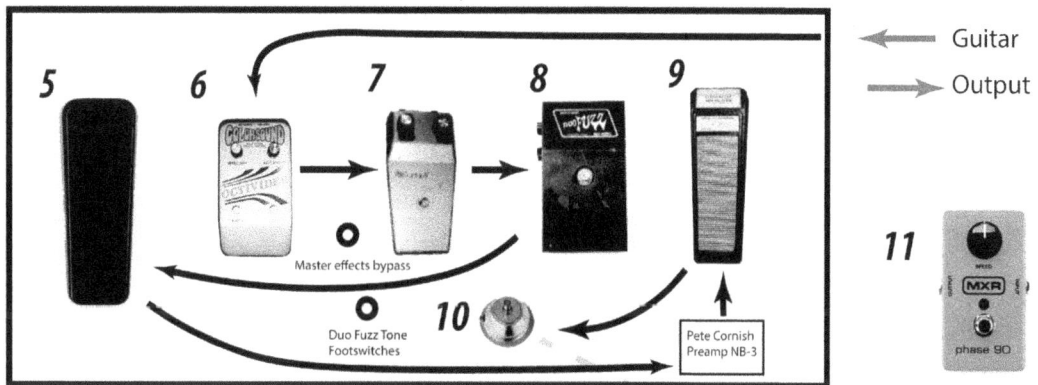

Guitar

Output

Master effects bypass

Duo Fuzz Tone Footswitches

Pete Cornish Preamp NB-3

1 - Gibson Les Paul Gold Top 1957
2 - Zemaitis Custom 12 String
3 - Yairi Nylon
4 - Mellotron
5 - Cry Baby Wah-Wah
6 - Colorsound Octivider
7 - Marshall Supa Fuzz
8 - Shaftesbury Duo Fuzz
9 - Schaller Volume Pedal F121
10 -Pedal Switch for Echoplex EP-3
11 - MXR Phase 90
12 - Echoplex EP-3 Tape Echo
13 - HH 100w IC100
14 - Hiwatt 150w 4x12 Cabinets SE 4123
15 - Autoharp
16 - Coloursound Tonebender (Fuzz)
17 - Tubular Bells

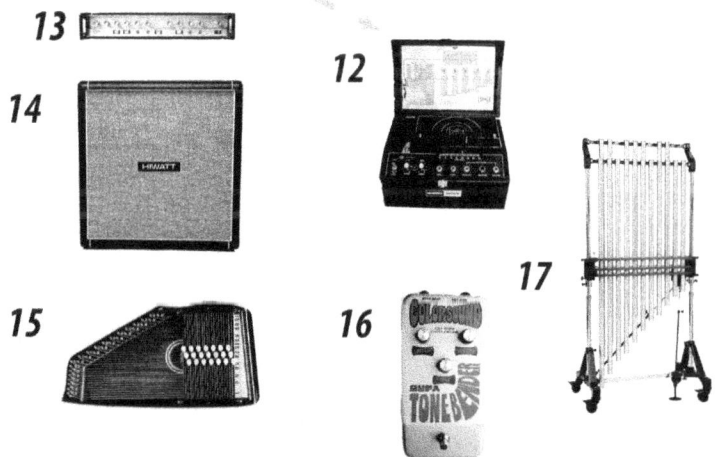

Signal Routing:

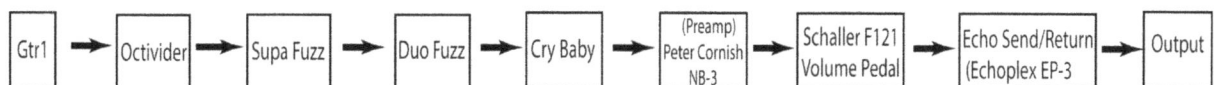

Gtr1 → Octivider → Supa Fuzz → Duo Fuzz → Cry Baby → (Preamp) Peter Cornish NB-3 → Schaller F121 Volume Pedal → Echo Send/Return (Echoplex EP-3 → Output

Intro of *Shadow of the Hierophant*: detail

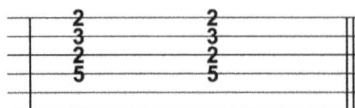

*Photo 56: Steve showing how he plays the D/G
in the intro of The Shadow of the Hierophant*

Photo by Paulo De Carvalho, 2017

from Steve Hackett - *Voyage of The Acolyte*

Shadow Of The Hierophant

by Steve Hackett, Mike Rutherford

Transcribed by Paulo De Carvalho

♩ = 54

* Gibson Les Paul Golden Top 1957

** Zamaitis Custom 12 strings

***Chords symbols reflect implied harmony

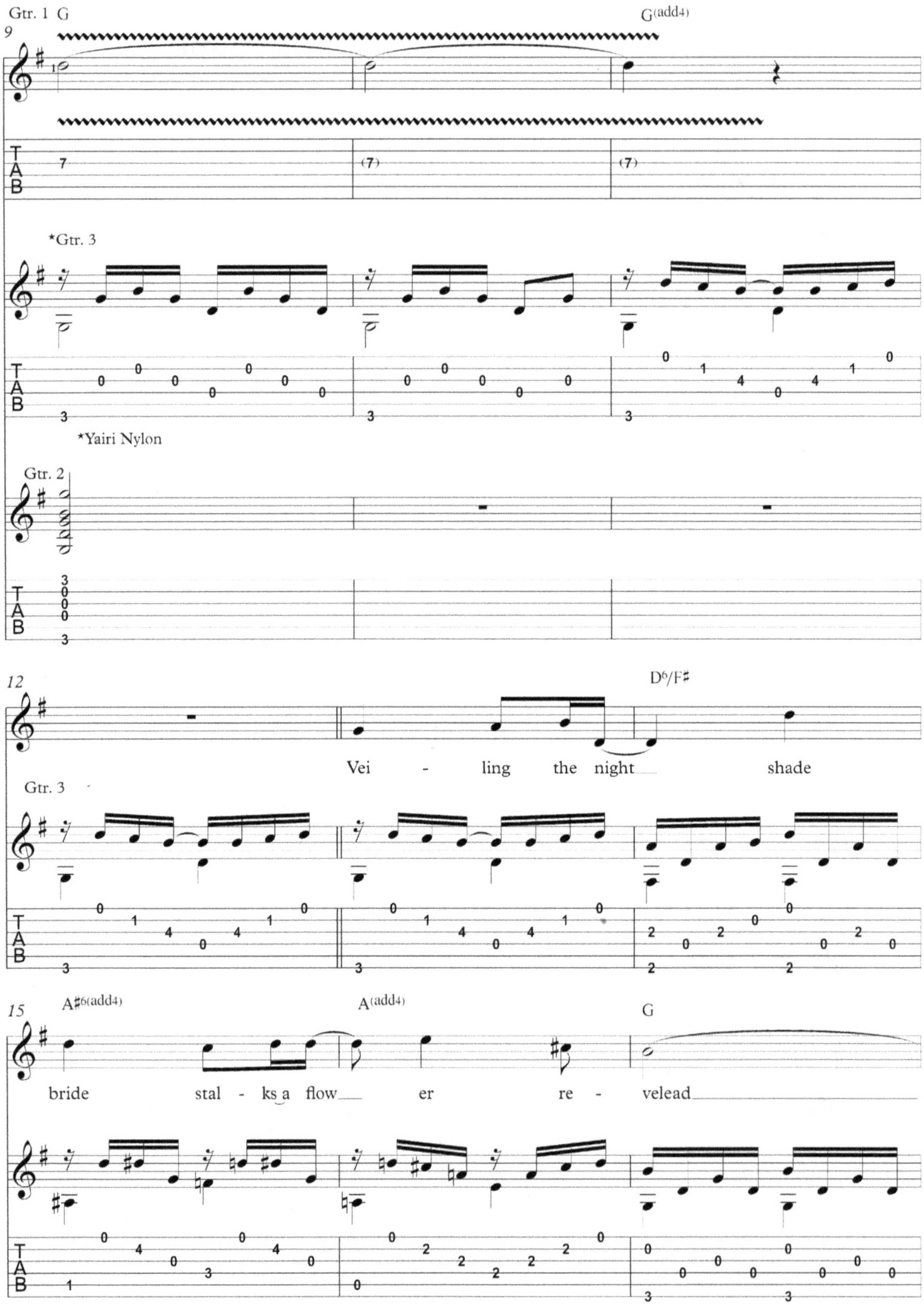
Gtr. 1
G
G(add4)
*Gtr. 3
*Yairi Nylon
Gtr. 2
D6/F♯
Gtr. 3
Vei - ling the night shade
A♯6(add4)
A(add4)
G
bride stal - ks a flow er re - velead

G(sus$^2_4$)
G(add4)
Nea - - ring the hour
*Gtr. 4
tr
* Flute arr. for gtr.
Gtr. 3
D6/F♯
A♯6(add4)
A(add4)
make haste to their thres - hold con -
Gtr. 3
G
Am11
G/B
G/C
C6/9
cealed

Lost in thought in search of vi - sion

Gtr. 2 and Gtr. 3

As the moon e -

clipsed the sun.

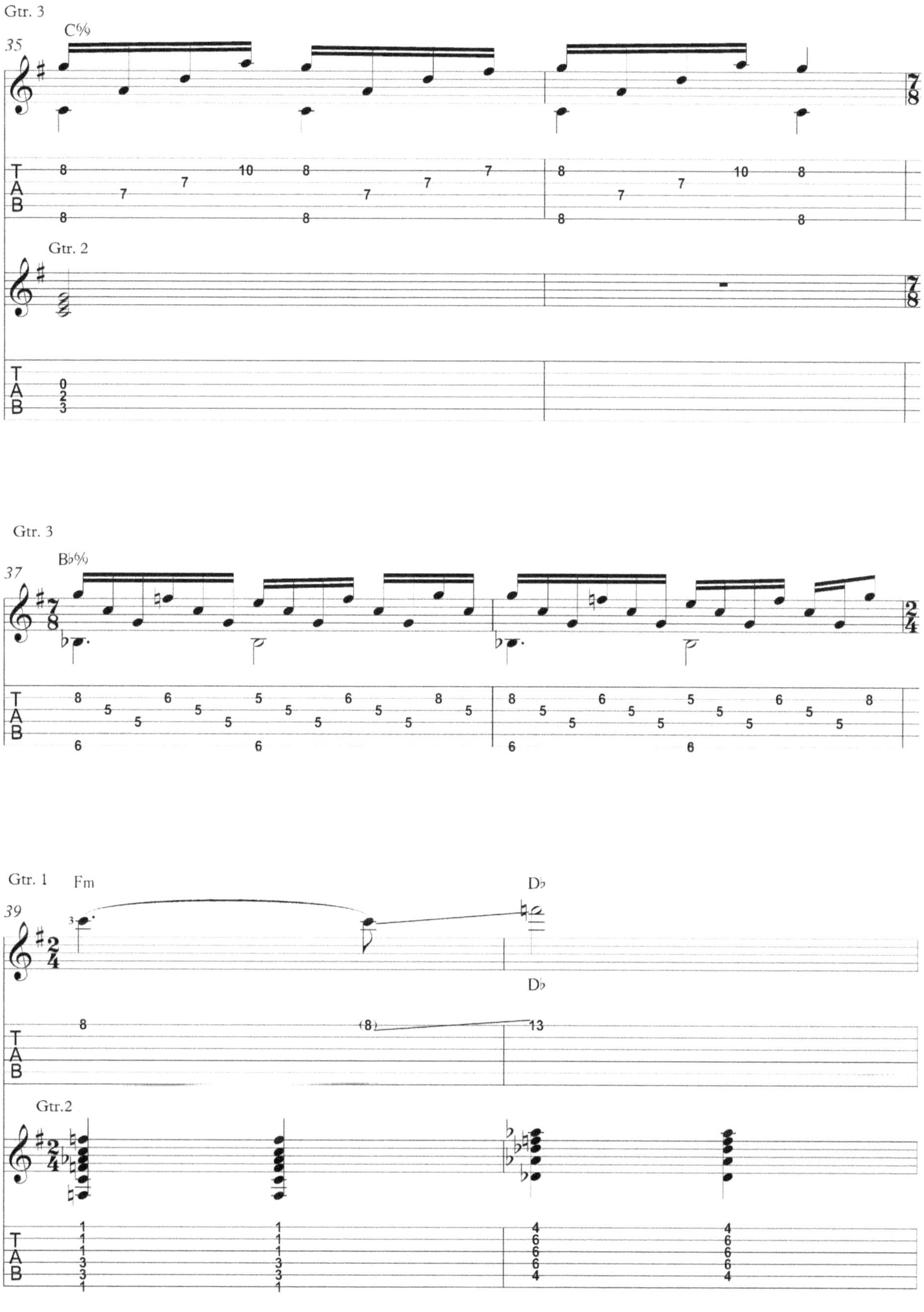
Gtr. 3
C6/9
35
Gtr. 2
Gtr. 3
B♭6/9
37
Gtr. 1
Fm
D♭
39
D♭
Gtr.2

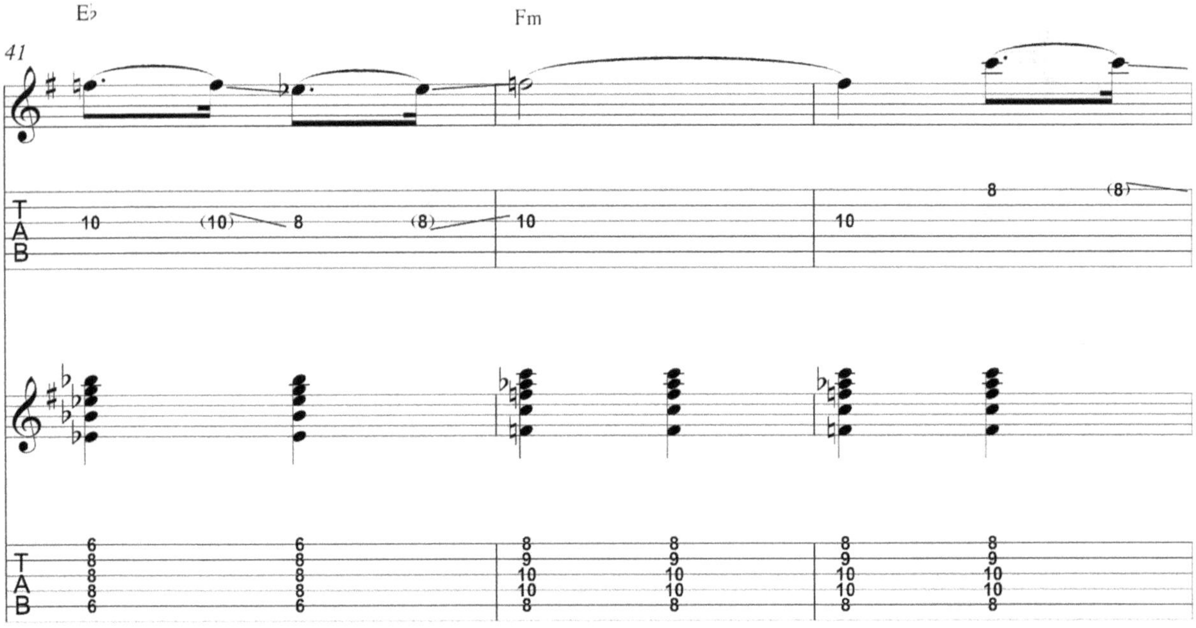
E♭
Fm
41

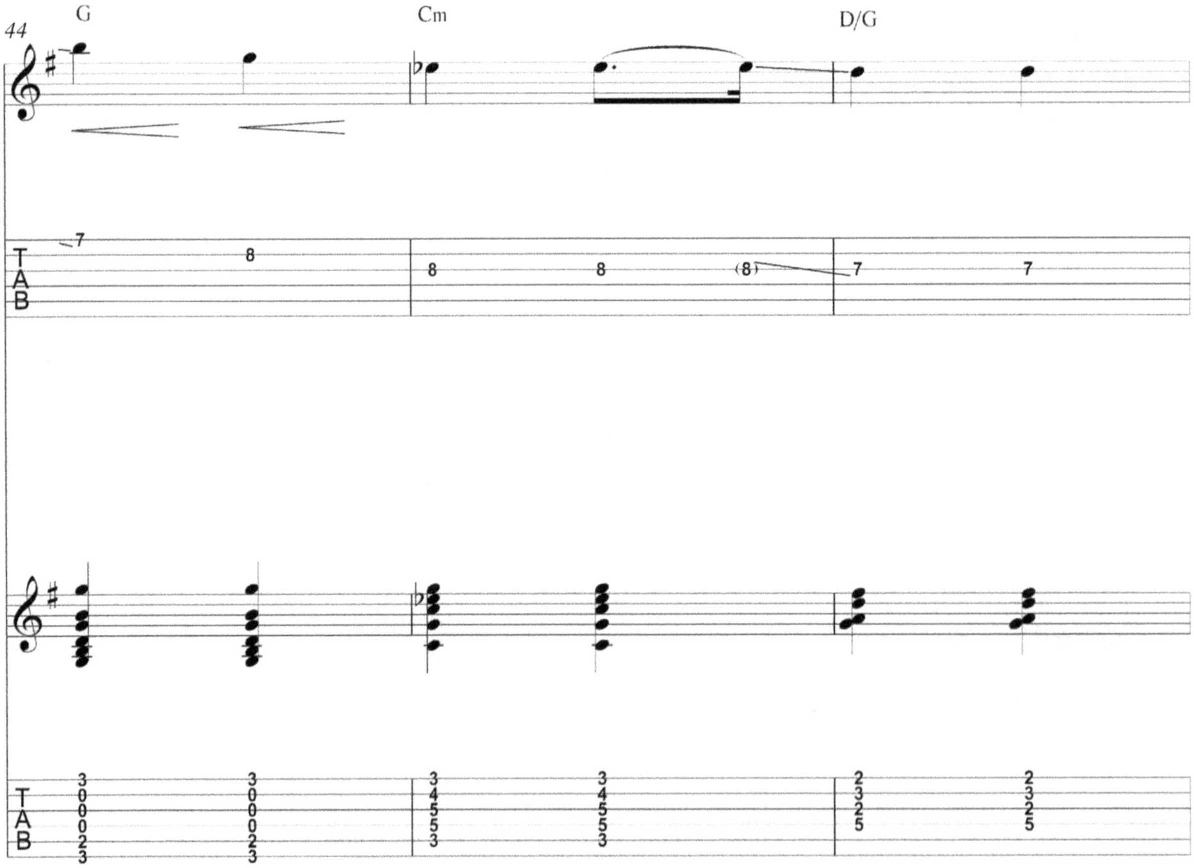
G
Cm
D/G
44

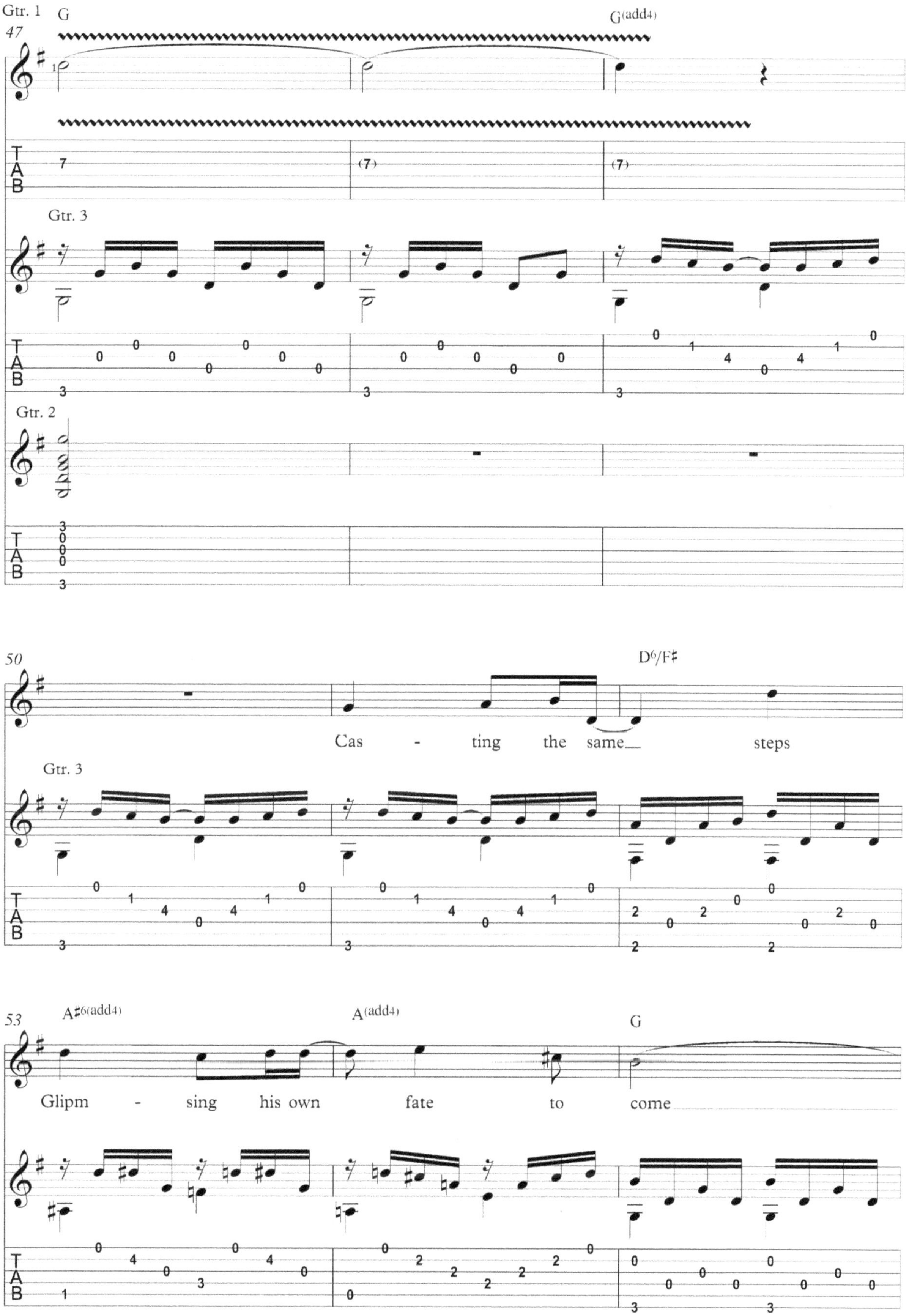
Gtr. 1
47
G
G(add4)
Gtr. 3
Gtr. 2
50
D6/F♯
Cas - ting the same steps
Gtr. 3
53
A♯6(add4)
A(add4)
G
Glipm - sing his own fate to come

56
G(sus4/3)
G(add4)
D6/F♯
Melt - in the dream___ void
Gtr. 4
tr
Gtr. 3
59
A♯6(add4)
A(add4)
G
Am11
from which he ne - ver can run
Gtr. 3
62
G/B
G/C
C6/9

Lost in thought in search of vi - sion

As the moon e - clipsed the

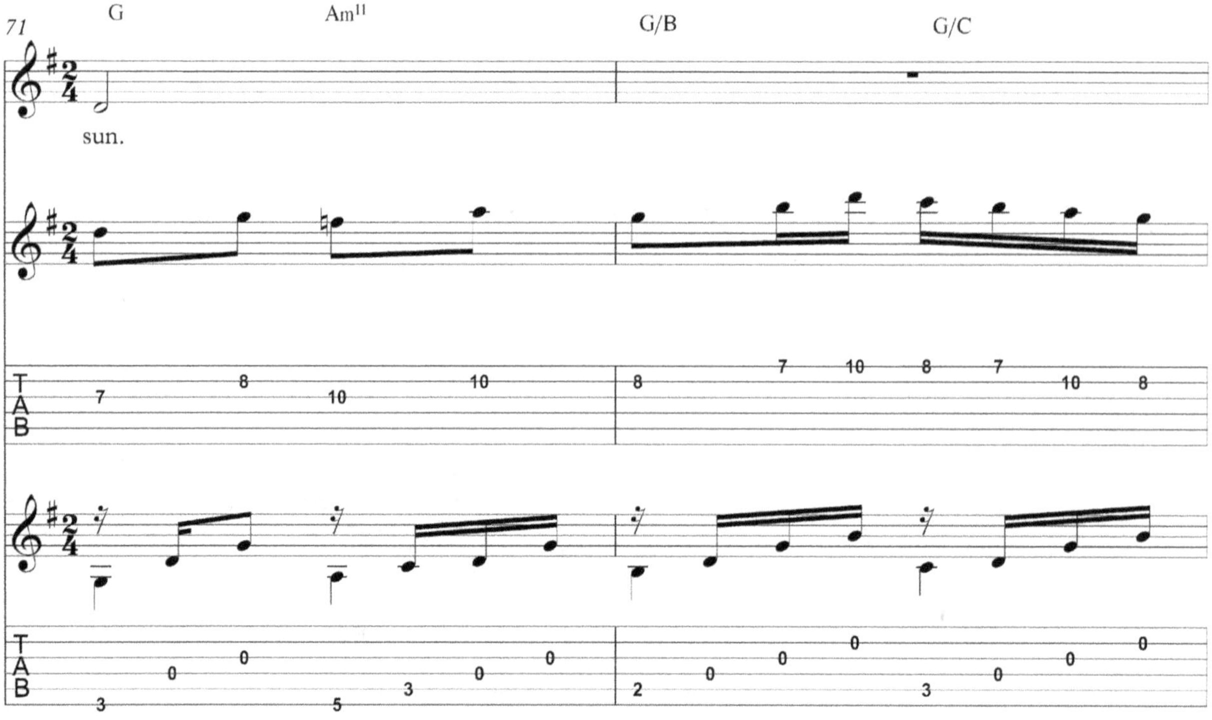
71
G
Am11
G/B
G/C
sun.

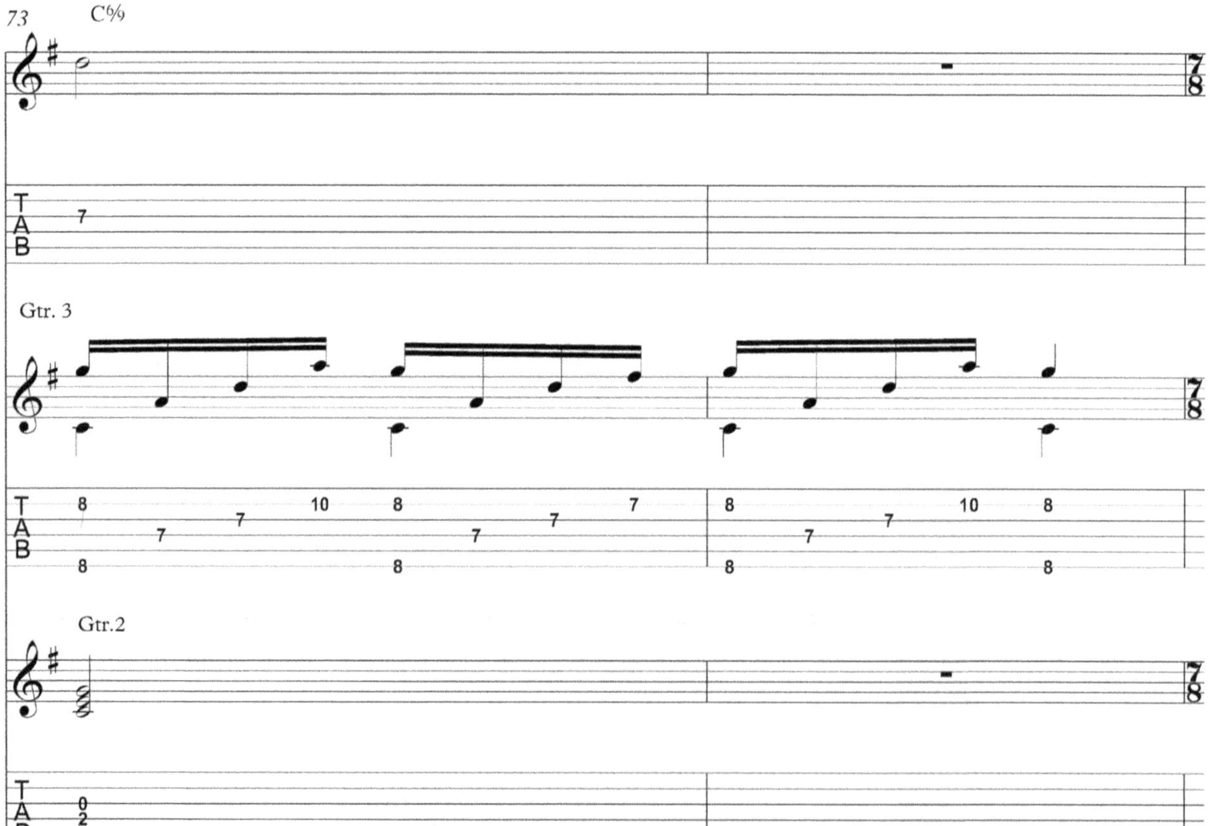
73
C6/9
Gtr. 3
Gtr.2

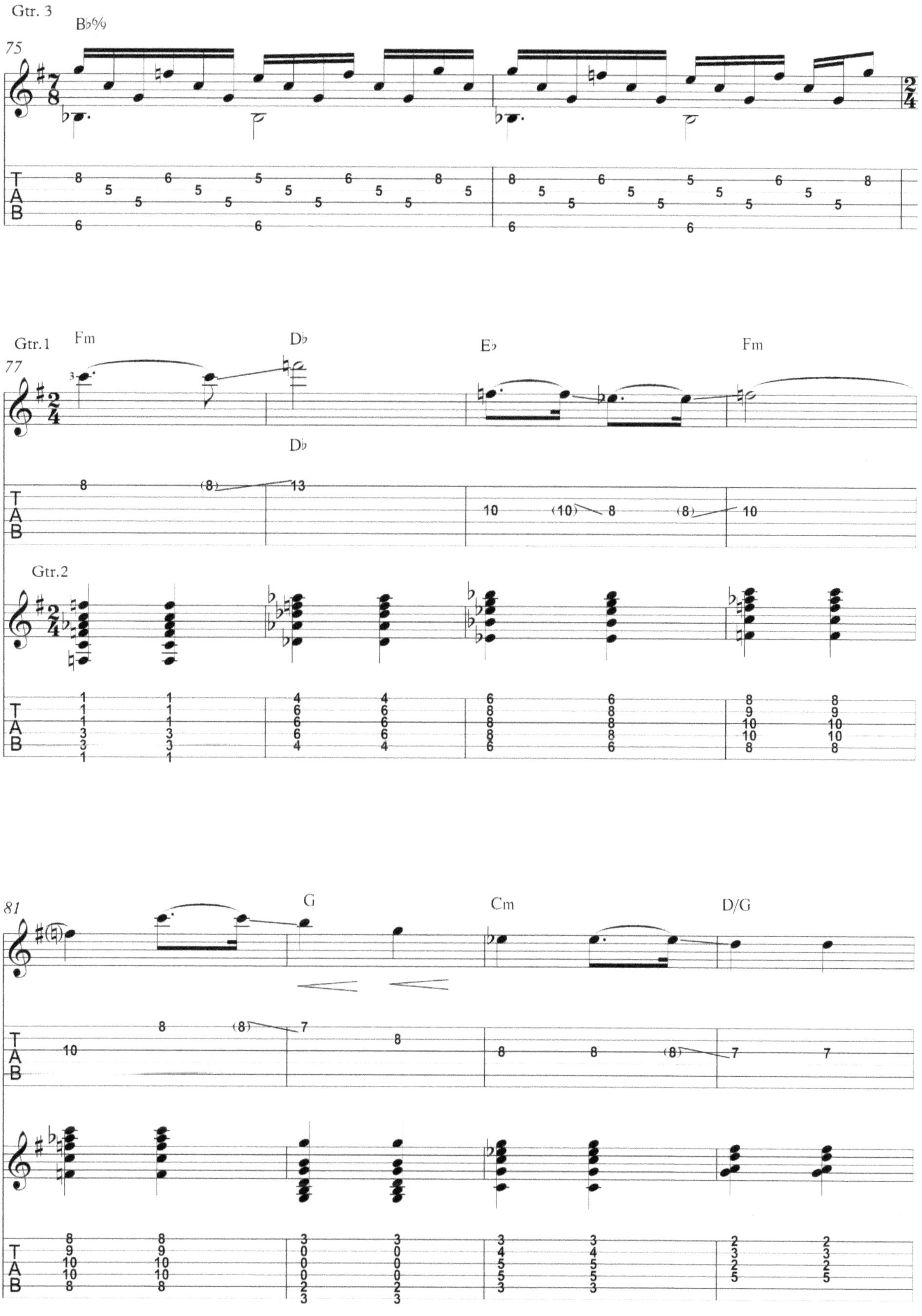
Gtr. 3
B♭6/9
75
Gtr.1
Fm
D♭
E♭
Fm
77
D♭
Gtr.2
81
G
Cm
D/G

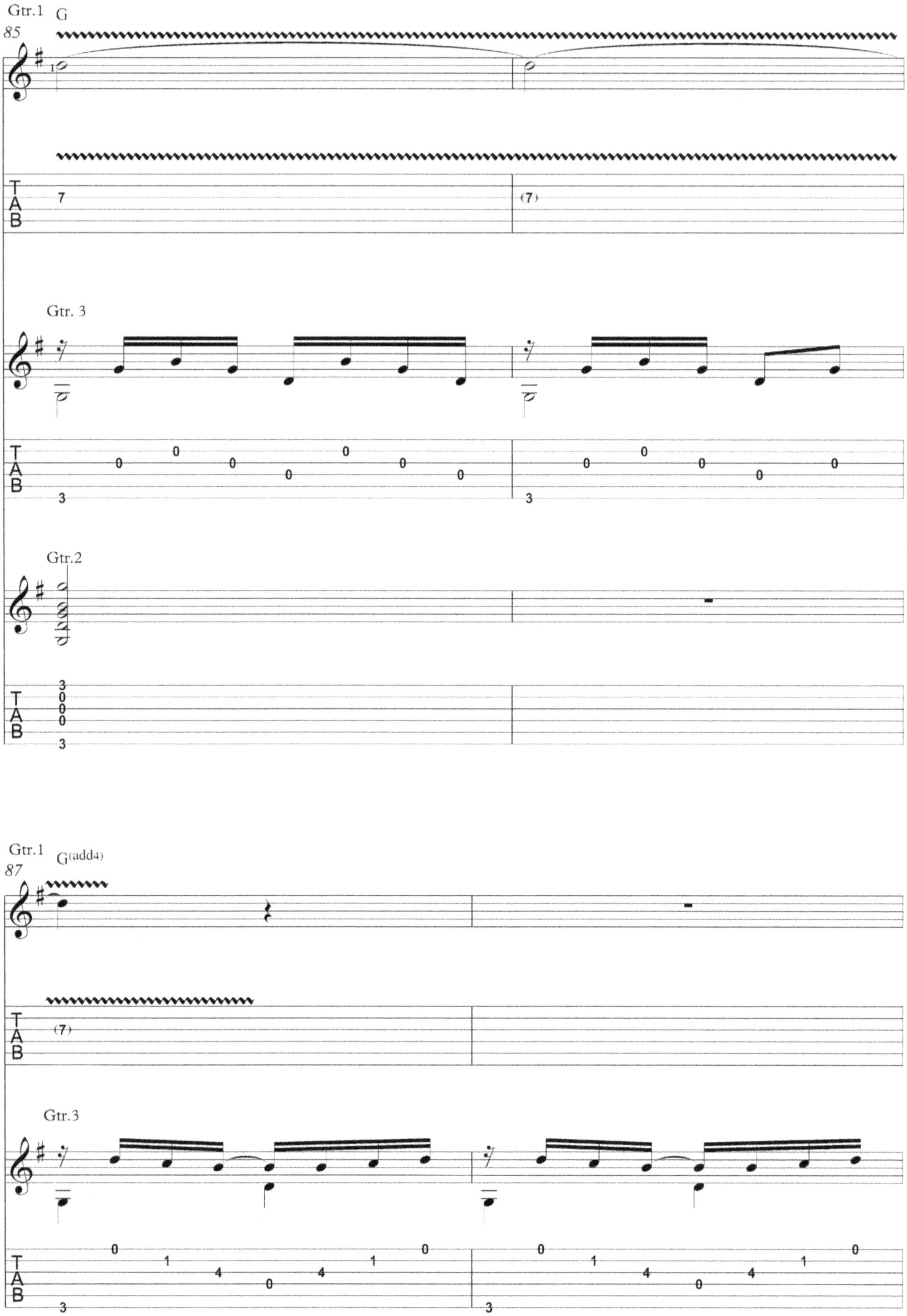
Gtr.1
G
85
Gtr. 3
Gtr.2
Gtr.1
G(add4)
87
Gtr.3

89
G(add4)
D6/F♯
A♯6(add4)
Tears fill the foun - - tains brea - king their pro
Gtr.4
Gtr. 3
92
A(add4)
G
G(add2add4)
- mise to heal
tr

Rip - pling the wa - - ters mir - ror an en-

- ded i - deal

100
G/B
G/C
C6/9
103
Em7
D/F♯
Bm
C(add9)
Deep in tought but rob - bed of vi - sion
Gtr. 2

As the moon e - clipsed the sun.

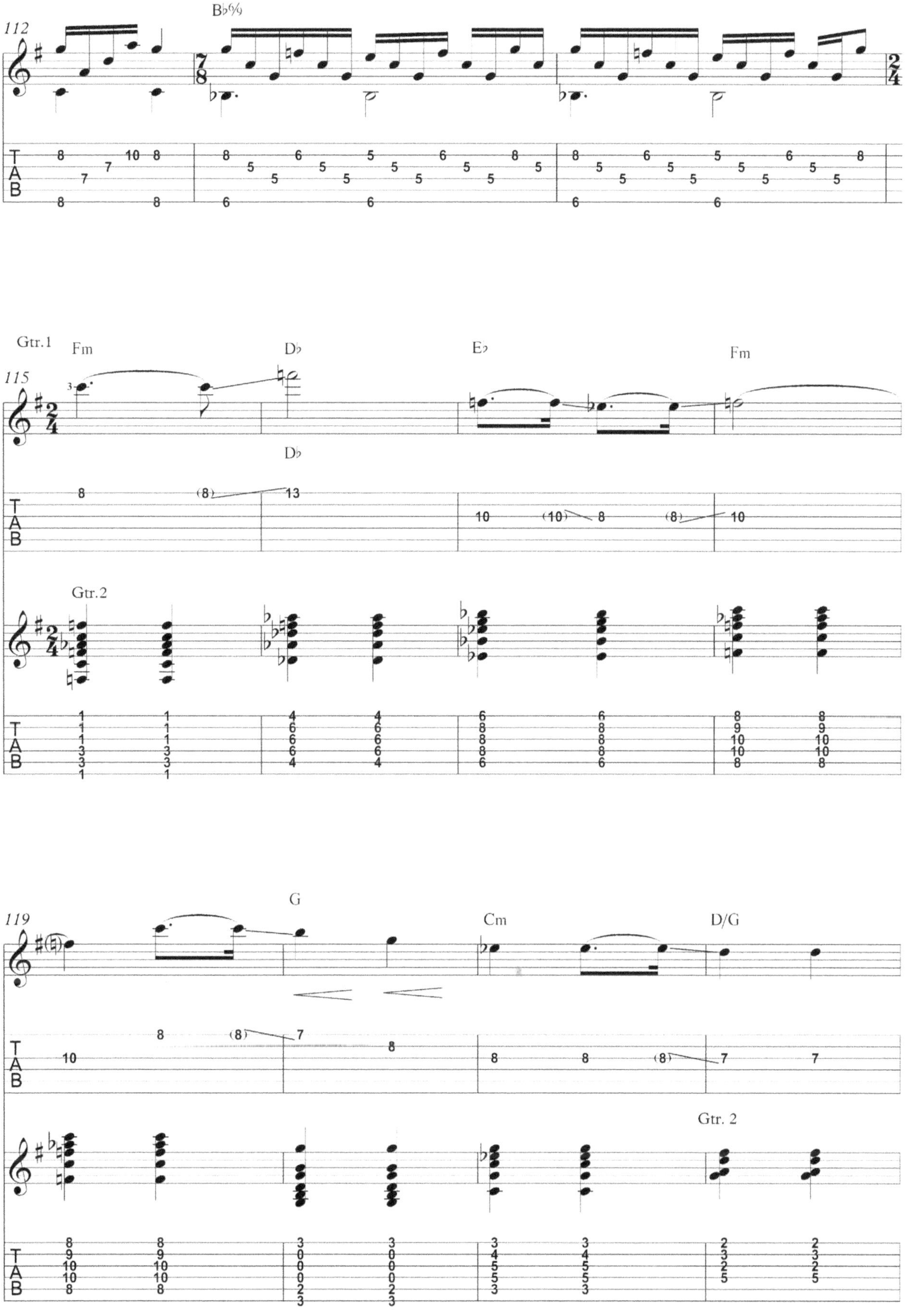
B♭6/9
Gtr.1
Fm
D♭
E♭
Fm
D♭
Gtr.2
G
Cm
D/G
Gtr. 2

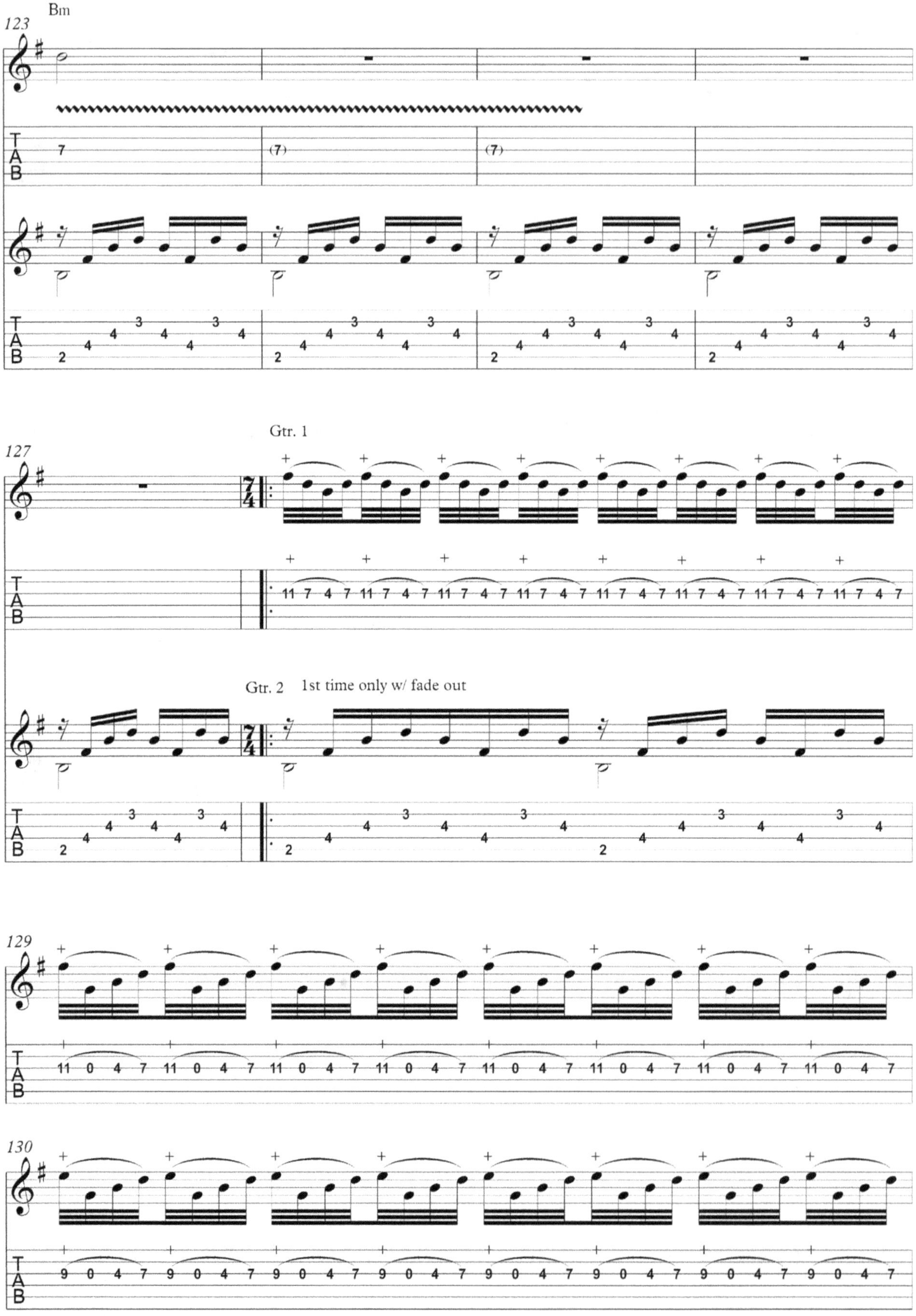
Bm
123
127
Gtr. 1
Gtr. 2
1st time only w/ fade out
129
130

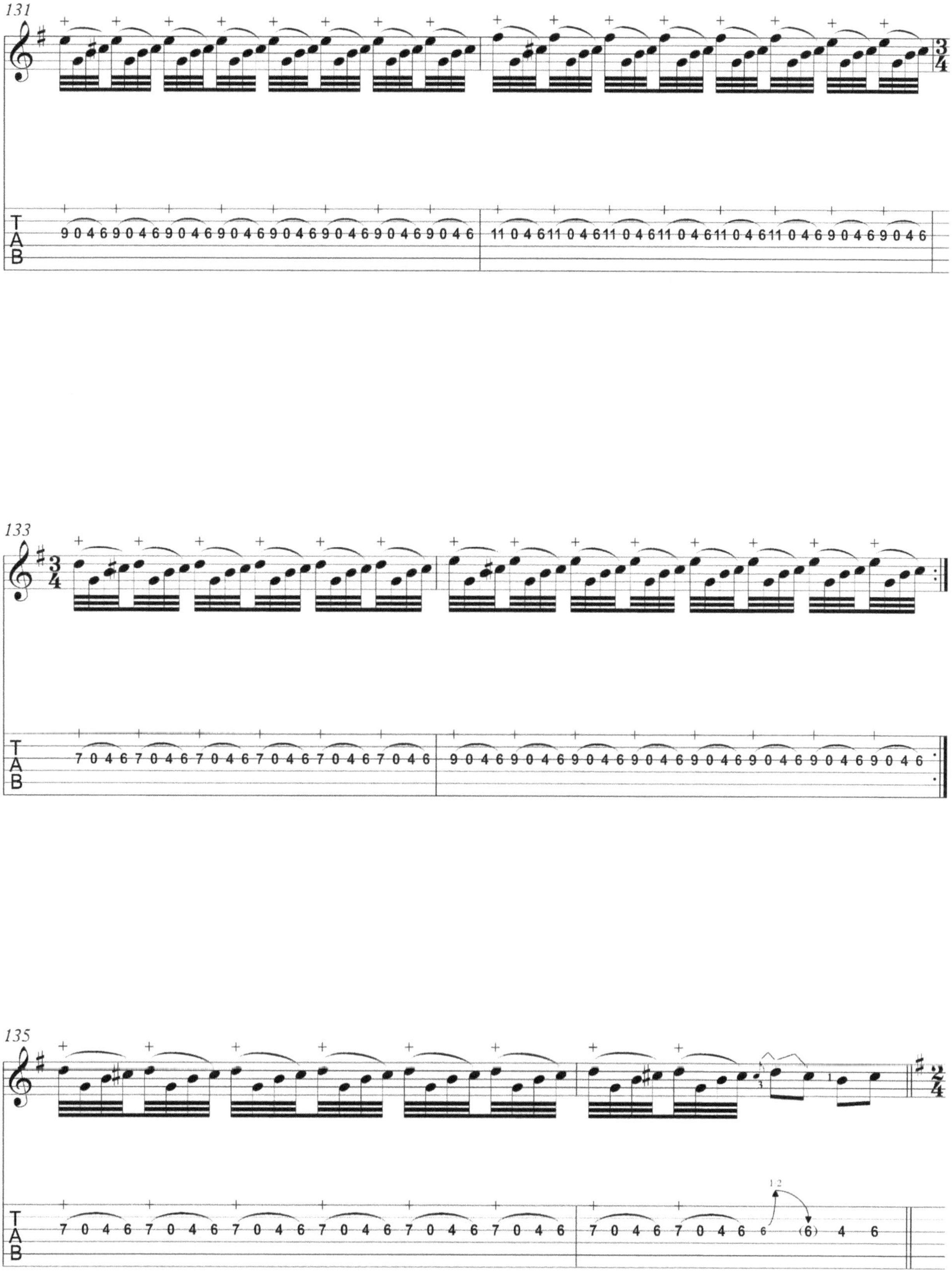
131
133
135

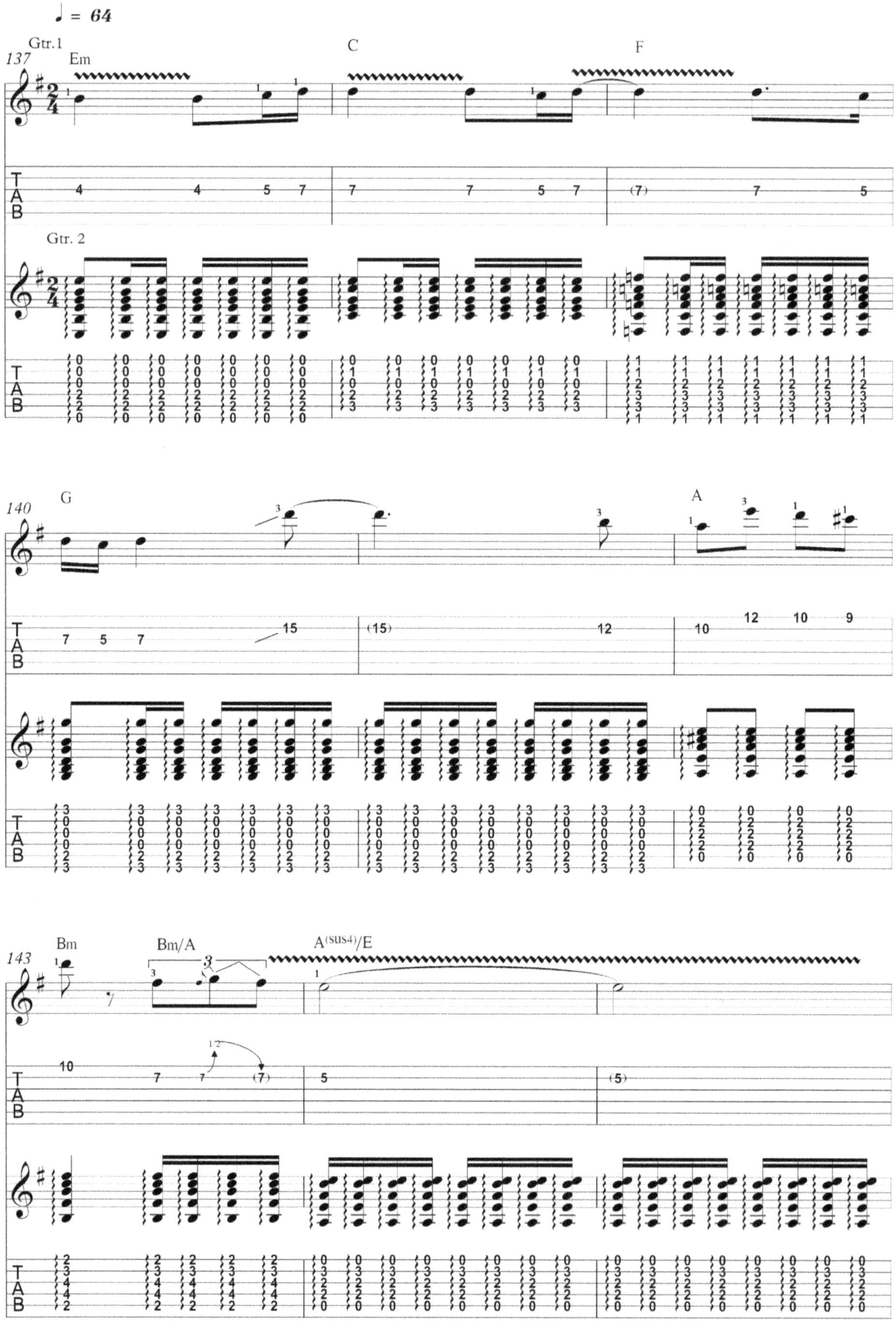
♩ = 64
Gtr.1
137
Em
C
F
Gtr. 2
140
G
A
143
Bm
Bm/A
A(sus4)/E

* Gibson Les Paul Golden Top 1957

152
*Gtr. 6
N.C.
Gtr. 1
D
*Vibraphone arr. for gtr.
Gtr. 5
Gtr. 2
Fade out
156

*Mellotron arr. for gtr.

*Vox Bass Pedal arr. for gtr.

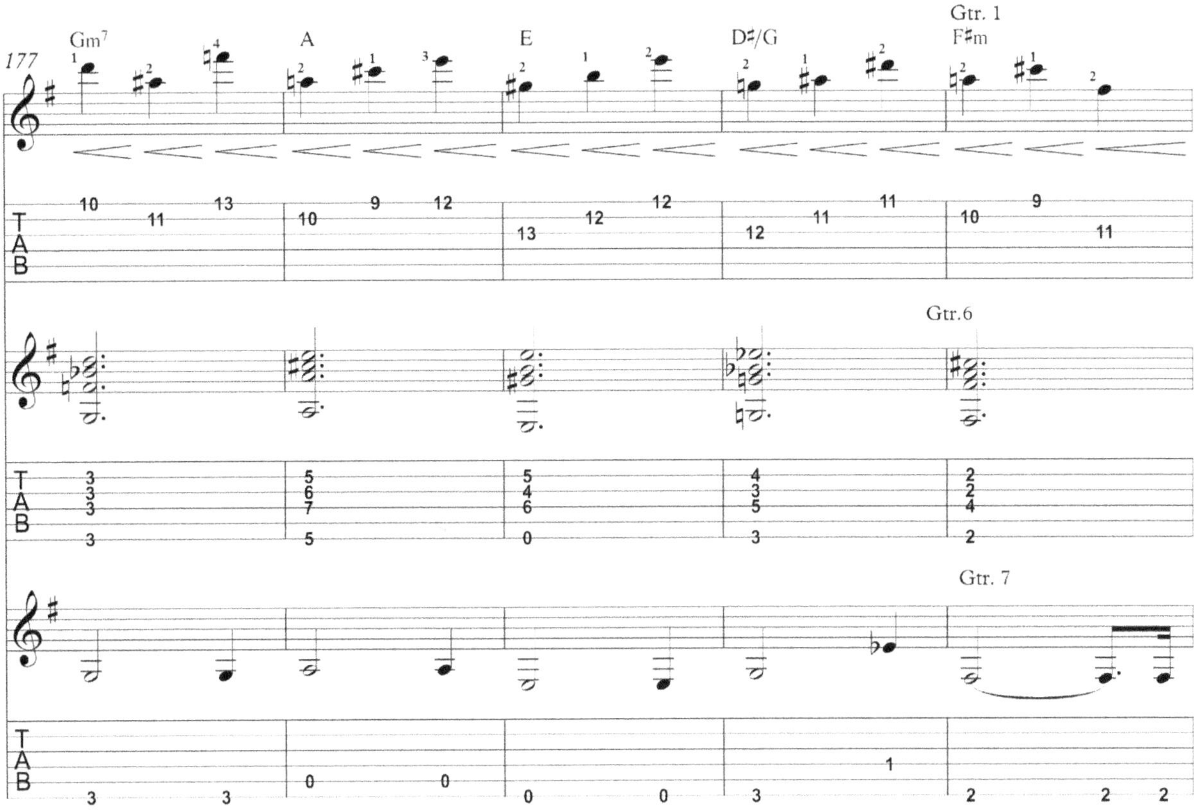
177
Gm7
A
E
D♯/G
Gtr. 1
F♯m
Gtr.6
Gtr. 7

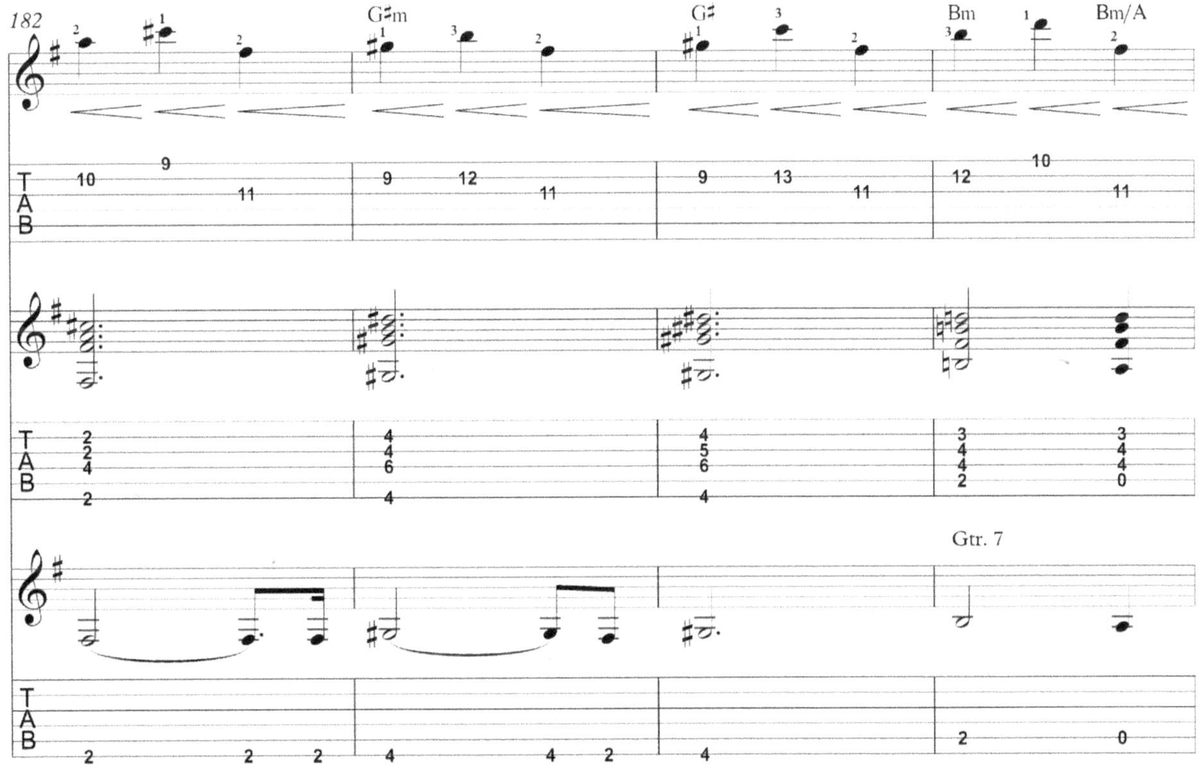
182
G♯m
G♯
Bm
Bm/A
Gtr. 7

* Gibson Les Paul Golden Top 1957

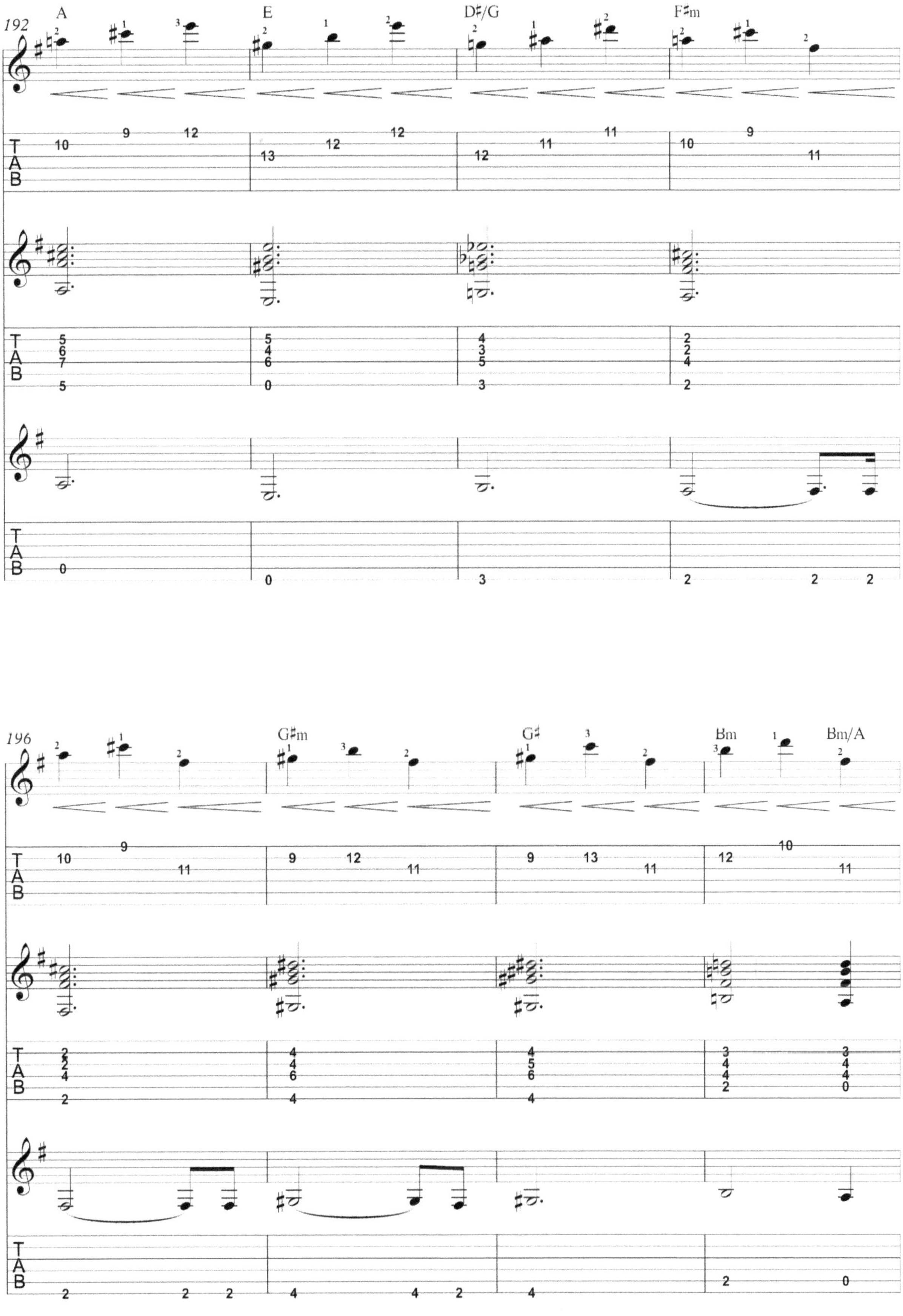
192
A
E
D♯/G
F♯m
196
G♯m
G♯
Bm
Bm/A

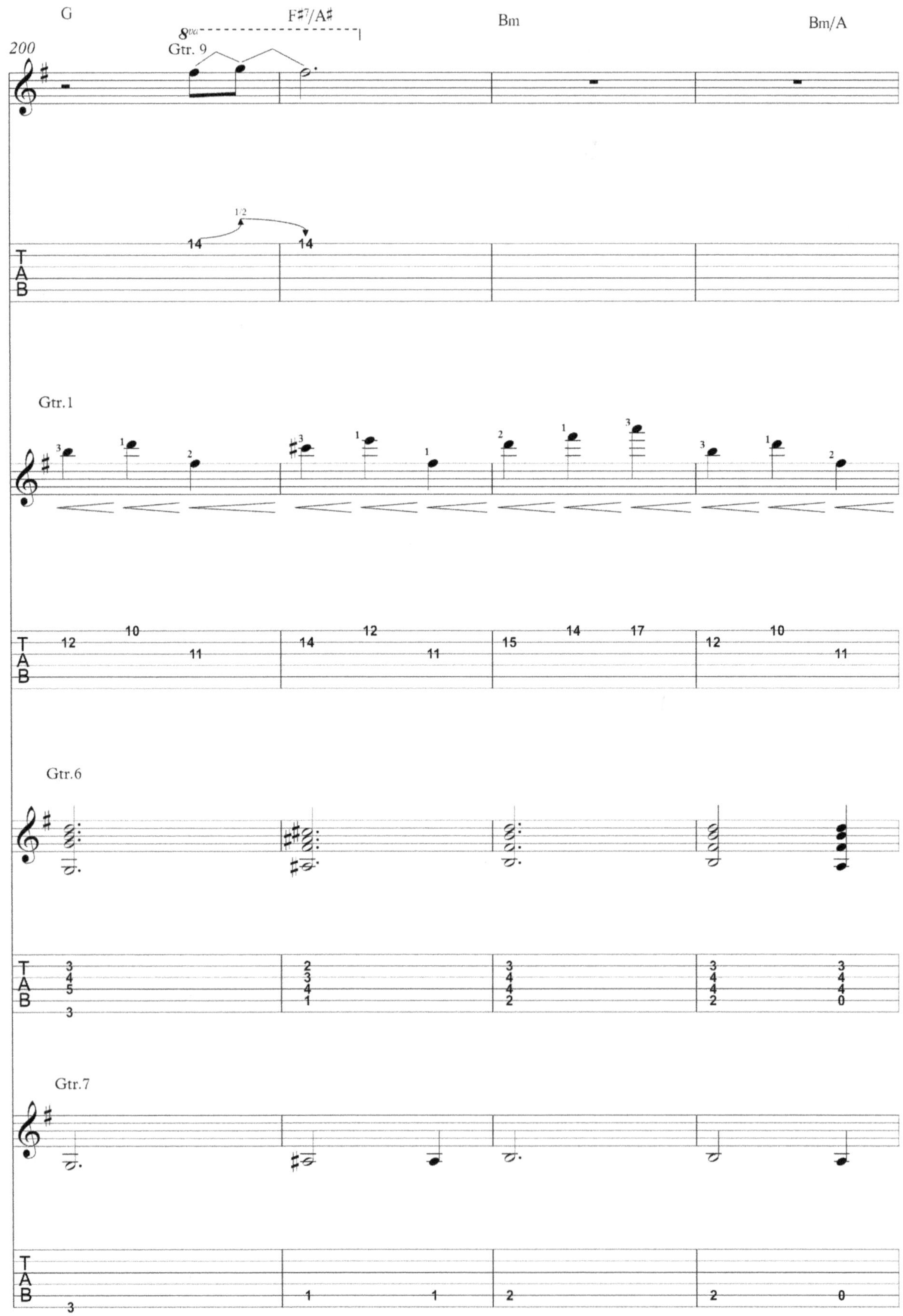
G
F♯7/A♯
Bm
Bm/A
200
8va
Gtr. 9
1/2
Gtr.1
Gtr.6
Gtr.7

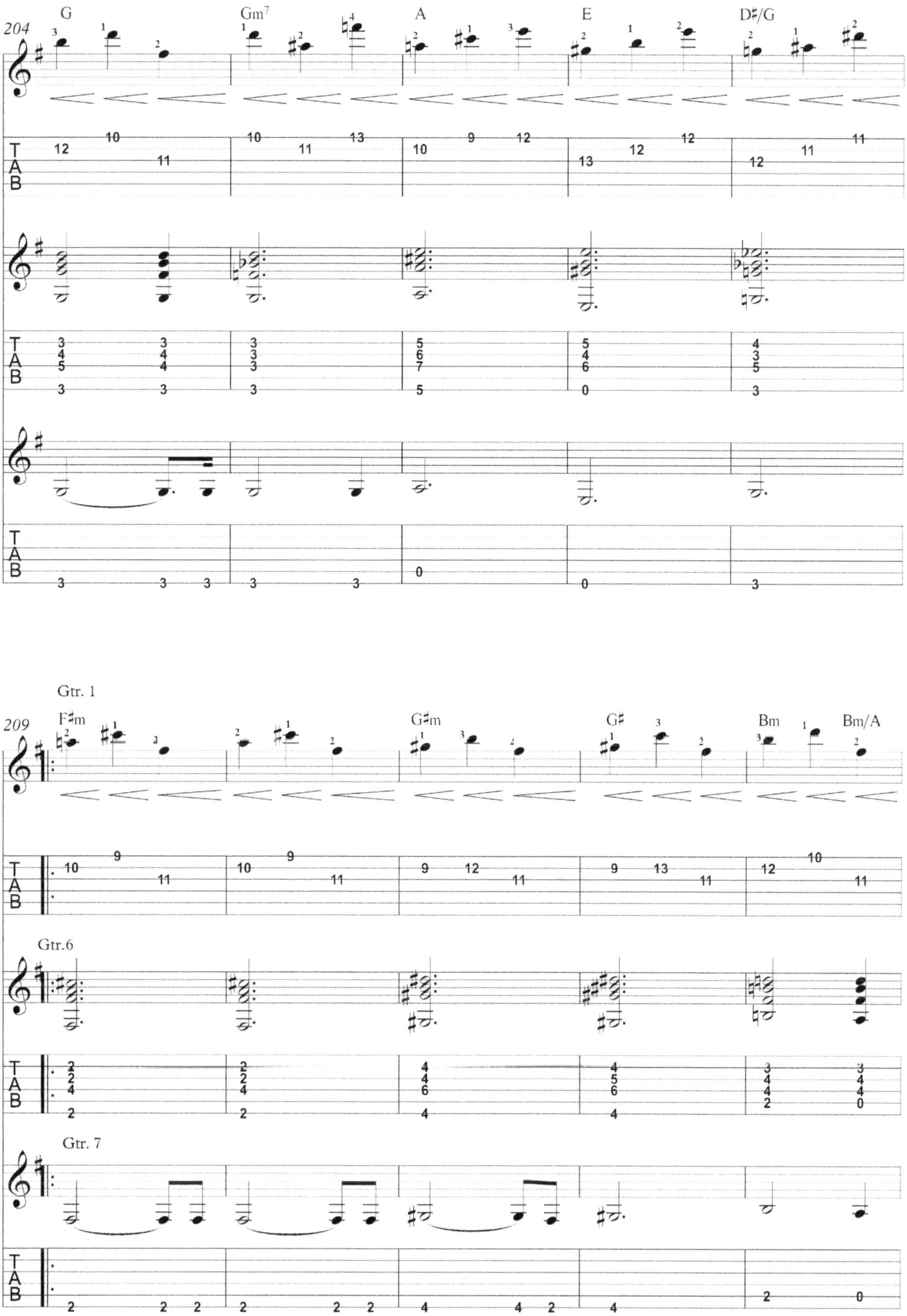
204
G
Gm7
A
E
D♯/G
Gtr. 1
209
F♯m
G♯m
G♯
Bm
Bm/A
Gtr.6
Gtr. 7

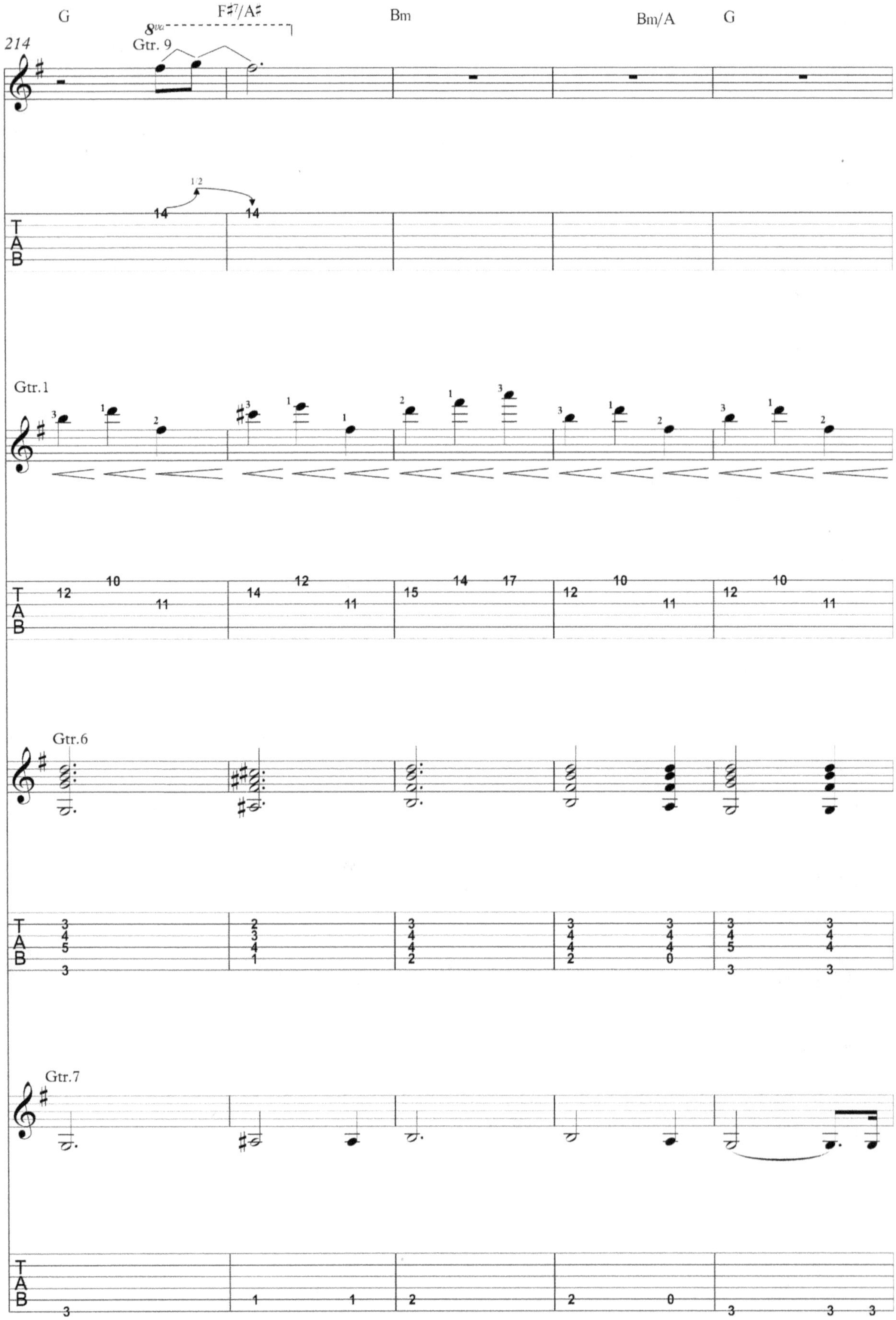
G
F♯7/A♯
Bm
Bm/A
G
8va
214
Gtr. 9
1/2
Gtr.1
Gtr.6
Gtr.7

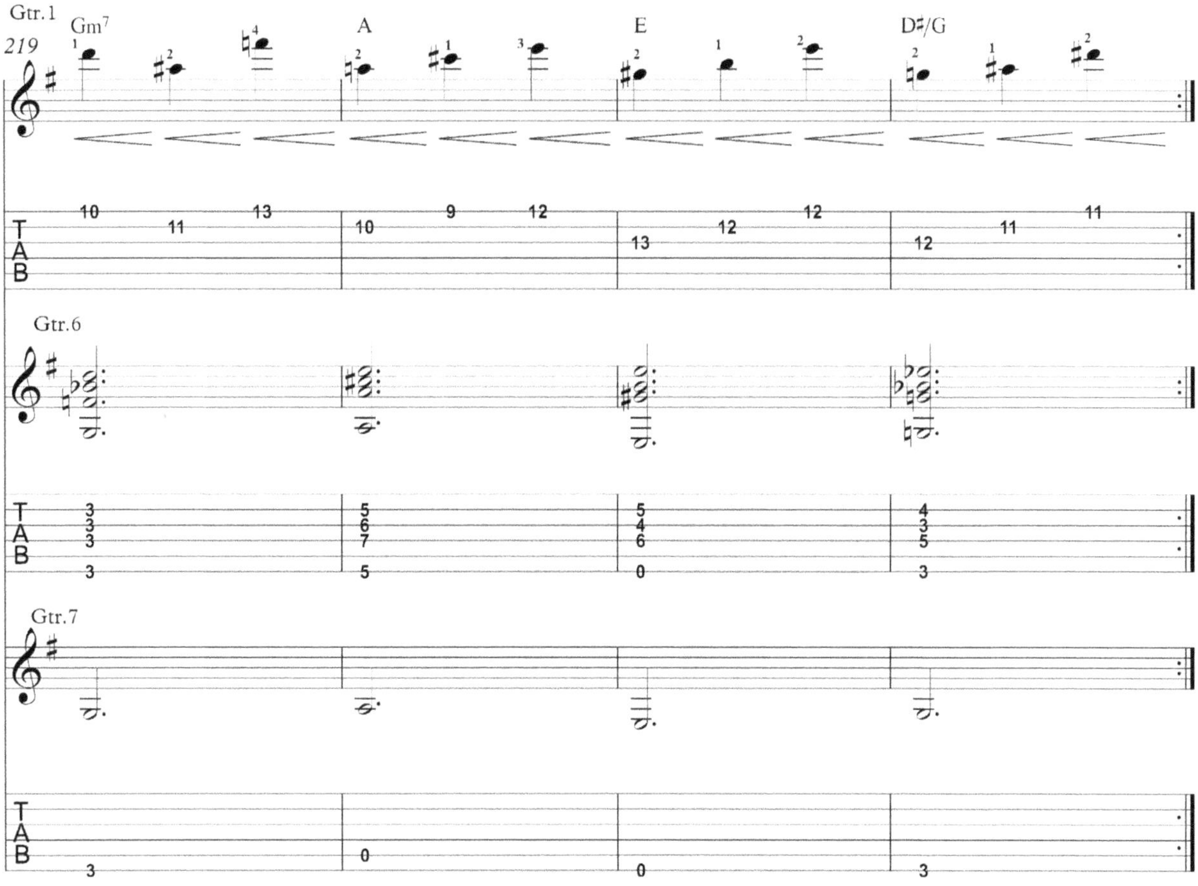
Gtr. 1
219
Gm7
A
E
D♯/G
Gtr. 6
Gtr. 7

SHADOW OF THE HIEROPHANT
BY STEVE HACKETT, MIKE RUTHERFORD

Intro:
|Fm |Db |Eb |Fm | |G |Cm |D/G |G | |G(add4) | | |

G(add4)   D6/F#
VEILING THE NIGHTSHADE

A#6(add4)   A(add4)   G   G(sus2 sus4)
BRIDE STALKS A FLOWER   REVEALED

G(add4)   D6/F#
NEARING THE HOUR MAKE

A#6(add4)   A(add4)   G   Am11 |G/B   G/C |C6/9 |
HASTE TO THEIR THRESHOLD   CONCEALED

Em7   D/F#   Bm   C(add9)
LOST IN THOUGHT IN SEARCH OF VISION

Am   Em   F   Am   G   Am11 |G/B G/C |C6/9 |
AS THE MOON ECLIPSED THE   SUN

|C/Bb |Bb6/9 |

Intro

G(add4)   D6/F#
CASTING THE SAME STEPS

A#6(add4)   A(add4)   G   G(sus2 sus4)
GLIMPSING HIS OWN FATE TO   COME

G(add4)   D6/F#
MELT IN THE DREAM VOID

A#6(add4)   A(add4)   G   Am11 |G/B   G/C |C6/9 |
FROM WHICH HE NEVER CAN RUN

Em7   D/F#   Bm   C(add9)
LOST IN THOUGHT IN SEARCH OF VISION

Am   Em   F   Am   G   Am11 |G/B G/C |C6/9 |
AS THE MOON ECLIPSED THE SUN

|C/Bb |Bb6/9 |

Intro

G   D6/F#
TEARS FILL THE FOUNTAINS

A#6(add4)   A(add4)   G   G(sus2 sus4)
BREAKING THEIR PROMISE TO   HEAL

G(add4)   D6/F#
RIPPLING THE WATERS

A#6(add4)   A(add4)   G   Am11 |G/B   G/C |C6/9 |
MIRROR AN ENDED   IDEAL

Em7   D/F#   Bm   C(add9
DEEP IN THOUGHT BUT ROBBED OF   VISION

Am   Em   F   Am   G   Am11 |G/B G/C |C6/9 |
AS THE MOON ECLIPSED THE SUN

|C/Bb |Bb6/9 |

Intro

Bridge Tapping

|G |C |F |G |G/B |A |Bm |A(sus4)/E | |D/F# |E/G# |

|D/F# |E/G# |A |F#m A/E D | | |

Solo Theme

Play 6 times:
F#m | |G#m |G# |Bm Bm/A |G |F#7/A# |
|Bm | Bm/A |G |Gm7 |A |E |D#/G |

F#m

PHOTO GALLERY

Photo 57: John Kackett (left) showing Paulo De Carvalho (right) how he composed "A Tower Struck Down" with his brother Steve Hackett. Northern England, 2017.

Photo 58: Paulo De Carvalho (left) with Steve Hackett's Yairi Nylon guitar and Steve Hackett (right) with his Zemaitis 12-String playing all the songs in Voyage of the Acolyte. London, 2017.

Photo 59: Steve Hackett (left) and Paulo De Carvalho (right). London, 2017

Photo 60: John Hackett (left) and Paulo De Carvalho (right), 2017.

Photo 61: the present location of De Lane Lea studio, former Kingsway Recorders, on Dean Street, London. Photo by Paulo De Carvalho, 2017.

ABOUT THE AUTHOR

PAULO DE CARVALHO is a guitar player, composer, arranger and audio engineer.

Author of **The Sound of Steve Hackett - A Selection of Guitar Transcriptions from His Solo Career** (2017).

Paulo earned a bachelor in musical composition through the Federal University of Rio de Janeiro, Brazil. He was granted the *Cultural Merit Award* from *Acontece Magazine* (2008, 2009, 2010) and he was nominated for the *Brazilian Press Award* as best Brazilian musician in the US (2008, 2009, 2010, 2011, 2012, 2013).

He performs and tours regularly playing Brazilian Jazz.

https://www.paulodecarvalhogtr.com